Software Testing

Software Testing
Testing Across the Entire
Software Development Life Cycle

Gerald D. Everett
Certified Senior Testing Education Specialist
IBM

Raymond McLeod, Jr.
University of Texas at Austin
Austin, TX

IEEE PRESS

WILEY-INTERSCIENCE
A JOHN WILEY & SONS, INC., PUBLICATION

Library of Congress Cataloging-in-Publication Data:

Everett, Gerald D., 1943-
  Software testing : testing across the entire software development life
cycle / by Gerald D. Everett, Raymond McLeod, Jr.
      p. cm.
  Includes index.
  ISBN 978-0-471-79371-7 (cloth)
1. Computer software–Testing.   2. Computer software–Development.   I.
McLeod, Raymond.
  II. Title.
  QA76.76.T48E94 2007
  005.1'4–dc22   2007001282

To my wife Nell and her steadfast encouragement during the relentless weekends and vacations while I wrote this book.

Jerry

To my good friend Carolyn, whose reminders, suggestions, and inspiration have made me a better person, father, and appreciator of the beauty that the world has to offer.

Ray

Contents

Preface

An informal survey of twenty-one U.S. universities by the authors found that nineteen were without any software testing courses. When talking with the faculty responsible for the software testing courses in three of the universities, we learned that the largest single impediment to creating a software testing course was the absence of a good textbook. We were told that the current selection of textbooks necessitated a combination of three or four to cover many of the topics, with some topics not even covered at all. This situation leaves much of the material coverage to the professor. If he or she does not have a background in software testing, the textbooks leave gaps that is hard to fill.

Whereas this situation is disconcerting, universities and businesses in Europe and Asia seem to value testing expertise more than in the US. Instead of only three of twenty-one universities delivering testing education as in the US, the ratio in Europe is more like seven out of ten. The reason for this discrepancy is because academic and business cultures that already value software testing do not need to be sold on the value of a comprehensive, basic textbook on the subject.

THE IMPORTANCE OF SOFTWARE TESTING

Software Testing: Testing Across the Entire Lifecycle provides the fundamental concepts and approaches to software testing. The topic is important for two reasons. First, according to US Government surveys there has been an estimated $59.5B in business losses since 2000 due to poor quality software. Second, based on the authors' inability to find experienced software testers to address some of the estimated $22.2B testing opportunity, the current pool of experienced software testers is already gainfully employed.

The topic merits a book because in the authors' opinion there is no single, comprehensive software testing textbook available that gives novice testers the whole picture. There are a large number of narrowly scoped, deep textbooks that are excellent for experienced testers, but they tend to leave the novice tester confused and discouraged. Our task is to provide the novice tester with a complete coverage of software testing as it is practiced today, as it will be practiced in the future, and as a viable career option.

THE APPROACH

Software Testing: Testing Across the Entire Lifecycle takes a four-fold approach. First, it examines the general mind-set of a tester using non-technical examples like buying a car. Second, it examines the structured approach that emphasizes test planning. Third, it examines the choices of software testing approaches and when during the software development cycle they are normally used. Finally, it walks the reader through a software development project from end to end, demonstrating appropriate use of the software testing approaches previously discussed on an individual basis.

DISTINCTIVE FEATURES

The most distinctive features of *Software Testing: A Comprehensive Software Testing Approach* are:

- A comprehensive treatment of what a technology professional needs to know to become a software tester. The presentation sequence builds from simple examples to complex examples. The descriptions and examples are directed toward practitioners rather than academicians.

- A chapter on analyzing test results effectively using simple math and complex math models. We have seen no other software testing textbook that treats test results analysis statistically. Quite to the contrary, other software testing textbook authors have expressed the opinion that statistics do not belong in a testing textbook.

- A choice of case studies.

  Case Study A   The first case study uses a popular Internet application called PetStore2 developed by Sun Microsystems to demonstrate best practices application development using Java. The textbook demonstrates through reader exercises how to plan and execute approaches described in Chapters 7 through 12 on this well-known application. The benefit to the reader is two-fold. First, the reader is given an application that is well suited for hands-on experience that reinforces the testing approaches described in the textbook. Second, when the reader successfully completes the case study exercises, she or he can claim resumé testing experience with an industry recognized application.

  Case Study B   The second case study is a step-by-step description and exercises that follows a successful testing project presented in Chapter 13.

Difficulties are encountered along the way because this is a real testing project. The case study unfolds in a manner that allows the authors to incorporate most of the testing concepts and approaches discussed individually in previous chapters and attempted hands-on in Case Study A.

ORGANIZATION

Chapter 1 provides an overview of testing, addressing such topics as the objectives and limits of testing, and the value versus the cost of testing. Chapter 2 describes the system development life cycle (SDLC) within which testing occurs. The major SDLCs, such as the waterfall cycle, prototyping, rapid application development, and the phased development methodology are described. This textbook uses the phased development methodology as its basic software development framework.

Chapter 3 provides an overview of structured testing, explaining a generic structured testing approach called SPRAE, which consists of the components of SPECIFICATION, PREMEDITATION, REPEATABAILITY, ACCOUNTABILITY, AND ECONOMY. Following, in Chapter 4, is an overview of four basic testing strategies—Static, White Box, Black Box, and Performance (Load) Testing. Both two- and three-dimensional "Chess Boards" are used to illustrate these basic strategies. Once the testing strategy has been devised, test planning can proceed and that is the subject of Chapter 5. Guidelines are offered for writing your Test Plan and Test Cases in the real world.

Chapters 6-9 explain the basic types of testing introduced in Chapter 4—Chapter 6 explains Static Testing, Chapter 7 explains Functional Testing, Chapter 8 explains Structural (Non-functional) testing, and Chapter 9 explains Performance Testing. As an example of the thoroughness of these explanations, the discussion of Structural Testing includes coverage of Interface Testing, Security Testing, Installation Testing, and the appropriately named Smoke Test.

With an understanding of the mechanics of testing, attention is directed in Chapter 10 to the testing environment, identifying both good and bad environments. Then, Chapter 11 describes the important topic of automated test tools, and Chapter 12 explains how to analyze and interpret test results.

With this foundation laid, Chapter 13 goes through a Full Software Development Lifecycle based on a project performed by the lead author for the State of Colorado.

The textbook concludes with coverage of Testing Complex Applications in Chapter 14, and identification of Future Directions of Testing in Chapter 15 that should prove helpful in considering a software testing career.

LEARNING AIDS

After the introductory chapter, Chapter 2 lays a conceptual foundation of methodologies and tools. This chapter relies heavily on diagrams that serve as frameworks, helping the reader successfully understand the concepts. Chapters that describe the testing process make substantial use of tables and sample printouts so that the reader can visualize the process.

THE COMPANION WEBSITE

The companion website ftp://ftp.wiley.com/public/sci_tech_med/software_testing/ provided by John Wiley & Sons, Inc. contains:

- A Study Guide with questions for each chapter, Case Study A, and Case Study B.
- An Instructor Guide with a course syllabus, textbook graphics for classroom projection, teaching objectives, teaching techniques, topics for discussion, questions for each chapter. To access the Instructor Guide, please contact Paul Petrali, Senior Editor, Wiley Interscience, at ppetrali@wiley.com.

ACKNOWLEDGMENTS

Throughout the text, the authors use the term "we." Although we take full responsibility for the material and the manner in which it is presented, we acknowledge that we have received much help along the way. First, we want to thank the thousands of students in academia and industry who have not only allowed us the opportunity to formulate and organize our material but to also provide valuable feedback that has served to keep us on course. Second, we want to thank our business clients who have provided real-world laboratories for us to apply our knowledge and experience. Lastly, we want to thank the people at John Wiley & Sons who provided their professional expertise to bring this book to reality. We especially want to thank Valerie Moliere, Paul Petrolia, Whitney Lesch, and Danielle Lacourciere.

Acknowledgments

We want to thank Kenneth Everett for spending many long hours challenging the testing approaches presented in the book. He won some. We won some. Several chapters were strengthened considerably by the intense discussions, regardless of who won. Ken is also responsible for the inclusion of case studies to provide more direct reinforcement of the reader's understanding and appreciation of testing techniques.

We want to thank Dr. Stephen Kan whose authorship discussions and professional, articulate writing style inspired us to write this book.

We want to thank our publication editor Paul Petralia and his trusty editorial assistant Whitney Lesch who deftly navigated us through the maze of publishing logistics to make this fine-looking textbook something you want to pick up and explore.

Chapter 1

Overview of Testing

LEARNING OBJECTIVES

- to identify the basic mindset of a tester, regardless of what is being tested
- to determine the correct motivations for testing in business
- to explain some of the reasons why testing is undervalued as a business practice
- to explain what differentiates software testers from software developers

1.1 INTRODUCTION

There were numerous spectacular magazine cover stories about computer software failures during the last decade. Even with these visible lessons in the consequences of poor software, software failures continue to occur on and off the front page. These failures cost the US economy an estimated $59.5 billion per year. [1] An estimated $22.2 billion of the annual losses could be eliminated by software testing appropriately conducted during all the phases of software development. [2]

"Software Testing: Testing Across the Entire Software Development Life Cycle" presents the *first* comprehensive treatment of all *21st Century* testing activities from test planning through test completion for every phase of software under development or software under revision. The authors believe that the cover story business catastrophes can best be prevented by such a comprehensive approach to software testing. Furthermore, the authors believe the regular and consistent practice of such a comprehensive testing approach can raise the industry level of quality that software developers deliver and customers expect. By using a comprehensive testing approach, software testers can turn the negative risk of major business loss into a positive competitive edge.

Many excellent textbooks on the market deeply explore software testing for narrow segments of software development. [3–5] One of the intermediate-level testing textbooks that the authors recommend as a follow-on to this textbook is Dr. James A. Whittaker's *Practical Guide to Testing*. [6] None of these textbooks deal with software testing from the perspective of the entire development life cycle, which includes planning tests, completing tests, and understanding test results during every phase of software development.

Readers who will benefit the most from this textbook include software professionals, business systems analysts, more advanced Computer Science students, and more advanced Management Information Systems students. The common experience shared by this diverse group of readers is an appreciation of the technology challenges in software development. It is this common experience in software development that will enable the readers to quickly gain a realistic expectation of testing benefits and acknowledge the boundaries of good software testing.

Although this textbook focuses specifically on software testing, fundamental testing concepts presented in the first section apply to all kinds of testing from automobiles to wine. This is possible because, to a large extent, testing is a mindset that anyone can practice on any professional task or pastime.

Computer hardware testers will find about 85% of this textbook directly applicable to their assignments. They should seek additional reference materials for information about the remaining 15% of the techniques they need.

Note: The easiest way to determine whether you are doing software or hardware testing is to examine the recommendation from the test outcome "this system runs too slowly." If the recommendation is to "tweak" the software or buy more/faster hardware, then you are doing software testing. If the recommendation is to reach for the soldering gun, then you are doing hardware testing.

Typically, a person interested in software testing as a profession will begin to specialize in certain kinds of testing like functional testing. Whittaker's textbook mentioned in the beginning of this section can serve as the logical next step for obtaining a deeper understanding of functional testing. The breadth of topics discussed in this textbook should serve as a reminder to the specialists that there are other aspects of testing that often impinge upon the success of their specialty.

1.2 OBJECTIVES AND LIMITS OF TESTING

There are many opportunities for testing in both professional and personal life. We will first explore some examples of non-computer-related testing that show patterns of thinking and behavior useful for software testing. Then we will examine some of the boundaries imposed upon testing by financial considerations, time constraints, and other business limitations.

1.2.1 The Mind of a Tester

Kaner, Bach, and Pettichord describe four different kinds of thinking exhibited by a good tester: [7]

1. Technical thinking: the ability to model technology and understand causes and effects

2. Creative thinking: the ability to generate ideas and see possibilities

3. Critical thinking: the ability to evaluate ideas and make inferences

4. Practical thinking: the ability to put ideas into practice

An example of these kinds of thinking is found in a fable called "The King's Challenge."

The King's Challenge (a fable)

Once upon a time, a mighty king wanted to determine which of his three court wizards was the most powerful.

So he put the three court wizards in the castle dungeon and declared whoever escaped from his respective dungeon cell first was the most powerful wizard in all the kingdom.

(Before reading on, decide what you would do.)

The first wizard immediately started chanting mystical poems to open his cell door.

The second wizard immediately started casting small polished stones and bits of bone on the floor to learn how he might open his cell door.

The third wizard sat down across from his cell door and thought about the situation for a minute. Then he got up, walked over to the cell door and pulled on the door handle. The cell door swung open because it was closed but not locked.

Thus, the third wizard escaped his cell first and became known as the most powerful wizard in all the kingdom.

What kinds of "tester" thinking did the third wizard exercise in solving the king's puzzle?

- Creative thinking: the ability to see the possibility that the door was not locked in the first place
- Practical thinking: the ability to decide to try the simplest solution first

1.2.2   Non-Software Testing at the User Level—Buying a Car

Next, we will use the automobile industry to find non-computer testing examples that can easily be related to software testing. Have you ever shopped for a car or helped someone else shop for a car? What shopping step did you perform first ?

One of the most obvious motivations for testing a car is to determine its quality or functionality before buying one. When you shop for a car, you typically have some pretty specific objectives in mind that relate either to your transportation needs for work or to your transportation needs for recreation. Either way, you are the person who will drive the car, you will be the car "user."

As a user, you are not interested in performing all possible kinds of tests on the car because you assume (correctly or incorrectly) that the manufacturer has done some of those tests for you. The important thing to realize is that you do limit your testing in some way. We will refer to this limited test as a "test drive," although some of the testing does not require driving the car per se. To better understand the *testing limits*, we will first examine what you do *not* test. Then, we will examine what you *do* test before you buy a car.

The following examples of test drive objectives are typically *not* those used for a personal test drive:

Objectives of a Test Drive are NOT

- **to break the car**
- **to improve the car's design**

You do not try to break the car or any of its components. Rather, you seek guarantees and warranties that imply the car manufacturer has already tried to break it and proven the car is "unbreakable" under normal driving conditions for x thousand miles or y years, whichever occurs first. In other words, you expect the car's reliability to have been already tested by others.

You do not typically try to improve the design of the car because you expect the car manufacturer to have employed a design goal that was reached by the particular model for which you are shopping. If you identify design changes you would like to make in the car, the normal reaction is to simply shop for a different model or for a different manufacturer to find a car with the desired alternative design already implemented.

A software analogy is to shop for a personal accounting package. For example, consider shopping for a home financial tool and finding Quicken by Intuit and Money by MicroSoft. As a user, you are not interested in a "test drive" to break the software. You expect (correctly or incorrectly) that the software is unbreakable. As a user, you are not interested in changing the software design. If you do not like the way Quicken selects accounts using drop-down menus, you consider the way Money selects accounts.

So what *do* you test during a car test drive? Typically, it is determined by your transportation needs (goals). The needs become *test* drive *objectives*. Test objectives are the measurable milestones in testing, which clearly indicate that the testing activities have definitely achieved the desired goals. You translate test drive objectives into testing approaches that validate whether the car on the dealer's lot meets your transportation objectives. Different objectives call for different test drive approaches. Next, we will look at examples of test drive objectives.

Objectives of a Test Drive ARE

- **to validate affordability**
- **to validate attractiveness**
- **to validate comfort**
- **to validate usefulness**
- **to validate performance**

Each of these testing objectives can be validated against the car without trying to break it or redesign it. Some of these testing objectives can be validated even before you get in the car and start the engine.

All of these objectives are personal. You are the only one who can prioritize these objectives. You are the only one who can evaluate the car against these objectives by a test drive, and decide whether to buy the car.

- *Affordability:* down payment, monthly payments, interest rate, and trade-in
- *Attractiveness:* body style, color scheme, body trim, and interior

- *Comfort:* driver or passenger height, weight, body shape, leg room, ingress or egress through a front door or back door, and loading or unloading through a hatchback or rear door.
- *Usefulness:* the number of seats versus the number of passengers, trunk space, convertible hauling space, on-road versus off-road, or trailer hitch weight capacity
- *Performance:* gas mileage, minimum grade of gas required, acceleration for freeway merging, acceleration to beat your neighbor, cornering at low speeds, cornering at high speeds, and the time or mileage between maintenance service

When you have your testing objectives clear in mind, you choose the testing approaches that best validate the car against those objectives. The following examples show some testing approaches and the kinds of testing objectives they can validate.

Testing Approaches Include

- **examining the sticker price and sale contract**
- **trying out the radio, the air conditioner, and the lights**
- **trying acceleration, stopping, and cornering**

These testing approaches are referred to by fairly common terminology in the testing industry.

- Examine = Static testing
  (*observe, read, review without actually driving the car*)
- Try out = Functional and structural testing
  (*work different features of the car without actually driving the car*)
- Try = Performance testing
  (*work different features of the car by actually driving the car*)

1.2.3 Non-Software Testing at the Developer Level— Building a Car

Now, we will switch from the user's, buyer's, or driver's perspective to the auto manufacturer's perspective. As with a shopper, it is important for a car builder to have specific testing objectives in mind and discard other testing objectives that are inappropriate for new car development.

Testing Objectives of a New Car to be Built

- **validate design via scale models.**
- **validate operation of prototypes.**
- **validate mass assembly plans from prototypes.**

The basis for this example is the normal progression of new car development that starts with written *requirements* for a new car such as

- seats six
- carries five suitcases
- runs on regular gas
- consumes gas at a rate of 25 miles per gallon at highway speeds
- has a top speed of 80 miles per hour

These requirements are the nonnegotiable design and manufacturing boundaries set by groups other than the designers such as marketing teams, Federal regulatory agencies, or competitors. It is the auto manufacturer's job to build a new car that does all these things to the letter of the requirements.

With the new car requirements in hand, the test objectives become more understandable. It is the job of the auto design tester to validate the current state of the new car against the car's requirements. If the new car does not initially meet the requirements (as few newly designed cars do), then it is the designer not the tester who must improve the design to meet the requirements.

After design changes are made, it is the tester's job to revalidate the modified design against the requirements. This design, test, correct, and retest cycle continues until the new car design meets the requirements and is completed *before* the car is manufactured.

Hopefully, this discussion points out the advantage of requirements for testing validation at every stage of creating the new car. One of the most pervasive software testing dilemmas today is the decision of companies to build Internet core-business applications for the first time without documenting any requirements. *Note*: Additional requirements testing approaches can be found in the Chapter 6 of this textbook.

As with the user test drive, the manufacture tester has many approaches that can be employed to validate the aspects of a new car against the car's requirements.

Testing Approaches Used While Constructing New Cars

- **plan the tests based on requirements and design specifications.**
- **examine blueprints and clay models.**
- **perform and analyze wind tunnel tests.**
- **perform and analyze safety tests.**
- **perform and validate prototype features.**
- **drive prototype and validate operations.**

This example implies an additional layer of documentation necessary for successful testing. As previously noted, requirements tell the designers what needs to be designed. Specifications (blueprints or models) are the designers' interpretation of requirements as to how the design can be manufactured.

When the specifications are validated against the requirements, all the subsequent physical car assembly validation can be performed against the specifications.

As with the test drive, the car builder testing approaches can be described by common testing terminology.

- Examine = Static testing
  (*observe, read, or review without actually building the car*)
- Perform = Functional and structural testing
  (*work different features of the car models, mock-ups, and manufactured subassemblies*)
- Drive = Performance testing
  (*work different features of the car in the prototypes*)

Because you have probably not built a car, it might be helpful to find examples from a book that details the car-building steps and the manner in which those steps are tested during real car development. [8]

Example of static testing

Read the description of wind tunnel testing that showed changing shapes on the wheel wells would allow the car to achieve 180 mph which became the target speed for road tests later.

Example of test planning

Read the estimate of the number of prototypes to be built for testing the C5, around one hundred, compared with the 300 or more expected to be built for normal car pre-production testing. These prototypes were expected to be used for all static and dynamic (road) testing prior to the start of assembly line production. In fact, some of the prototypes were used to plan and calibrate assembly line production steps.

Read the description of final prototype endurance tests that include driving the test car on a closed track at full throttle for a full 24 hours, stopping only for gas and driver changes.

Examples of functional and structural testing

Read the description of heater and air conditioner testing in which drivers would see how soon the heater made things comfortable in freezing weather. In summer, one internal environment test would let a Corvette sit under the desert sun for 3 hours, then the test driver would get in, close the doors, start the car and air-conditioning to monitor the system until the driver stopped sweating.

Read the description of body surface durability testing which involved driving into a car-wash solution of corrosive salt and chemicals that caused the car to experience the equivalent of a decade of corrosion exposure.

Example of performance testing

Read the description of travel weather testing extremes. Some cars were taken to frigid climates and forced to operate in sub-zero temperatures. Some cars were taken to extremely hot climates and forced to operate in 120+ degree Fahrenheit temperatures.

Read the description of road grade conditions testing that required a driver to pull up a short on a steep slope, set the parking brake, turn off the engine, wait a few moments, then restart the engine and back down the slope.

Read the description of road surface conditions testing where drivers raced over loose gravel to torture the underside of the car and wheel wells.

Read the description of road surface conditions testing that employed long sequences of speed bumps to shake the car and its parts to an extreme.

The book traces all the steps that the General Motors Corvette development team took to create the 1997 model C5 Corvette. It is interesting from the manufacturing standpoint as well as the organizational intrigue standpoint because 1996 was supposed to be the last year the Corvette was made and sold. The C5 became the next-generation Corvette and was brought to market in 1997. The C5 design was manufactured until 2004. Perhaps you have seen the C5 flash by on the highway. It looks like Figure 1.1.

Figure 1.1   1997 Corvette C5 Coupe

1.2.4   The Four Primary Objectives of Testing

Testing can be applied to a wide range of development projects in a large number of industries. In contrast to the diversity of testing opportunities, there is a common underpinning of objectives. The primary motivation for testing all business *development* projects is the same: to reduce the *risk* of unplanned development expense or, worse, the risk of project failure. This development risk can be quantified as some kind of tangible loss such as that of revenue or customers. Some development risks are so large that the company is betting the entire business that the development will be successful. In order to know the size of the risk and the probability of it occurring, a *risk assessment* is performed. This risk assessment is a series of structured "what if" questions that probe the most likely causes of development failure depending on the type of development and the type of business the development must support. This risk motivation is divided into four interrelated testing objectives.

Primary objectives of testing

Testing objective 1: Identify the magnitude and sources of development risk reducible by testing.

When a company contemplates a new development project, it prepares a business case that clearly identifies the expected benefits, costs, and risks. If the cost of the project is not recovered within a reasonable time by the benefits or is determined to be a bad return on investment, the project is deemed unprofitable and is not authorized to start. No testing is required, unless the business case is tested. If the benefits outweigh the costs and the project is considered a good return on investment, the benefits are then compared to the risks. It is quite likely that the risks are many times greater than the benefits. An additional consideration is the likelihood that the risk will become a real loss. If the risk is high but the likelihood of the risk occurring is very small, then the company typically determines that the risk is worth the potential benefit of authorizing the project. Again, no testing is required.

If the risk is high and the likelihood of its occurrence is high, the questions "Can this risk be reduced by testing?" and "If the risk can be reduced, how much can testing reduce it?" are asked. If the risk factors are well known, quantifiable, and under the control of the project, it is likely that testing can reduce the probability of the risk occurring. Fully controlled tests can be planned and completed. If, on the other hand, the risk factors are not under control of the project or the risk factors are fuzzy (not well known or merely qualitative), then testing does not have a fair chance to reduce the risk.

Testing objective 2: Perform testing to reduce identified risks.

As we will see in subsequent chapters, test planning includes positive testing (looking for things that work as required) and negative testing (looking for things that break). The test planning effort emphasizes the risk areas so that the largest possible percentage of the test schedule and effort (both positive testing and negative testing) are dedicated to reducing that risk. Very seldom does testing completely eliminate a risk because there are always more situations to test than time or resources to complete the tests. One hundred percent testing is currently an unrealistic business expectation.

Testing objective 3: Know when testing is completed.

Knowing that 100% testing of the development is unachievable, the tester must apply some kind of prioritization to determine when to stop testing. That determination should start with the positive test items in the test plan. The tester must complete the positive testing that validates all the development requirements. Anything less, and the tester is actually introducing business risk into the development process.

The tester must then complete as much of the risk-targeted testing as possible relative to a cost and benefit break-even point. For example, if there is a $10,000 business risk in some aspect of the development, spending $50,000 to reduce that risk is not a good investment. A rule of thumb is a 10–20% cost to benefit break-even point for testing. If the same $10,000 business risk can be thoroughly tested for $1000–2000, then cost to benefit is very favorable as a testing investment.

Finally, the tester must complete as many of the negative test items in the plan as the testing budget allows after the positive testing and risk testing are completed. Negative testing presents two situations to the test planner:

- The first situation is the complement of the positive test items. For example, if a data field on a screen must accept numeric values from 1 to 999, the values 1, 10, 100, 123, 456, 789, and 999 can be used for positive test completion while the values −1, 0, and 1000 can be used for negative test completion.

- The second situation is the attempt to anticipate novice user actions that are not specified in the requirements or expected during routine business activities. Planning these kinds of tests usually takes deep insight into the business and into the typical ways inexperienced business staff perform routine business activities. The time and expense necessary to test these "outlier" situations often are significantly out of proportion to the likelihood of occurrence or to the magnitude of loss if the problems do occur.

Testing objective 4: Manage testing as a standard project within the development project.

All too often, testing is treated as a simple skill that anyone can perform without planning, scheduling, or resources. Because business risk represents real dollar loss, real dollar testing is required to reduce the risk. Real dollar testing means that personnel with testing expertise should be formed into a testing team with access to the management, resources, and schedules necessary to plan and complete the testing. The testing team, as any other business team, can deliver the testing results on time and within budget if the team follows good standard project management practices.

The benefit of this observation is the reassurance that testing does not have to be hit or miss. It can be planned and completed with the confidence of any other professional project to achieve its objectives. The liability of this observation is the realization that testers are a limited resource. When all available testers are scheduled for an imminent testing project, further testing projects cannot be scheduled until you find additional qualified testers.

When you run out of time to test

As with all project schedules, it is possible to run out of testing time. If that situation arises, what can be done to make the most of the testing that you can complete? When approaching the end of the testing schedule, consider doing a quick prioritization of the outstanding defects. Place most of the testing and correction emphasis on the most severe defects, the ones that present the highest possible business risk. Then review the testing plans that you will not have time to complete and assess the risk that the incomplete testing represents.

Present the development manager with an assessment of the risks that are expected due to the premature halting of testing. The development manager must then decide whether to halt the testing to meet project schedules or to seek additional time and resources to complete the testing as planned.

When you know you can not test it all—positive testing objectives
When you know you can not test it all, review all the completed testing results and compare them with the application or system functionality that the customer has deemed most important. The object of this review is to determine the features to test with your remaining schedule and resources that would make the largest positive impact on the customer's function and feature expectations.

When you know you can not test it all—hidden defect testing objectives
When you know you can not test it all, review the completed testing results and determine if there are trends or clusters of defects that indicate more defects are likely to be found in the same area. Then request a review of that area of code by the development team to determine if additional, hidden defects can be corrected by minor development rework. With minimal additional effort on the part of the developer and tester, likely trouble spots can be addressed before the last remaining testing resources are expended.

1.2.5   Development Axiom—Quality Must Be Built In Because Quality Cannot Be Tested In

Testing can only verify the product or system and its operation against predetermined criteria (requirements). Testing neither adds nor takes away anything. Quality is an issue that is determined during the requirements and design phases by the development project stakeholders or requesting customers. It is not decided at testing time.

1.3   THE VALUE VERSUS COST OF TESTING

Most business decisions are based on a comparison of the value of doing something versus the cost of doing something, typically called the *return on investment* (*ROI*). ROI is the calculation of how quickly and how large the "payoff" will be if a project is financed. If the project will not quickly provide a payoff or the payoff is too small, then the ROI is considered bad. The business motivation for doing something is to receive more benefit than the investment necessary to realize that benefit.

Testing requires the same ROI decision as any other business project. The implication is that testing should be done only when the test results can show benefit beyond the cost of performing the tests. The following examples demonstrate how businesses have placed value on testing results.

1.3.1 Non-Software Testing at the Marketing Level— Auto Safety versus Sales

Auto manufacturers determined a long time ago that thoroughly testing their new car designs was a safety risk management value that far outweighed the cost of the tests. As a result, the descriptions of new car development safety testing such as those in the Corvette story are found in the literature of all major car manufacturers.

There are two possible outcomes of safety testing and the management of the risk that the tests reveal. The first outcome is the decision whether or not to correct a safety problem before the first newly built car is manufactured and sold in large numbers. The input for this decision is the cost of the safety repair versus the perceived risk of the safety to the public in terms of lawsuits and penalties for the violation of regulations.

The second outcome is the decision whether or not to recall a car already manufactured and sold to many customers in order to fix the safety problem. The inputs for this decision are the presales cost figures and risks and the added cost of retrofitting safety solutions to cars that are already manufactured and sold.

The Ford Pinto is one example of safety risk versus cost to mitigate the risk decision. [9] Ford started selling Pintos in 1971. Later that same year, one of the engineers' testing scenarios discovered that when the Pinto is rear-ended in a collision, the gas tank is punctured which causes an explosion and subsequent fire that can trap occupants in the flaming vehicle. Ford assigned a risk probability to such a rear-end collision and to the subsequent fatalities along with a cost of the risk that would be incurred if families of the fatalities sued Ford.

From the risk assessment, Ford assigned a $25,000 value to a human life lost in a car fire. Then, they estimated the number of car fires that could be expected from the Pintos based on a vast number of car sales statistics. From these two numbers, Ford calculated the break-even settlement cost resulting from faulty gas tank litigation at approximately $2.20 per car. From the manufacturing assessment, Ford calculated the cost of retrofitting every Pinto with a gas tank bracket to be $8.59–11.59 per car. At the end of 1971, Ford decided that the best ROI decision was to refrain from retrofitting the gas tank brackets and pay all faulty gas tank lawsuits.

In nonlife-threatening industries, this risk management strategy might have worked well. In this situation, the families of the fatalities caused by the exploding gas tanks foiled Ford's risk mitigation strategy. Instead of suing Ford individually, the grieving families filed a class action suit after the third such fatality. That forced Ford to reveal its testing discoveries and risk mitigation plan. Instead of the expected $5M–10M in wrongful death lawsuit settlements, an incensed jury hit Ford with a $128M settlement.

1.3.2 Estimating the Cost of Failure

As we saw in the failure example for the Ford Pinto, there are different kinds of business risks and different kinds of business losses that can occur from these risks.

It is important for the tester to understand the different kinds of business losses in order to identify the most appropriate kinds of testing that can mitigate the losses.

Different Kinds of Business Losses

- **revenue or profit**
- **testing resources (skills, tools, and equipment)**
- **customers**
- **litigation**

One of the first measures used by a business to put boundaries around testing is the cost of testing. Regardless of the size of the risk to be reduced by testing, there is a cost associated with performing the tests. Testing does not contribute directly to the bottom-line of a business. Spending $5M on more car testing does not result in an offsetting $5M in increased car sales; therefore, regardless of how well planned and executed the tests are, testing reduces the total profit of the final product.

Unfortunately for project budgets, the cost of testing goes beyond the immediate testing efforts. As the authors of this textbook advocate, good testers need good training, good tools, and good testing environments. These resources are not one-time expenses. Most of these costs are ongoing.

The final two kinds of business losses (customer and litigation) typically represent the highest risk because the cost to the company cannot be forecast as accurately as tester salaries, tools, and facilities. The loss of customers due to perceived issues of poor quality or unsafe products can directly affect the bottom-line of the company, but how many customers will be lost as a result? Part of the answer lies in how the customer developed the negative perception, that is, by trade journal, magazine, newspaper, or TV news commentator, to mention a few ways. To complete the loss cycle, if enough customers develop a negative perception, then large numbers of individual lawsuits or class action suits might result. The loss from litigation might be beyond anyone's ability to imagine, much less to forecast. Finally, at some level the tester must realize that, for test planning purposes, an unhappy customer can do a company as much financial damage as an injured customer.

1.3.3 Basili and Boehm's Rule of Exponentially Increasing Costs to Correct New Software

Managers and executives of companies that develop computer software have perpetuated the myth that quality can be tested into a software product at the end of the development cycle. Quality in this context usually means software that exhibits *zero* defects when used by a customer. It is an expedient myth from a business planning perspective, but it ignores two truths: (1) Testing must be started as early as possible in the software development process to have the greatest positive impact on the quality of the product and (2) You can not test in quality … period!

The reluctance of many managers to include testing early in the development cycle comes from the perception of testing as a "watchdog" or "policeman" ready to pounce on the tiniest product flaw and cause expensive delays in making the product deadline. Ironically, just the opposite is true. The longer the delay in discovering defects in the software under development, the more expensive it is to correct the defect just prior to software release.

After spending a professional career measuring and analyzing the industry-wide practices of software development, Drs. Basili and Boehm computed some industry average costs of correcting defects in software under development. Figure 1.2 is an irrefutable proof of the axiom "test early and test often." [10A] The numbers first published in 1996 were revalidated in 2001.

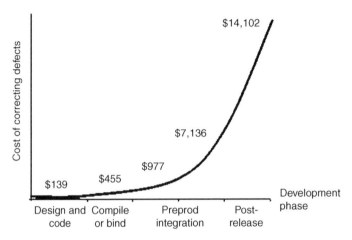

Figure 1.2   Defect correction cost profile for the software industry

At the beginning of a software development project, there is no code, just design documentation. If the design documentation is properly tested (called static testing, see Chapter 6), then the cost of correction is the cost of revising the documentation. This is typically done by a technical writer at relatively small personnel cost after the application-knowledgeable development management provides the correction. Basili finds the average cost to revise a document defect is $25.

As software code (considered fair game for static testing) is written and code execution begins, the cost of a correction rises to $139, primarily due to the expense of programmer effort. Several kinds of testing can be done; however, the code defect resolution at this development phase is correcting the code.

As pieces of program code are completed and tested, they are knitted together, or integrated into larger program modules that begin to perform meaningful business tasks. The cost of correcting these larger units of code more than doubles to $455 due to the additional time it takes to diagnose the problem in more complex code and the additional time needed to disassemble the code module into correctable pieces, correct the code, and then reassemble the code module for retesting.

As the software development team draws closer to the application or product completion, more program modules are brought together into the final delivery package. Capers estimates the cost of defect correction at this stage doubles to $7,136 per defect, primarily due to the increased difficulty in defect diagnosis and correction for this larger aggregation of code that has been packaged for delivery.

Does it really save money to wait and test the software application or product just before it goes out the door? Thirty years of industry statistics say a resounding "NO!"

The story gets worse. If the development manager decides to scrimp on testing or skip testing completely to save a few thousand dollars and "let the customers help test it," the manager will experience the largest project defect correction cost. Capers concludes that it costs on average $14,102 to correct each defect that got past the development team entirely, and that is detected by the customer who receives the application or product. Now the cost of defect correction must also include diagnosis at a distance, package level correction, and the delivery of the correction fixes to *all* customers of the product, not only to the customer who found the defect. If the customer has already installed the application or product and is using it in mission critical situations, then the developer's challenge to fix the customer's code is somewhat like trying to fix a flat tire on a car... while the car is going 50 miles per hour.

1.3.4 The Pot of Gold at the End of the Internet Rainbow

Software that provides businesses with a presence on the Internet can represent billions of dollars in new revenue to a company. This truly staggering business sales increase is possible because the Internet immediately expands the businesses' customer base from a local or regional base to a worldwide base. This phenomenal business sales increase is further possible because the Internet immediately expands the store hours from an 8-hour business day in a single time zone to 24 hours, 7 days per week.

1.3.5 The Achilles Heel of e-Business

The lure of a staggering business sales increase causes business executives to drive a company into its first Internet ventures with a haste born of a king's ransom promise. Everything done by the software development team is scrutinized to find ways to cut corners and save *time-to-market*, to cash in on the king's ransom before the competition does. One of the first software development steps to succumb to the "gold rush" is the proper documentation of requirements. The mandate is, "Just do something ... now !!!" Testing takes on the appearance of a speed bump as the executives race toward going live on the Internet.

These business executives either forget or disregard the other side of the equation, that is, the amount of risk in completing such a venture with a new, untried (from the company's perspective) technology. If the company stands to gain billions by the successful completion of the first Internet venture, the company also stands to lose billions if the first Internet venture fails. And failed they did, in droves, during 2000 through 2002.

So, two lessons can be learned from what is known as the "dot.bomb" crash. These lessons can be related surprisingly easily to other instances of companies rushing into new technology markets. First, you can take too many shortcuts when developing software. Second, you will pay for testing now or later, but the cost of testing is unavoidable. Testing now is always less expensive than testing later.

1.4 RELATIONSHIP OF TESTING TO THE SOFTWARE DEVELOPMENT LIFE CYCLE

Software testing and software development are not totally unrelated activities. The success of both processes is highly interdependent. The purpose of this section is to examine the interdependency of testing and development. Additionally, both testing and development processes are dependent on other support management processes such as requirements management, defect management, change management, and release management. Some of the ancillary management processes that directly impact the effectiveness of testing will be discussed further in Chapter 10.

1.4.1 The Evolution of Software Testing as a Technology Profession

Back in the 1950s and 1960s, software quality was a *hit-or-miss* proposition. There were no formal development processes and no formal testing processes. In fact, the only recorded testing activity during that time was reactive debugging, that is, when a program halted (frequently), the cause was sought out and corrected on the spot.

One of the more famous industry legends of that era was Captain Grace Murray Hopper, the first programmer in the Naval computing center. At that time, computers were composed of vacuum tubes and mechanical switches. One day, Captain Hopper's computer program halted abruptly. After several hours of testing the vacuum tubes and checking the mechanical switches, she found a large moth smashed between two contacts of a relay switch, thereby causing the switch fault that stopped the computer program. She "debugged" the program by removing the moth from the switch. The moth is still on display in the Naval Museum in Washington, DC.

Captain Hopper rose in military rank and professional stature in the software community as she led efforts to standardize software languages and development processes. She was still professionally active and a dynamic speaker in the 1990s.

As more and more software applications were built in the 1960s and 1970s, their longevity enabled many corrections and refinements that yielded very stable, very reliable software. At this juncture, two events occurred that are of interest to testers. First, customers began to expect software to be highly reliable and stable over extended periods of time. Software developers, sensing this growing customer expectation for extremely high-quality software, began to examine the development processes in place and refine them to shorten the incubation time of new software to attain the same stability and reliability as that found in the older, more mature systems.

Software developers of the 1970s and 1980s were, for the most part, successful in capturing their best development practices. These captured practices did provide a repeatable level of software reliability and stability. Unfortunately for customers, the level of software reliability and stability provided by these captured corporate processes was far below the level of software reliability and stability of the earlier systems. It is informed conjecture that the missing ingredient was a comparable software testing process. For unexplained reasons, this new, lower quality software became acceptable as the industry norm for a large number of computer users. [11]

Testing did not become a recognized formal software process until the 1990s when the Y2K Sword of Damocles threatened all industries that relied on computer power for their livelihood. Testing was thrust to the forefront of frantic software activities as the savior of the 21st century. Billions of dollars were spent mitigating the possible business disasters caused by the shortcuts programmers had taken for years when coding dates. These shortcuts would not allow programs to correctly process dates back and forth across the January 1, 2000 century mark or year 2000 or "Y2K" in the vernacular. The authors think that it is to the credit of the professional testing community that January 1, 2000 came and went with a collective computer whimper of problems compared to what could have happened without intervention. Thousands of businesses remained whole as the calendar century changed. Although some executives mumbled about the cost of all the Y2K testing, wiser executives recognized how close to disaster they really came, and how much of the ability to do business in the 21st century they owed to testers and testing processes.

1.4.2   The Ten Principles of Good Software Testing

Y2K testing did not start in a vacuum. Several groups of computer professionals realized the need to develop a full repertoire of software testing techniques by the mid-1980s. By the 1990s, software testing whitepapers, seminars, and journal articles began to appear. This implies that the groups of the 1980s were able to gain practical experience with their testing techniques.

Although Y2K testing did represent a very specific kind of defect detection and correction, a surprising number of more general testing techniques were appropriate for retesting the remediated (Y2K-corrected) programs. Thus, the Y2K testing frenzy directed a spotlight on the larger issues, processes, and strategies for full development life cycle software testing. These principles are an amalgam of the professional testing experience from the 1980s and 1990s and the Y2K experience to yield the following underlying software testing principles.

Principles of good testing

Testing principle 1: *Business risk can be reduced by finding defects.*
    If a good business case has been built for a new software application or product, the majority of the uncontrolled risks can be limited. Indeed, a large part of a good business case is the willingness to chance the risk of failure in a certain market space based on the perceived demand, the competition for the same market, and the timing of the market relative to current financial indicators. With those limits well established, the focus is on the best way and most timely way to capture the target

market. The cost of the needed software development is forecast, usually with some precision, if the effort is similar to prior software development efforts. The question typically missed at this juncture is, "What will it cost if the software does not work as it is advertised?" The unspoken assumption is that the software will work flawlessly this time, even though no prior software development has been flawless. Therefore, a strong connection should be made early in the process between looking for defects and avoiding risk.

Testing principle 2: *Positive and negative testing contribute to risk reduction.*
    Positive testing is simply the verification that the new software works as advertised. This seems like common sense, but based on the authors' experience with software during the past 20 years, new off-the-shelf software continues to have defects right out of the package that scream, "Nobody tested me!" There is no reason to expect that new corporate software systems have a better track record. Similarly, negative testing is simply the verification that customers can not break the software under normal business situations. This kind of testing is most often omitted from the software development because it is more time consuming than positive testing; it requires more tester creativity to perform than positive testing, and it is not overtly risk-driven.

Testing principle 3: *Static and execution testing contribute to risk reduction.*
    The preponderance of software testing conducted today involves executing the program code under development. Functional, structural (nonfunctional), and performance testing must execute program code to complete the tests. A small but growing number of testing teams and organizations have awakened to the fact that there are a large number of documents produced during software development that, if reviewed for defects (static testing), could significantly reduce the number of execution defects *before* the code is written. The corollary statement is that the best programmers in the organization cannot overcome bad requirements or bad specifications by writing good code.

Testing principle 4: *Automated test tools can contribute to risk reduction.*
    As software has become orders of magnitude more complex than the COBOL, PL/1, or FORTRAN systems of yesterday, new types of business risks have arisen. These new risks are most often found in the performance area where system response times and high volumes of throughput are critical to business success. This makes them impossible to test manually. It is true that performance testing tools are quite expensive. It is also true that the potential risk due to poor performance can exceed the cost of the performance test tools by several orders of magnitude. As of 2004, some companies still consider a performance test that involves calling in 200 employees on a Saturday, feeding them pizza, and asking them to pound on a new application all at the same time for several hours. As we will discuss in Chapter 9, this kind of manual testing has severe limitations, including typically an inadequate number of employees that volunteer to test (What happens if you need to test 3000 users and have only 200 employees?) and the nonrepeatability of test results because no one performs a manual test exactly the same way twice. The last 5 years of automated performance test tool maturity has prompted the strong consideration of testing tools to replace other kinds of manual testing when conditions are favorable.

Testing principle 5: *Make the highest risks the first testing priority.*

When faced with limited testing staff, limited testing tools, and limited time to complete the testing (as most testing projects are), it is important to ensure that there are sufficient testing resources to address at least the top business risks. When testing resources cannot cover the top business risks, proceeding with testing anyway will give the system stakeholders the false expectation that the company will not be torpedoed and sunk by software defects.

Testing principle 6: *Make the most frequent business activities (the 80/20 rule) the second testing priority.*

Once you have the real business killers well within your testing sights, consider the second priority to be the most frequent business activities. It is common industry knowledge that 80% of any daily business activity is provided by 20% of the business system functions, transactions, or workflow. This is known as the *80/20 rule.* So concentrate the testing on the 20% that really drives the business. Because the scarcity of testing resources continues to be a concern, this approach provides the most testing "bang for the buck." The other 80% of the business system typically represents the exception transactions that are invoked only when the most active 20% cannot solve a problem. An exception to this approach is a business activity that occurs very seldom, but its testing importance is way beyond its indication by frequency of use. The classic example of a sleeper business activity is a year-end closing for a financial system.

Testing principle 7: *Statistical analyses of defect arrival patterns and other defect characteristics are a very effective way to forecast testing completion.*

To date, no one has reported the exhaustive testing of every aspect of any reasonably complex business software system. So how does a tester know when the testing is complete? A group of noted statisticians observed a striking parallel between the defect arrival, or discovery patterns in software under development, and a family of statistical models called the Weibull distribution. The good news is that the intelligent use of these statistical models enables the tester to predict within 10%–20% the total number of defects that should be discovered in a software implementation. These models and their ability to predict human behavior (software development) have been around for at least 20 years. The bad news is that we have not found any significantly better ways to develop software during the same 20 years, even though programming languages have gone through multiple new and powerful paradigms. Chapter 12 takes a closer look at these models and how they can assist the tester.

Testing principle 8: *Test the system the way customers will use it.*

This principle seems so intuitive; however, the authors see examples of software every year that simply were not tested from the customer's perspective. The following is a case in point. A major retail chain of toy stores implemented a Web site on the public Internet. Dr. Everett attempted to buy four toys for his grandchildren on this toy store Internet Web site with catalog numbers in hand. Finding the toys to purchase was very difficult and took over 45 min to achieve. When he finally found all four toys and placed them in his shopping cart, Dr. Everett was unable to complete the purchase. The web page that asked for his delivery address continually responded with the nastygram, "City required, please provide your city name," even though he entered his city name in the appropriate field several different ways, including lowercase, uppercase, and abbreviated formats. In frustration, he abandoned the incomplete purchase. Thinking that he would at least alert the toy store to their Internet problem, Dr. Everett clicked the *Help* button. In the field entitled, "Give us your comments," he described his roadblock to completing the purchase. When he clicked the *Submit* button, a name and address page appeared. Upon completion of the name and address page, he clicked the next *Submit* button, only to receive the "City required, please provide your city name" nastygram again. The application programmers earned an "A" for city field code reuse and an "F" for not testing the city field code in the first place.

An address is a pretty basic piece of customer-supplied business information. The company had a software defect in the customer address code that resulted in the direct loss of business. The defect was such that the company also could not easily learn why they were losing business from their customers. It took this company less than a year to close their Web site because it was unprofitable … perhaps all because nobody tested a city field code routine.

Testing principle 9: *Assume the defects are the result of process and not personality.*

This principle presents an organizational behavior challenge for the tester. Good software developers naturally feel a sense of ownership regarding the programming they produce. Many aspects of the ownership can be positive and can motivate developers to do their best possible work. At least one aspect of the ownership can be negative, causing the developer to deny less-than-perfect results. The tester must find a way to focus on the software defect without seeking to place blame.

Many organizations have started tracking the source of software defects to verify proper matching of programming task with programmer skills. If a mismatch exists, the management process responsible for assigning development teams is truly at fault, not the programmer who is working beyond his or her skill level. If the skills are well matched to the tasks, the question becomes one of providing processes that assist the developer in writing error-free code, that is, programming standards, design walkthroughs, code walkthroughs, and logic-checking software tools. If the execution phase is the first time anyone else on the development team sees the code, the development process provided no safety net for the developer before the code has been executed. In this case, the tester can wear the white hat and, by identifying defects, ultimately assist the improvement of the development process that helps the developers write better code.

Testing principle 10: *Testing for defects is an investment as well as a cost.*

Most executives, directors, and managers tend to view testing only as an expense, and to ask questions such as "How many people? How many weeks delay? How much equipment? and How many tools?" Although these cost factors represent a legitimate part of the overall business picture, so do the tangible benefits that can offset the testing costs, business risk reduction notwithstanding. Some of the benefits can be realized during the current testing projects by the intelligent use of automated testing tools. In the right situations, automated testing tools can reduce the overall cost of testing when compared with the same testing done manually. Other benefits can be realized on the next testing projects by the reuse of testing scripts and the reuse of defect discovery patterns. When testing scripts are written, validated, and executed, they constitute reusable intelligence for the system being scripted. This "canned" knowledge can be applied to the next version of the same system or to new systems with similar functionality. The technique of reusing test scripts on a subsequent version is called *regression testing*. Defect discovery patterns, when collected over a number of development projects, can be used to more accurately forecast the completion of testing. These same testing histories can also be used to verify that improvements in development processes really do improve the system being developed. Historical defect patterns and their usefulness are explored in Chapter 12.

1.4.3   The Game of "Gossip"

Capers Jones, has some revealing information about the source of software defects. Figure 1.3 shows a plot of his findings on the same software development axis as the defect correction cost plot. [10B]

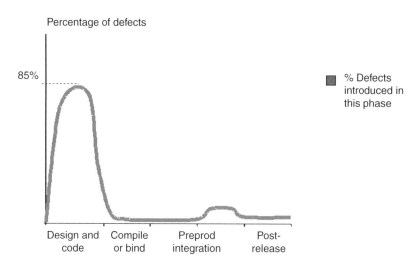

Figure 1.3   Percentage of defects. Applied Software Measurement, Capers Jones, 1996

The findings tell us that 85% of all software defects are introduced at the earliest phase of development before any code has been executed ! If there is no code execution, then what is the source of this mountain of defects? The answer is the documentation, that is, the requirements, the specifications, the data design, the process design, the interface design, the database structure design, the platform design, and the connectivity design. Intuitively, this seems reasonable. If the system design documentation is incorrect or incomplete, then no programmer can overcome a bad design with good code. A dearth of requirements, the most fundamental development documentation, is endemic to software development. The typical developer's attitude is, "Just tell me what you want and I'll build it."

To demonstrate the fallacy of bypassing requirements documentation, recall the children's game called "Gossip" in which everyone stands around in a circle, and the game leader whispers something to the person on his or her right. That person then whispers the same thing to the person on his or her right, and so on around the ring. When the whispered message makes it around the ring to the last person, the person says the message aloud, and the leader compares it to the original message. Usually, the whole circle of children burst out laughing because the original message was twisted and turned as it went around the circle. Now replace the children in the circle with a business manager who wants a new software system or another product, a director of software development, a software development manager, and say four senior software developers. The director starts the game by whispering his/her new software application requirements to the nearest manager in the circle. Would you bet your company's future on the outcome of the gossip circle? Many companies still do.

1.5   TESTER VERSUS DEVELOPER ROLES IN SOFTWARE TESTING

In the beginning, there was the software developer and he was mighty. He could write specifications, could code programs, could test programs, and could deliver perfect systems. Testers were nontechnical employees who volunteered to come into the office on a weekend and pound on a computer keyboard like a trained monkey in exchange for pizza and beer. The emergence of a massive Y2K catastrophe threat changed technical perceptions forever. The software developer's shiny armor of invincibility was considerably tarnished, whereas the tester's technical acumen rose and shone like the sun. It is now very clear that both the developer and the tester have specific, complementary, highly technical roles to fulfill in the development of good software. This section examines some of the issues around these new roles.

1.5.1   A Brief History of Application Quality Expectations, or "Paradise Lost"

The first software development and operation environments were closed to the end-user. These systems were predominantly batch processing, that is, end-users fed the systems boxes and boxes of daily transactions on punch cards or paper tape and then received the reports the next day or the next week. What happened in between the submissions of batches and the production of reports was considered magic.

If problems occurred on either the input or output side during the batch runs, the end-user never knew it. This closed environment enabled programmers to correct a defect without the end-user's knowledge of the nature of the defect, the nature of the correction, or the amount of time necessary to perform the correction. Therefore, the end-user perceived the system to be perfect. Continued system maintenance over a number of years did, in fact, yield software that was incredibly stable and defect-free.

As the closed system was opened to the end-user via dumb terminals (data display only, no process intelligence like personal computers), the end-user saw how flawlessly this mature software worked. When newer software systems were developed, the systems' immaturity was immediately evident by comparison with the tried and true older systems. Initially, some developers lost their jobs over the poor quality of the new software. End-user pressure to return to the quality of the older systems prompted software development groups to seek and employ development processes for delivering the same software quality. This software was not necessarily better, just consistent in quality. Testing was considered "monkey-work." The authors of this textbook contend that, because testing was held in such low esteem, developers with the best processes soon hit a quality brick wall. The developers' response to end-user complaints of software defects, instability, and unreliability became, "We are using the best development processes in the industry. This is the best we can do."

After a couple of decades of hearing "This is the best we can do," end-users and software customers apparently began to believe it. Still, no professional testing was done. Several books were published about the phenomenon of end-user quality expectations converging downward to meet the software developers' assurance of best effort. Mark Minasi's book, *The Software Conspiracy*, notes the resurging consumer awareness of the relatively poor quality of the new century software. Mark documented a growing consumer constituency that started sending the message, "You *can* do much better" to the software industry through selective product boycotts. [11] Smart software developers began to realize that if they were going to survive in the marketplace, they must team with professional testers to get over the quality brick wall.

To illustrate the point, ask yourself how many times you must reboot your business computer each year. If you reboot more than once or twice a year and have not complained bitterly to your business software retailer, welcome to the world of lower software expectations.

1.5.2 The Role of Testing Professionals in Software Development

Many software professions require very sophisticated technical skills. These professions include software developers, database developers, network developers, and systems administrators. The authors contend that the best software testers must have advanced skills drawn from all of these software professions. No other software professional except the software architect has a similar need for such a broad range of technical skills at such a deep level of understanding. Without this breadth of technical knowledge and advanced skills, a senior-level software tester could not design, much less execute, the complex testing plans necessary at system completion time for e-business applications.

What does the accomplished software tester do with this broad technical knowledge base? The software tester's singular role is that of a verifier. The tester takes an objective look at the software in progress that is independent of the authors of development documents and of program code and determines through repeated testing whether the software matches its requirements and specifications. The tester is expected to tell the development team which requirements and specifications are met and which requirements and specifications are not met. If the test results are descriptive enough to provide clues to the sources of defects, the tester then adds value to the developer's effort to diagnose these defects; however, the full diagnosis and correction of defects remain solely the developer's responsibility.

What else does a tester do besides validating software? The professional answer is plan, plan, and plan. Testing activities are always short of time, staff, equipment, or all three; therefore, the expert tester must identify the critical areas of software to be tested and the most efficient ways to complete that testing. As with all technical projects, these kinds of decisions must be made and cast into a plan and schedule for testing. Then, the tester must manage the plan and schedule to complete the testing.

1.5.3   The Role of Test Tool Experts in Software Development

Mature automated test tools began to arise in the marketplace around 1995. The good news is that these tools enable software testers to do testing more effectively than by using any manual procedure. In many cases, these tools have enabled software testers to do testing that is impossible to perform manually. Although manual testing still has a place in the software tester's folio of approaches, the use of automated test tools has become the primary strategy.

With over 300 automated test tools in the market, a new testing role emerged that is responsible for identifying the right tool for the right testing, installing the tool, and ensuring that the tool is operating correctly for the test team. The first testing professionals to fill this role tended to specialize in certain kinds of tools from just one or two vendors. As the tool suites grew and matured, the test tool experts found it necessary to broaden their specialty across more tool types and tool vendors. The testing paradigms behind these test tools is examined in Chapter 11.

The impetus behind test tool experts expanding their tool expertise is the software testing community's recognition that no single test tool can support all the different kinds of tests that are necessary across the entire development life cycle.

1.5.4 Who Is on the Test Team?

As with all other software professions, the software testing profession has entry-level skills, intermediate-level skills, and advanced skills. A good test team has a mix of skill levels represented by its members. This enables the more experienced testers to be responsible for the test planning, scheduling, and analysis of test results. The intermediate-level testers can work within the test plan to create the test scenarios, cases, and scripts that follow the plan. Then, with the advice and mentoring of the senior testers, a mix of intermediate-level and entry-level testers executes the tests.

1.6 PUTTING SOFTWARE TESTING IN PERSPECTIVE

Billions of dollars in business are lost annually because companies and software vendors fail to adequately test their software systems and products. These kinds of business losses are expected to continue as long as testing is considered just another checkmark on a "To-do" list or a task given to employees who are on the bench and have nothing else to do.

Testing is, in fact, a professional role that requires technical skills and a mindset that encourages the early discovery of the problems that represent real business risks. Although this textbook covers software testing in detail, many of the testing concepts and techniques it presents can be applied to other engineering disciplines and professions, as well as many personal pursuits.

1.7 SUMMARY

There are many opportunities for testing in both professional and personal life. We first explored some examples of non-computer-related testing that show patterns of thinking and behavior useful for software testing. Then, we examined some of the boundaries imposed upon testing by financial considerations, time considerations, and other business limitations.

1.7.1 The Four Primary Objectives of Testing

Testing can be applied to a wide range of development projects in a large number of industries. In contrast to the diversity of testing scenarios and uses is a common underpinning of objectives. The primary motivation for testing all business development projects is the same: to reduce the risk of unplanned expense or, worse, the risk of failure. This primary motivation is divided into four interrelated testing objectives.

1. **Identify the magnitude and sources of development risk reducible by testing**
2. **Perform testing to reduce identified risk**
3. **Know when testing is completed**
4. **Manage testing as a standard project within the development project**

1.7.2   Development Axiom—Quality Must Be Built In Because Quality Cannot Be Tested In

Testing is concerned with what is in the product or system and what is missing. Testing can only verify the product or system and its operation against predetermined criteria. Testing neither adds nor takes away anything. Quality is an issue that is decided upon during the requirements and design phases by the development project owners or requesting customers. Quality is not decided at testing time.

1.7.3   The Evolution of Software Testing as a Technology Profession

Back in the 1950s and 1960s, software quality was a hit-or-miss proposition. There were no formal development processes and no formal testing processes. Software developers of the 1970s and 1980s were, for the most part, successful in capturing their best development practices. This capture provided a repeatable level of software reliability and stability. Unfortunately for customers, the level of software reliability and stability provided by these repeatable corporate processes was far below the level of software reliability and stability of the earlier systems. It is an informed conjecture that the missing ingredient was a comparable software testing process. For unexplained reasons, this new, lower quality software became acceptable as the norm to a large number of computer users.

Testing did not become a recognized formal software process until the 1990s when the Y2K Sword of Damocles threatened all industries that somehow relied on computer power for their livelihood. Then, testing was thrust to the forefront of software activities as the savior of the 21st century. Billions of dollars were spent mitigating the possible business disasters caused by the shortcuts programmers had taken when coding dates.

1.7.4   The Ten Principles of Good Software Testing

Y2K testing did not start in a vacuum. Several groups of computer professionals realized the need to develop a full repertoire of software testing techniques by the mid-1980s. By the 1990s, software testing whitepapers, seminars, and journal articles began to appear. This indicates that the groups of the 1980s were able to gain practical experience with their testing techniques.

Although Y2K testing did represent a very specific kind of defect detection and correction, a surprising number of more general testing techniques were appropriate for retesting the remediated (Y2K-corrected) programs. Thus, the Y2K testing frenzy directed a spotlight on the larger issues, processes, and strategies for full development life cycle software testing. These principles are an amalgam of the professional testing experience from the 1980s and 1990s and the Y2K experience to yield the following underlying software testing principles.

Principles of good testing

1. **Business risk can be reduced by finding defects.**
2. **Positive and negative testing contribute to risk reduction.**
3. **Static and execution testing contribute to risk reduction.**
4. **Automated test tools can substantially contribute to risk reduction.**
5. **Make the highest risks the first testing priority.**
6. **Make the most frequent business activities (the 80/20 rule) the second testing priority.**
7. **Statistical analyses of defect arrival patterns and other defect characteristics are a very effective way to forecast testing completion.**
8. **Test the system the way customers will use it.**
9. **Assume that defects are the result of process and not personality.**
10. **Testing for defects is an investment as well as a cost.**

KEY TERMS

Test limits	Testing completion	Risk assessment
Testing objectives	Verifier	Return on investment
Multiple testing	Requirements	(ROI)
approaches	Development risk	80/20 rule

KEY CONCEPTS

- Testing is a technical profession with a significantly different mindset, and with significantly different concepts and skills from those of the technical developer profession.
- All engineering projects introduce defects into the new system or product. Making a business decision not to find the defects, by not testing, will not make them go away.

- Testing should start at the beginning of a development project because everything produced by the project is an excellent test candidate.

- To be most effective, testing plans and activities should focus on known business risk.

- No business testing project can ever exhaustively test for every possible defect in a product or service because of finite limitations in funds, skills, and resources.

- The real challenge for experienced testers is to identify what can go untested with the least impact to the business.

Chapter 2

The Software Development Life Cycle

LEARNING OBJECTIVES

- to recognize that an information systems development project follows a well-defined system development life cycle (SDLC) methodology
- to examine the separate data and process models within an SDLC
- to identify the more popular SDLC methodologies
- to list the key features of the phased development methodology (PDM)
- to identify where software testing occurs in the PDM

2.1 INTRODUCTION

The development of an information system demands the commitment of valuable company resources and time. Large projects often require millions of dollars of effort and take years to complete. Specific sequences of activities have been devised to guide developers along a path that repeatedly delivers quality software on time and within budget. In this chapter, we describe how collections of the more popular software activities have evolved, and then focus on one collection named the PDM, which is especially effective in providing an overall framework for software development.

2.2 METHODOLOGIES AND TOOLS

Two terms that one often hears in relation to information systems development are methodologies and tools. A *methodology* is a recommended way of doing something, and a *tool* is a device for accomplishing a task. Relating these terms to the

Software Testing: Testing Across the Entire Software Development Life Cycle, by G. D. Everett and R. McLeod, Jr.
Copyright © 2007 John Wiley & Sons, Inc.

building of a house, the arhchitect's blueprint is a methodology (the architect's recommended way of building the house), and the tools are what the construction workers use to actually build the house (nail guns, circular saws, and electric drills).

An *information system methodology* is a recommended way to develop an information system. A System Development Life Cycle (SDLC) is a series of stages within the methodology that are followed in the process of developing and revising an information system. A *stage* is a segment of an SDLC that consists of certain types of activity. Stages are usually completed in a certain sequence using software development tools.

Developers use system design tools for data, process, and object modeling. Data modeling tools include entity-relationship diagrams (ERDs) and data dictionaries. Process modeling tools include data flow diagrams (DFDs) and use case diagrams. Object modeling tools include class and sequence diagrams. Business processing uses workflow diagrams (WFDs).

2.3 THE EVOLUTION OF SYSTEM DEVELOPMENT LIFE CYCLES

When the first business computer was installed at General Electric in 1954, the developers had no previous experiences to guide them in the right direction. They were forced to use trial and error. Gradually, the developers compiled a list of Do's and Don'ts to cut down on the errors and increase the likelihood that the next development project would be more successful.

2.3.1 The Classical SDLC

The lists of Do's were the beginning of an SDLC. The first SDLC structure, which we will call the *classical SDLC*, consisted of four stages—planning, analysis, design, and implementation. Planning consisted of such things as defining the problem to be solved or specifying the objectives of the new system. Analysis consisted of conducting a system study for the purpose of thoroughly understanding the existing system. Design consisted of defining the processes and data to be used in the new system. Implementation consisted of preparing the software, building the data files, assembling the hardware, and cutting over to the new system. Figure 2.1 illustrates how these stages were intended to be taken in sequence. The term *waterfall development life cycle* is used today to describe the classical SDLC because it was based on the assumption that each stage would be executed a single time in a specific sequence.

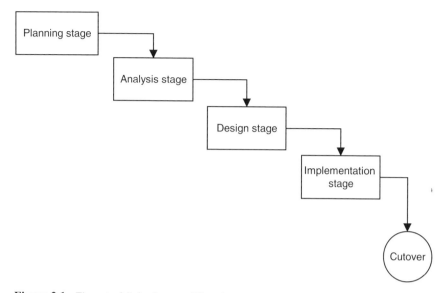

Figure 2.1   The waterfall development life cycle

2.3.2 Prototyping

Although the sequence of the classical SDLC stages was intuitively logical, there were two major weaknesses. First, it took from 3 to 5 years to go through the stages in order. All too frequently, the business market targeted by the new system had time to move out from under the new system. Second, there was invariably a need to backtrack and repeat stages or portions of stages to accommodate changes in business requirements or changes in the business market.

Developers came to the conclusion that a better approach would be to expect that interim changes would be the rule rather than the exception. The result was *prototyping:* the development of a system by means of a series of iterations to incorporate midstream changes until the system meets all the business requirements. Figure 2.2 shows how the prototyping stages are arranged with any of the first four stages repeated until the user approves the prototype. Stage names different from those in the classical SDLC are used in the figure, but they continue the logical sequence that begins with planning and concludes with implementation.

In some projects, the user is unable to specifically define what the system will accomplish and how it will accomplish it. In these cases, developers use prototyping to define the user's needs. This kind of prototype is called a *requirements prototype.* The prototype is often just a nonoperational shell of the intended system. Once it is approved, it serves as the blueprint for development of the system following an

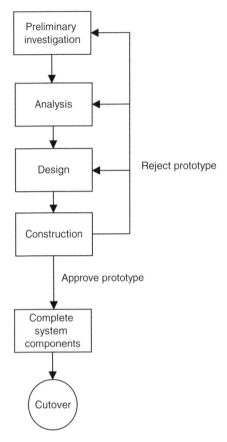

Figure 2.2   The prototyping development life cycle

SDLC methodology. Figure 2.2 also illustrates the requirements prototype by virtue of the design iteration, with the blueprint serving as the basis for completing the system components such as software, hardware, and data. In other cases, a prototype called an *evolutionary prototype* is built to contain all of the operational features of the system and is put into use upon approval.

Although the classical SDLC has been largely replaced, prototyping continues to be used in many development projects, especially those of relatively simple PC-based systems like electronic spreadsheets and database management systems.

2.3.3   Rapid Application Development

Computer consultant James Martin conceived of the *rapid application development* (*RAD*) in an effort to expand the classical SDLC to larger scale projects while substantially reducing the implementation time by 2–3 years. [12] RAD consists

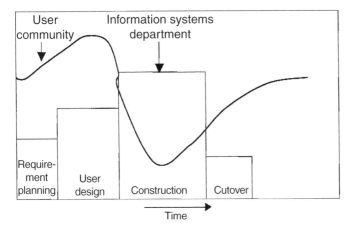

Figure 2.3   The RAD life cycle compared with a classical SDLC. *Source:* James Martin, *Rapid Application Development*, Prentice Hall, New York, 1991, page 127. Reprinted by permission of Pearson Education, Inc, Upper Saddle River, NJ.

of basically the same stages as the classical SDLC, but they are augmented with heavier user involvement, use of computer-based development tools, and skilled with advanced tools (SWAT) teams. Figure 2.3 compares RAD with the classical approach and illustrates how users play much greater roles, especially during the early stages.

The information systems developers are able to spend less effort to complete tasks because they use computer-aided software engineering (CASE) tools. Sometimes the information systems developers are organized into specialized teams, called SWAT teams, such as those specializing in activities like economic justification and systems designs like those involving Web sites and wireless communications. Many large firms using large computer systems today are committed to RAD as their primary SDLC.

An SDLC that incorporates the best features of prototyping and RAD is the phased development methodology (PDM). Because it is the methodology that we will use in this text, it is described in detail on the remaining pages of this chapter.

2.4   THE PHASED DEVELOPMENT METHODOLOGY

The main underlying concept of phased development is that the system can be subdivided into subsystems or modules. Each subsystem represents the objective of a separate development phase. A *phase* is a series of SDLC stages that are completed for a subset of a system, a subsystem, or module. Once work on the individual phases is completed, the subsystems are integrated to form a whole solution.

2.4.1   Life Cycle Stages

Figure 2.4 illustrates how the project begins with a preliminary investigation. Then the analysis, design, and preliminary construction stages are executed in an iterative manner for each phase until that phase receives user approval. Then, the two final stages complete the project. This entire process represents the first cycle in the life of the system being developed. The next releases of the system will follow the same process paths to produce the second-third, and fourth cycles in the life of the system. The life cycle is not considered complete until the system is sunset.

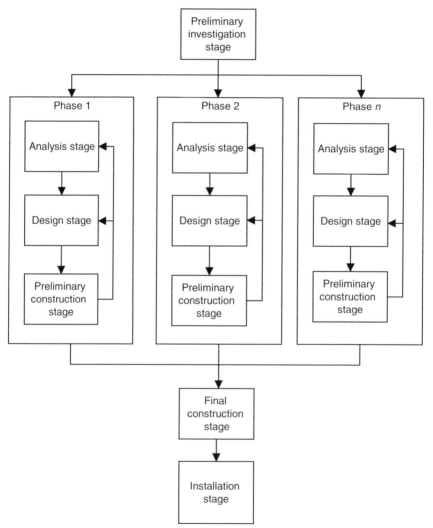

Figure 2.4   PDM stages and phases

2.4.2   System Development Phases

Figure 2.5 shows how the analysis, design, and preliminary construction stages are repeated for a data warehousing project, assuming that the subsystems include a staging area, the warehouse data repository, and an information delivery system. The work on each subsystem is a phase.

2.4.3   Software Testing in the Stages

Some kind of software testing is normally performed in every development phase except Installation. The Preliminary INVESTIGATION, Analysis, and Design phases are "paper and pencil" exercises because all of these phase results are documents. No code is written in these phases, so no test executions can be performed.

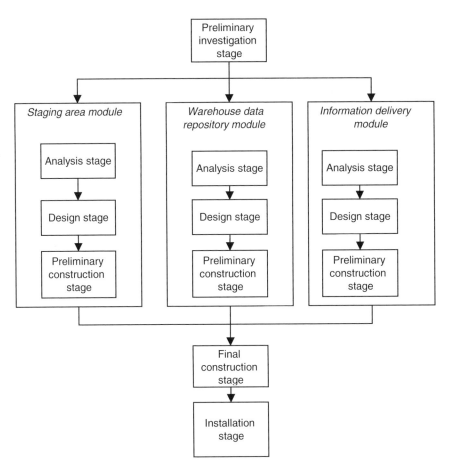

Figure 2.5   PDM phases of a data warehousing project

That is ok because there is plenty to test in the documentation of the first three phases. Documents are tested to verify they are correct, complete, accurate, use good spelling, use good grammar, and are properly formatted. This kind of manual testing is sometimes called "paper and pencil testing" because computer execution is not required. The more formally recognized term for this document testing is *static testing*. As we have seen in Chapter 1, if the system requirements are not static tested, then errors in the requirements will show up later as expensive programming defects. The PDM demonstrates that there are documents written *before* the requirements documents that can, in fact, cause the requirements documents to have errors. This documentation dependency further underscores the importance of the tested correctness of the earliest documents written.

Programmers do not normally refer to their code as "documentation," but in fact it needs to be static tested like a document. If you have ever participated in code inspections or code walk-throughs, these are some of the ways code is static tested before it is executed for functional, structural, and performance verification.

As the development progresses, other documents are produced that need to be static tested as well. Examples of these later documents are End User Guides, Operator Guides, Training Manuals, and Installation Guides.

Once the development staff begins to write program code, additional kinds of testing are needed as the code begins to work and are successively larger components or modules of the application. Chapters 7–9 will provide a detailed treatment of the code execution kinds of testing. The majority of this execution testing is considered "active" testing because the tests intentionally cause the code to behave in certain expected ways. Once the new system is installed, some kind of monitoring will probably be employed to verify the continued operation of the system as designed and tested. This kind of testing is considered "passive" testing because the tests do not cause the code to behave in certain ways; rather, the tests only observe and report the behavior of the system doing routine business.

The Installation phase of the PDM is the only phase in which no testing occurs. This phase presents its own challenges to the development and production teams but not the testing team. The testing team has already validated that the system will successfully install and that the persons responsible for operating the system can perform the install correctly. This installation verification is accomplished in the last steps in the Final construction phase. To understand this approach better, place yourself in the role of the new system owner who must sign a document saying that the new system is ready for installation in production. Remember that production is the way your company sustains daily business on the computer. Putting anything untried in production is playing Russian Roulette with your entire business. Are you really going to agree that the new system is ready for installation in production without seeing proof that the new system passed all Final construction tests? We hope not.

Table 2.1 is a summary of the above testing discussion by PDM phase with a little additional detail in the code producing phases to set the stage for the Chapters 7–9 presentations.

Table 2.1   Testing in the PDM

Stage	Type of testing
Preliminary investigation	None
Analysis	• Static testing of requirements
Design	• Static testing of all design documents
Preliminary construction	• Static testing of all codes
	• Functional tests
	• Performance tests
Final construction	• Static testing of users guide, operators guide, installation guide, and training material
	• Performance tests
	• Load tests
	• User acceptance testing
	• Installation testing
Installation	None
Postimplementation evaluation	• Monitoring of operation and performance within prescribed boundaries

We will now describe each stage of the PDM.

2.5   THE PRELIMINARY INVESTIGATION STAGE

During preliminary investigation, the developers perform an enterprise analysis. From this analysis the developers define system goals, objectives, and performance criteria. The developers evaluate system and project risk. Finally, the developer evaluates system and project feasibility. The stage is completed when the developers receive user approval of their findings and recommendations to proceed.

2.5.1   Perform Enterprise Analysis

As the developers seek to become familiar with the organization and its environment, two graphical diagrams can provide a framework. Figure 2.6 is the general systems model of an example called the "firm," which contains all of the required components and flows of an organization functioning as a closed-loop, managed system. The developers can ensure that all process components and data flows are present and performing as intended. For example, does the firm have standards of performance that managers are to achieve ? Another example, does information flow directly to management from the physical system of the firm where the firm's operations are performed?

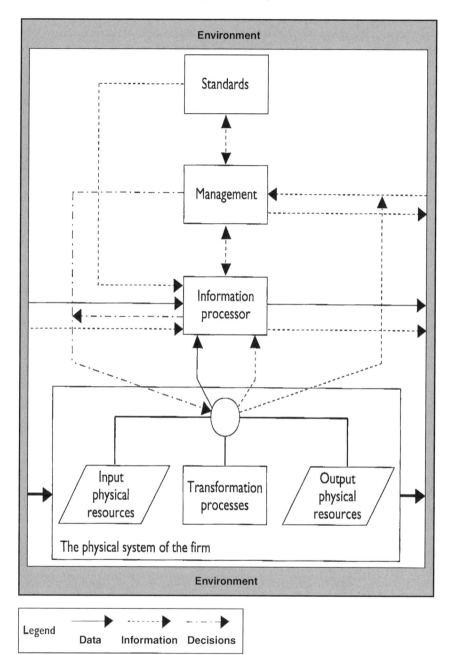

Figure 2.6 The general systems model of the firm

A similar framework is the model of the firm in its environment in Figure 2.7. This diagram shows eight elements that exist in the firm's environment. The firm is connected to the elements by resource flows of personnel, materials, machines, money, data, and information. This model enables the developers to recognize all of the environmental elements and consider their relationships within the firm.

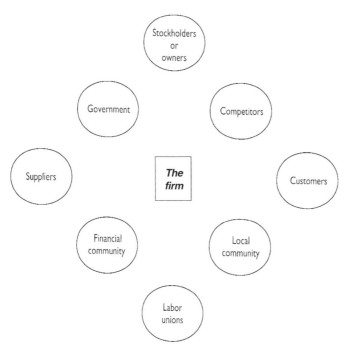

Figure 2.7   The firm in its environment

With this understanding of the enterprise and its environment, the developers can turn their attention to the system and project at hand.

2.5.2   Define System Goals, Objectives, and Performance Criteria

System goals are conditions or situations of great business importance that are to be attained. They are the reason for the project and take such forms as improved responsiveness, increased quality, and improved decision making. *System objectives* are more specific targets that, when achieved, should lead to accomplishment of the goals.

Figure 2.8 is a goal analysis form that the developers can complete to address three main goal categories:

1. system quality,

2. project management, and

3. relevance of the system to the organization.[13]

	Current context and requirements	Actions needed to meet goals
System quality		
Functionality	Frequent out-of-stock conditions, excessive inventory costs.	Implement computed - reorder points and economic order quantiy.
Maintainability		
Portability/Scalability		
Project management		
Timeliness	Management wants new inventory system as soon as possible.	Manage project with Gantt chart and milestone dates report.
Cost		
Client commitment		
Organizational relevance		
Decision-making effectiveness	Buyers have incomplete information for supplier selection.	Maintain data for each supplier on cost, quality, and shipping response.
Operations efficiency		
Competitive advantage		

Figure 2.8   A goal analysis form

The left-hand side of the form lists these main goals and their subgoals. In the center column, the developers can enter notes that describe the current situation and/or the requirements to be met by the system and project. In the right-hand column, the developers can enter actions that will be needed to meet the goals. This example contains only entries for a sampling of the cells. For a project, the developers make entries in all cells.

It is always a good idea to identify quantitative measures of the new system performance so as to avoid the risk of failing to create a system that satisfies the users' perception of the system goals. The term *performance criteria* is used to describe these quantitative measures for specific objectives. For example, if a goal of the new system is to process customer sales orders faster, then a performance criterion could be to process a customer sales order within 3 hours after receipt in the sales department if it currently takes 4 hours. With the goals quantified in such a specific way, it will be relatively easy to test the extent to which the system meets these objectives during development. If the system achieves the performance criteria objectives, then achievement of the more general goals is assured.

2.5.3   Evaluate System and Project Risk

As the developers embark on the project, they should identify any risks that they might face in terms of project or system failure. The project risk evaluation form in Figure 2.9 shows how attention can be directed at four categories that can influence risk:

1. characteristics of the organization,

2. the information system being developed,

3. the developers, and

4. the users.

Factors affecting project risk	Rating (−1, 0, +1)	Comments
Organization		
Has well-defined objectives?	+1	Has strategic business plan
Is guided by a strategic information system plan?		
Proposed system supports achievement of organizational objectives?		
Information system		
Existing model? Clear requirements?	+1	Existing system well documented
Automates routine, structured procedures?		
Affects only a single business area?		
Uses proven technology?		
Can be implemented in less than 3 months?		
Installation at only a single site?		
The developers		
Are experienced in the chosen methodology?	−1	First time to use object-oriented methodology
Are skilled at determining functional requirements?		
Are familiar with information technology?		
The users		
Have business area experience?	0	Some are experienced; some are new to the area
Have development experience?		
Are committed to the project?		
Total points	+1	

Figure 2.9   Project risk evaluation form

The form lists specific characteristics for each category that are rated and described by the developers. When a characteristic (such as the *absence* of well-defined objectives) is considered to offer a risk, it receives a rating of −1. When it does not offer a risk (such as the *presence* of well-defined objectives), it is rated +1. When the situation is borderline, it receives a rating of 0. In this example, only a sampling of the cells is completed. The rating points are summed, and the total provides an indication of the degree of risk to be faced. This total is not an absolute indicator: if the total points are positive, there may still be unacceptable business risk in the project, or if the total points are negative, the business risk may be acceptable. It usually takes the tracking and comparison of risk evaluation and actual risk results from several projects to be able to accurately interpret the meaning of the total risk points for a particular development organization for future projects.

The developers should address any characteristics receiving a rating of 0 or −1 by specifying one or more risk reduction strategies to be taken. Good risk reduction strategies are matched resources and skills with project needs, realistic completion schedules, sufficient budget, milestone reports, prototyping, documentation, education, training, and software testing.

2.5.4   Evaluate System and Project Feasibility

At this point the developers seek to confirm that the system and its project are feasible. Feasibility studies are conducted to

- evaluate technical feasibility (Does the required technology exist? Does the firm know how to develop in that technology?),
- economic feasibility (Can the system and project be justified economically from the additional revenue it will provide?),
- operational feasibility (Is the system workable considering the skills and attitudes of the people who must make it work?),
- legal and ethical feasibility (Does the system fit within legal and ethical constraints of the business? Does the system conform to local and international trade agreements?), and
- schedule feasibility (Can the system be developed in the allotted time with the proposed resources and budget?).

2.5.5   Conduct Joint Application Design (JAD) Sessions to Confirm Preliminary Findings

Having gathered much information to guide the remainder of the project, the developers must share their findings with the users before proceeding. This sharing can be accomplished by means of a JAD session. A *JAD session* is a joint meeting of developers and users, directed by a trained facilitator, where project-related findings and questions are openly discussed, making liberal use of visual aids. [14] JAD sessions are a good risk mitigation process.

The purpose of this particular JAD session is to get the information from the preliminary investigation out on the table so that developers and users agree on what the system will do (requirements) and how it will be developed (specifications).

2.5.6 Receive Approval to Proceed

The firm's top-level managers and those managers who have been directly involved with the project determine whether to proceed. Three choices are available:

1. proceed to the analysis stage;
2. repeat some of the preliminary investigation steps to provide better information for the decision; or
3. scrap the project.

When the approval to proceed is received, the next stage is analysis.

2.6 THE ANALYSIS STAGE

Each subsystem is analyzed for the purpose of determining its functional (business) requirements and then documenting those requirements.

2.6.1 Analyze Functional Requirements

The *functional requirements* are the business functions that the system is to perform. These requirements are defined by analyzing existing system documentation, conducting personal interviews and surveys with business management and staff, conducting JAD sessions, and observing the existing system in action.

2.6.2 Analyze Existing System Documentation

Documentation of the existing system can provide a valuable source of information about what the new system must do. This is especially true when the new system is a replacement or enhancement of the existing one. Existing system documentation takes the form of flowcharts, dataflow diagrams, entity-relationship diagrams, screen shots, example reports, and workflow diagrams.

2.6.3 Conduct Personal Interviews

In-depth interviews with key business owners who understand and use the existing system can represent the best source of information for the existing functional requirements. Many but not all of these same business process owners will also be an excellent source of information for the new functional requirements. Others like marketing or research executives who may have been the source of the new functional requirement requests also need to be included in the interview schedule.

2.6.4 Conduct Surveys

When information sources cannot be interviewed personally (perhaps there are too many or they are spread over a wide geographic area), surveys can be designed to gather the information in the form of mail or telephone questionnaires.

2.6.5 Conduct JAD Sessions

Another round of JAD sessions can be conducted, this time for the purpose of enabling groups to address and define the functional requirements.

2.6.6 Observe the Existing System

The developers should spend time in the user area, observing the existing system in operation and the use of on-line help or printed user guides.

2.6.7 Document Functional Requirements

Any number of documentation tools can be used to document the functional requirements, but an excellent one is the functions components matrix, illustrated in Table 2.2.

The matrix lists the functions that the system must perform (input, processing, output, storage, and control) across the top as column headings and lists the components of the system (its resources) as row headings down the left-hand side. The resource rows include people, data, information, software, and hardware. The matrix shows what resources will be used to perform what functions and is prepared for each subsystem. The sample in Table 2.2 consists of only a sampling of entries. On the People row you specify the titles of the people and the functions that they perform. Data specifications can be in the form of data tables, files, records, or elements. Information usually needs to

Table 2.2 Functions components matrix

	Input	Processing	Output	Storage	Control
People	Data entry operator enters sales order data				Sales order clerk batches sales orders
Data				Customer master file Inventory master file Accounts receivable master file	
Information			Customer invoices Customer statements		
Software tools	Order entry program	Inventory program Accounts receivable program	Billing program	Access	
Software functions	Conduct credit check	Compute new balance on hand Determine new receivable amount			
Hardware	Data entry workstations	Server	Printers	Direct access storage devices	

be displayed as some form of output. The software is specified in terms of its components (names of programs and prewritten packages) and the functions that they perform.

All of the documentation that is accumulated in a project forms the *project dictionary*. Figure 2.10 lists the contents at this point.

I.   Problem definition

II.   System goals
a. Goal analysis form

III.   System constraints

IV.   System objectives

V.   System performance criteria / quantifiable system
objectives

VI.   Existing system documentation
   a.   Process models
      1.   Entity-relationship diagrams
      2.   Work flow diagrams
      3.   Pseudocode
   b.   Data models
      1.   Data flow diagrams
      2.   Data dictionary
   c.   Object models
      1.   Class diagrams
      2.   State diagrams

VII.   New system functional requirements
   a.   Functions components matrix
   b.   Use cases

VIII.   Development plan
   a.   Project risk evaluation form
   b.   Risk reduction strategies
   c.   Gantt chart
   d.   Computer configurations
   e.   Network diagrams
   f.   Resource availability schedule
   g.   Schedule of activities / work plan
   h.   Milestone report

IX.   Appendix
   a.   Working papers

Figure 2.10   Sample contents of the project dictionary at the end of the analysis stage

2.7   THE DESIGN STAGE

With the functional requirements specified, the developers now prepare the logical design of the new system. *Logical design* is technology independent and consists of modeling the data and the processes of the new system. Logical design consists of four basic steps:

1. Identify the feasible designs.
2. Evaluate the feasible designs.
3. Conduct JAD sessions to confirm designs and evaluations.
4. Select the best design.

The project dictionary provides the starting point for taking these steps.

2.7.1 Identify the Feasible Designs

Modern computer technology provides many possible approaches to design-ing a system configuration. For example, should the user interface employ a graphical user interface or a text-only screen layout ? Should output informa-tion be displayed on the screen or printed? Should the output be tabular or graphic? The developers consider the possible designs that are feasible in terms of the user needs, and, *for each*, consider the six types of design illustrated in Figure 2.11.

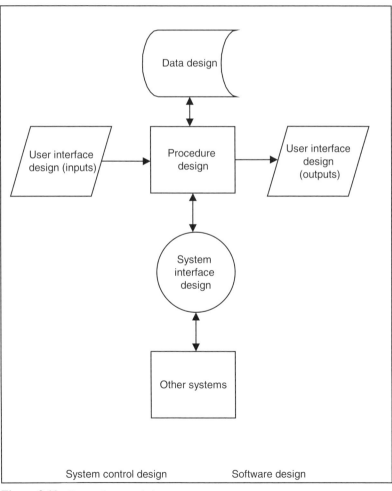

Figure 2.11   Types of system design

Design the user interfaces (*input and output*)

User interfaces often take the form of an interactive dialog consisting of both input and output. Within this framework, the output is a logical place to begin because the fundamental purpose of the system is to produce some type of output. In considering both output and input interface design, the developers evaluate the various display devices and how they are to be used.

Design the procedures

This design considers all of the functions both from the business perspective (sales, orders, and payments) and the technology perspective (shared data, security, and backup/recovery).

Design the data

Attention is given to the nature of the data that the system must store and how it will be stored (the structure and the devices).

Design the interfaces with other systems

With the input, procedure, output, and storage components designed, attention can turn to how the system will interface with other systems on the same computers, on other computers operated by the firm, and on other computers external to the firm (suppliers, vendors, shippers, and large customers).

Design the system controls

Controls must be built into each component to ensure that at audit time it can be proven by update logs that the system performs as intended.

Design the software

Determinations are made concerning how the component designs will be carried out with software. Both the processes and data of the new system are documented using the same tools that were used in documenting the existing system in the analysis stage. Then, programming languages and standards are chosen that afford the developers the best ways to express the new processes and data in lines of computer code. Both language richness and maintainability are factors in this determination.

2.7.2 Evaluate the Feasible Designs

When the Figure 2.11 framework has been followed for each of the feasible designs, they are then evaluated collectively by comparing and contrasting the advantages and disadvantages of each. An effective approach to this collective evaluation task is to prepare a table such as the one pictured in Table 2.3. The alternative designs occupy the columns, and the rows address the relevant points. Sample entries illustrate how each alternative design is evaluated and how notes are made of questions to be answered. The last row contains the user choice and the rationale that supports that choice.

Table 2.3   Alternative designs evaluation table

	Alternative 1 GUI interface and access back end	*Alternative 2 Web interface and access back end*	*Alternative n Web interface and oracle back end*
Key features	Custom-tailored interface to user needs Good relational database model		
Advantages	Developers knowledgeable in technology		Relational database with capacity for future expansion
Disadvantages		Relational database with limited capacity for future expansion	
Questions	Will this configuration be sufficient in meeting user current and future needs?		Could firm outsource oracle implementation?
User choice		This alternative preferred based primarily on functionality and ability to meet target cutover date	

This is only one of many possible approaches to feasibility evaluation. Other approaches can evaluate the systems based on how well each meets the goals specified in the goal analysis form, employ quantitative evaluations of weighted criteria, and so forth. [15]

2.7.3 Conduct JAD Sessions to Confirm Designs and Evaluations

The developers meet with the business owner managers and senior business users to confirm that all of the feasible designs were considered and that each was thoroughly evaluated. Business users and developers have worked together throughout the entire design process. This is the final, formal review before taking the design to top management for approval.

2.7.4 Select the Best Design

Armed with the evaluation data, business owner management and executives can select the best design. The management group can include project sponsors in the form of the firm's executive committee and MIS steering committee, information systems managers, and user area managers working with members of the project team who provide technical expertise. With the design selected and approved, the developers can turn their attention to preliminary construction.

2.8 THE PRELIMINARY CONSTRUCTION STAGE

During preliminary construction, the logical design is converted to a physical design. *Physical design* consists of assembling the components of people, data, information, software, hardware, and facilities that comprise a functioning system or subsystem. These components are brought to the construction as needed. For some items such as hardware, personnel, and facilities, planning can begin immediately with actual arrival coming in later stages. For example, planning can begin for user training that will actually take place close to the date when the new system is put into operation.

The preliminary construction stage is primarily concerned with software development and consists of two major steps:

1. Construct the software and test data for each module.
2. Demonstrate the modules to users and project sponsors.

This is the key user decision point in the phased development methodology pictured in Table 2.4. The user acceptance of this completed preliminary phase work determines whether analysis, design, and preliminary construction will proceed to final construction. If the preliminary phase work is not accepted by the users, the developers must iterate back thru the earlier phases making the modifications necessary to gain user acceptance the next time around.

2.8.1 Construct the Software for Each Module

The software development unfolds during this and the two final stages of the phased development. During this stage the software for each module is prepared, tested, and approved by the users. In the final construction stage, the tested modules from the preliminary construction stage are integrated to form the whole system and are tested as such. During the installation stage the system receives final user approval and is put into operation.

Table 2.4 Software development environments

	Development sandbox environment	Development integration environment	Production staging environment	Production environment
Hardware	Individual developers' workstations or designated individual server areas	Shared server space	Staging server(s)— maybe externally hosted	Production server(s)—maybe externally hosted
Access	Developers access their own hardware	Project team members, project managers	Review team, project managers	Public—might include worldwide use or limited use to enterprise intranet or other security boundaries
Activities	Coding Prototyping Individual component and page development Unit testing	Component and page integration Integration testing Integration problem resolution	System testing User acceptance testing	Public operation

Across this life cycle process, the development of custom software evolves through four environments, illustrated in Table 2.4. The software for each module is prepared and tested in the development sandbox environment. The software for the integrated system is assembled and tested in the development integration environment. User acceptance testing occurs in the production staging environment. The approved system goes into operational use in the production environment. The flow of purchased or packaged software through the environments usually starts with the production staging environment because there is no source code for the firm's programmers to develop or integrate.

A *development sandbox* consists of the required software development tools and preliminary test data that developers use in "building sandcastles." This is a term used by developers to denote trying out creative designs without constraints imposed by a rigid production environment. Locally duplicated sandboxes, called *variant sandboxes*, enable team members to simultaneously work on different releases of the same project. In this environment, developers use their own desktop or laptop computers and engage in coding, prototyping, individual component and page development, and unit testing. The important ingredients of the development environment include

- copies of the latest software files by version number prepared by the module team,
- short test data files,
- copies of all system documentation, and
- a change log that identifies the version, author, and date for each software module revision.

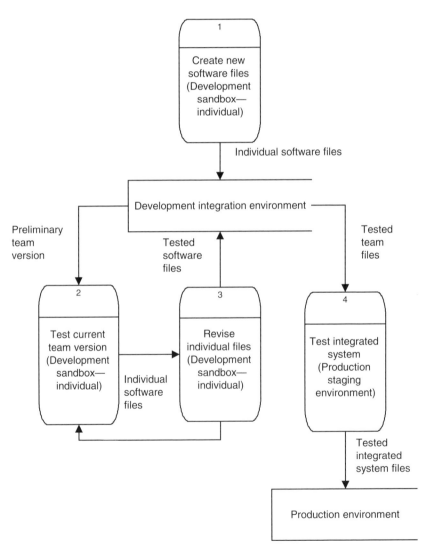

Figure 2.12   Software flow to the production environment

Figure 2.12 shows how the software flows from the development environments to the production environment. As developers complete copies of their software (Step 1), it is loaded into the development integration environment where it is made available to the members of all module teams. Each member can load the software from the development integration environment into their own sandboxes so that they can test their software to ensure that it works with the team software (Steps 2 and 3). The developers revise their software as needed and copy it back to the development integration environment (Step 3). The integrated system software is tested before entering the production environment (Step 4).

2.8.1.1 *Test the Components of Each Module*

Testing usually brings to mind software testing first, which is certainly important. But, attention should also be given to testing the other system components like the hardware, the data, and the personnel.

- *Unit tests*: The tests that are conducted on the module software are called *unit tests* or *module tests*.

- *Data tests*: Creation of the data component is so important that teams often designate it as a separate phase. Planning for the database or warehouse data repository to be used by the system must begin early in the project, perhaps as early as the Preliminary investigation stage. In the Preliminary construction stage, data testing takes the form of building subsets of the database or warehouse repository and confirming that the data structures and contents perform as anticipated by the system design independent of the software that must maintain it.

- *Hardware tests*: When the system module utilizes new hardware, tests should be conducted to ensure that the hardware operations conform to the manufacturer's promises and the module's operational requirements (processor speed, screen resolution, data storage capacity, memory capacity for multiple concurrent tasks, and so on).

- *Personnel tests*: Testing the personnel component is intended to determine whether the personnel already have sufficient skills to use the new system. The new system may require more detailed business knowledge than the old system. How does the business manager measure his or her staff's readiness? What training is available to close any skill gaps before the system "goes live?"

2.8.2 Demonstrate the New System Modules to Users and Project Sponsors

As the software modules successfully pass the tests, they are demonstrated to users and project sponsors. There are three possible outcomes of these demonstrations.

1. If significant changes are considered to be necessary, an on-the-spot feasibility study can be conducted to determine whether to scrap the project or repeat the analysis, design, and Preliminary construction stages.

2. If only minimal changes are identified, the project reverts back to the analysis stage and the changes are incorporated in the design.

3. When the users and project sponsors accept the module as demonstrated, the next step is the Final construction stage.

2.9 THE FINAL CONSTRUCTION STAGE

This is the stage where all of the components of the new system are brought together to verify readiness for installation and operation. Eight activities are performed.

1. Construct and test production-ready software.

2. Construct and test a production-ready database or warehouse data repository.

3. Install any required new hardware and connectivity.

4. Make available the physical facility.

5. Test the hardware configuration.

6. Complete the documentation.

7. Gain user acceptance to "go live."

8. Train participants and users.

With so many activities going on usually at the same time, it is important that they be well planned and managed. By virtue of being close to the cutover to the operational system, it is possible to plan the remaining tasks with considerable accuracy. It is common to revise the original implementation plan at this point to take advantage of the additional, more precise planning information available from completing the other development phases.

2.9.1 Construct and Test Production-Ready Software

The tests that are conducted of the entire system are called *system tests*. One purpose of the tests is to validate the integrated modules to ensure that they function as a system. A second purpose of the tests is to validate that the new system will correctly interact/interface with other firm systems as needed. The goal of system testing is to locate system errors before the system is put into production.

2.9.2 Construct and Test a Production-Ready Database or Warehouse Data Repository

The creation of a database or warehouse data repository can be as challenging as creation of software. This is especially true for such organizations as insurance companies and banks that maintain data for long periods of time. In addition to the type of organization, other factors that contribute to a challenging effort include the size of the firm, whether the data are already available in a computer-readable form and whether existing data are in the format required by the new system. For projects with complex data efforts, firms often outsource the development activity.

2.9.3 Install Any Required New Hardware and Connectivity

Planning for acquisition of additional hardware should begin early in the project so that the hardware is delivered, tested, and available when needed. Some new hardware might be needed as early as unit testing in the preliminary construction stage. Considerable lead time needs to be expected in order to identify potential hardware vendors, get competitive bids, complete the purchase, and physically receive the hardware.

2.9.4 Make Available the Physical Facility

Planning for any construction of new or remodeled facilities must also begin early in the project. Preparation of facilities for large-scale systems demands inclusion of features that provide for the necessary temperature and humidity controls, pollutant controls, uninterrupted power, fire detection and suppression, and security measures. Such communications-oriented systems as local and wide area networks add still another layer of complexity and importance to physical facility planning and construction.

2.9.5 Test the Hardware Configuration

Common hardware tests include testing the system to ensure its ability to access data, process data, communicate with other hardware, and handle forecast peak loads.

2.9.6 Complete the Documentation

As the project has unfolded, documentation has been added to the project dictionary. The conclusion of the Final construction stage is a good point to complete any process and data models and other documentation that will be necessary for any future system revision or reengineering efforts. This is also the time that the training material and operation guides are written and published.

2.9.7 Gain User Acceptance to "Go Live"

During this activity, the system components are installed; the user acceptance test is designed and conducted. The *user acceptance test* is the final test of the system to determine whether it meets the users' perceived needs. Acceptance by both users and system sponsors is required before the development team can proceed to the installation stage. In the event that all of the functional or performance criteria are not satisfied, the project sponsors can demand that the system be revised or modified so as to meet the standards. This rejection will require that the project revert back to previous stages.

2.9.8   Train Participants and Users

Users are typically the business managers and staff who will provide the system inputs and use the system outputs to complete daily business activities. Participants are those persons who work within the system but do not use its output for business. Logically, you want to provide training as close to the cutover date as possible so that the information will be fresh on the minds of the recipients as they put it into use. However, planning for training development and delivery must begin earlier, perhaps as early as the beginning of the project.

At this point, the developers are satisfied that the system accomplishes its objectives. The remaining step is to obtain approval from the system users and project sponsors that the system is acceptable. With that approval in the next stage, the system can be put into operational use.

2.10   THE INSTALLATION STAGE

During this stage the system components are installed, cut over to the new system is accomplished, and a postimplementation evaluation is conducted.

2.10.1   Install System Components

The unit testing and system testing in earlier stages focused on the software and data components. The user acceptance test should encompass all of the components: hardware, information, personnel, and physical facility along with the tested and verified software and data.

2.10.2   Cutover to the New System

With user approval, the system is put into use. Cutover can be immediate (for small-scale systems), phased (for larger scale systems), or parallel (where the old system is continued as the new system is gradually phased in).

2.10.3   Conduct the Postimplementation Evaluation

Some time after cutover and after the system has had time to settle down, an evaluation is made to determine whether the new system did, in fact, meet the functional and performance criteria. The evaluation can be made by users and such unbiased third parties as internal auditors and consultants. The findings of these evaluations can determine whether additional systems work is necessary.

Over time as the system is used, both formal and informal additional evaluations can be made. These evaluations form the basis for future redevelopment and reengineering projects.

2.11   PUTTING PHASED DEVELOPMENT IN PERSPECTIVE

The classical SDLC was not that bad from a logical standpoint. It is hard to find fault with a repeatable sequence of planning, analysis, design, and implementation that worked. The big weakness was that the continual need to repeat stages was not anticipated in a proactive way and had to be handled in a reactive way. Prototyping excels when it comes to the iterative design and development because that is the main idea of that methodology. The PDM is a blending of the logical sequence of the classical SDLC and proactive iterative prototyping. The main strength of the PDM is the fact that it subdivides the system into modules and then regards each as a separate phase of Analysis, Design, and Preliminary construction. It is an extremely flexible methodology that is applicable to all but exceptionally small projects, where prototyping can fulfill the need.

2.12   SUMMARY

An information system methodology is a recommended way to develop an information system. This methodology is known as an SDLC. SDLCs have evolved from classical to prototyping to RAD to phased development.

Phased development consists of six stages: Preliminary investigation, Analysis, Design, Preliminary construction, Final construction, and Installation. The Analysis, Design, and Preliminary construction stages are repeated for each subsystem, or module, of the system being developed. Each sequence of analysis, design, and preliminary construction for a module is called a phase.

During Preliminary investigation, an enterprise analysis is conducted; system objectives, goals, and performance criteria are defined; system and project risk are evaluated; and system and project feasibility are evaluated. Findings are reviewed with users in JAD sessions and approval to proceed is received.

During the analysis stage, functional requirements are analyzed using a variety of data gathering techniques and are then documented. During the Design stage, the logical design is developed by identifying feasible designs, evaluating them, conducting JAD sessions to confirm designs and evaluations, and selecting the best. Six types of design include user interface, procedure, data, interfaces with other systems, controls, and software.

During Preliminary construction, efforts proceed through three environments leading to production: development sandbox, development integration, and production staging. Development sandboxes provide all of the tools necessary for software development and are duplicated in the form of variant sandboxes to facilitate parallel software development for the multiple modules. Unit tests are conducted of not only software but the other components as well. New modules are demonstrated to users and project sponsors.

When approval to proceed is received, the Final construction stage is executed, bringing together all of the components to form an integrated system and conducting system tests of each. When the developers, users, and system sponsors are convinced that the system is performing as intended, proceed to the final stage Installation. Installation is where the system components are installed in the user area and cutover to the new system is executed. Some time after cutover, a postimplementation evaluation is conducted to verify the capability of the system to satisfy the performance criteria.

The structure of phased development that consists of separate phases for each system module is its main strength.

KEY TERMS

Methodology,
    information system
    methodology
Tools
Stage
Phase
Static testing

System goals
System objectives
Performance criteria
Joint application design
    (JAD) session
Functional
    requirement

Logical design
Physical design
Development
    sandbox
Unit test, module test
System test
User acceptance test

KEY CONCEPTS

System development life cycle
    (SDLC)
Classical SDLC
Prototyping

Rapid application development (RAD)
Phased development methodology (PDM)
Multiple software development
environments

Chapter 3

Overview of Structured Testing

LEARNING OBJECTIVES

- to recognize the value of checklists for technology processes
- to simplify the plethora of testing checklists
- to examine the usefulness of a robust, generic testing checklist

3.1 INTRODUCTION

The introduction to this book uses examples from the automobile industry to illustrate how testers think. This chapter will use examples from the aircraft industry to illustrate how testers plan.

In the mid-1930s, aircrafts were complex machines with metal skins and powerful engines that could fly high (10,000 ft) and fast (100 mph) for a substantial distance (500 miles). War clouds began to form over Europe. In preparation for possible involvement in a European conflict, the U.S. Army Air Corps asked the American aircraft manufacturers to build a "multi-engine bomber" that would fly higher (20,000 ft) and faster (250 mph) and farther (1000 miles) than any aircraft in existence. The new aircraft needed to do all these things *and* carry a 2-ton payload (bombs). Martin, Douglas, and Boeing aircraft manufacturers responded with plans and subsequent hand-built flying prototypes. The first flight tests revealed the Boeing Model 299 to perform better than Martin's 146 or Douglas's DB-1; furthermore, the Model 299 exceeded all government specifications. Jumping ahead in the story, one final compulsory flight for all competitors stood between Boeing and a business-rescuing government contract for 18 of these new bombers.

On October 30, 1935, the Boeing Model 299 prototype took off for its final acceptance flight...and promptly plunged to earth, killing all on board and completely destroying the prototype. In accordance with government bidding rules, the contract for new bombers was given to second place Martin whose prototype did finish the mandatory final acceptance flight. [16]

Software Testing: Testing Across the Entire Software Development Life Cycle, by G. D. Everett and R. McLeod, Jr. Copyright © 2007 John Wiley & Sons, Inc.

What happened to the Boeing Model 299 prototype? It is not hard to imagine how quickly Boeing wanted an answer to that question. From an economics viewpoint, losing the government contracts could force Boeing into bankruptcy because Boeing was already in dire financial straits. From an engineering point of view, an unseen design flaw could make Boeing a pariah of new aircraft designs for the government and commercial markets alike.

Boeing did discover the cause of the Model 299 prototype crash after a very intensive investigation. The good news was that the crash was caused neither by faulty design nor by faulty construction. Review of the crash revealed no inappropriate pilot action. The prototype's test pilots were the best in the industry.

The crash was caused by elevator (tail control) locks that were not removed before takeoff. These control locks are normally placed on all control surfaces (ailerons, rudder, elevators) when an aircraft is parked at an airport to prevent wind damage by moving these hinged surfaces. At the time of the crash, there was no standard understanding among the ground crew and pilots as to who was responsible for removing these control locks, either after landing or before the next takeoff. So, if both groups assumed that the other group removed the control locks, the control locks remained in place, thereby freezing the controls during takeoff with deadly consequences.

The solution to this problem was as profound as it was simple: the now ubiquitous pilot's preflight *checklist*. The preflight checklist guarantees that if an *experienced* pilot verifies each action on the checklist has been accomplished before takeoff, the takeoff can be successfully accomplished repeatedly with minimal safety risk.

3.2 CHECKLIST MENTALITY FOR SOFTWARE TESTERS

Professional software testers have found the concept of a "preflight" checklist with the same professional caveats to be an excellent way of ensuring a successful testing project.

What are the professional caveats? Before you pick up a checklist either for a pilot or a tester and attempt to fly a plane or test software, consider the professional prerequisites. The goal of the checklist is to be able to say "Yes, I have verified that" to every checklist question. For example, the following question does appear on aircraft preflight checklists: "flight controls free and correct?" It is just one short question in the middle of a list of 15 or 20 questions. If you hold a pilot's license, then your flight *experience* (2 weeks of ground school, 40 hours of flight instruction, pilot's license, and 100–5000 hours of flight as pilot in command) tells you what stick to wiggle and what wing surface movement to expect before you say to yourself, "Yes, I have verified that."

The following question appears on all professional software testing checklists: "testing success defined?" It is just one short question in the middle of a list of 15–20 questions. If you have successfully completed several major testing projects, then your testing *experience* tells you the importance of knowing how to tell when you are done testing before you can plan a successful testing project so that you can say, "Yes, I have verified that."

The pilot's preflight checklist comes from the aircraft manufacturers. Where does the software testing checklist come from? Unlike aircraft, software does not normally come with a testing checklist from the factory. Software testing checklists have historically come from three other sources.

1. A corporation's custom checklist developed by trial and error (pain and suffering) over years of internal organization experience.

2. A consulting company's commercially offered standard checklist—usually called a "methodology" or a "method" or a "process" or a "framework" developed over years of experience with many customers.

3. A consulting company's commercially offered customized checklist with the customization process developed over years of experience with many customers.

These three sources have produced more than a dozen testing checklists that the authors have professionally encountered. The number is surprising at first because 12+ is more than the three or four main ways of developing software (see Chapter 2) and less than the different kinds of software products on the commercial market. The answer lies more toward the software development side of the equation than the product side. Approximately 90% of the steps in the three or four different software development approaches are common, step sequencing notwithstanding. So a single software testing checklist with a few alternative steps could conceivably fill the bill for all software development projects.

Examine closely any number of different testing checklists and two observations will quickly arise. First, the superficial comparison of checklists causes one to conclude that they are all very unique. Further research will show the uniqueness arising primarily from differences in terminology and development stages that different organizations choose. The testing terminology is usually tightly bound to the organization's development terminology. This binding does not necessarily make testing any more effective or unique. This binding does make testing more understandable to its associated development team.

Second, deep at the core of each testing checklist you will find the same questions. Most professional testers are, in effect, using a common checklist for successful testing. To the inquiring reader, the assertion that all software testing can be done using one robust, generic testing checklist needs proof. The remainder of this chapter introduces an example of a robust, generic testing checklist called SPRAE. SPRAE is then used as the presentation vehicle for the remainder of the textbook topics that cover the software development life cycle end to end. Q.E.D.

3.3 SPRAE—A GENERIC STRUCTURED TESTING APPROACH

Dr. Edward L. Jones, Florida A&M University, developed and published a simple, five-step checklist for software testing. His intended audience is software developers with the expectation that software developers who know how to test make better software developers. We agree with Dr. Jones' expectation and subscribe to his statement:

"... SPRAE is general enough to provide guidance for most testing situations." [17]

We also believe that Dr. Jones' statement intimates that the greater value of SPRAE is in the hands of experienced software testers.

Our professional examination of SPRAE has revealed SPRAE to be as robust as the checklists available from the three common sources of testing methods previously mentioned. This implies a double benefit for those software professionals and students who invest the time and effort to learn SPRAE. The first benefit is core testing concepts and a checklist that does deliver good testing. The second benefit is substantially transferable skills from testing job to testing job, regardless of the customized testing checklists used by the new employer. Recall that most of the differences among commercial testing methods are found in the development cycle terminology and milestone positioning. Learn the new development life cycle and terminology and prior testing checklist experience can be leveraged in the new development organization.

The SPRAE checklist has five items. The acronym "SPRAE" is derived from the first letter of each checklist item.

*S*pecification

*P*remeditation

*R*epeatability

*A*ccountability

*E*conomy

3.3.1 Specification

The *specification* is a *written* statement of expected software behavior. This software behavior may be visible to the end user or the system administrator or someone in between. The intent of the testing specification is to give focus to all subsequent test planning and execution. Dr. Jones states the corollary of this principle to be "no specifications, no test." This is the pivotal concept most often misunderstood about software testing. Dr. James A. Whittaker at the Florida Institute of Technology reinforces Dr. Jones' criticality of specifications as a prerequisite for successful testing by continuously asking his testing students, "Why are you testing that?" [18]

3.3.2 Premeditation

Premeditation is normally expressed as *written* test plans, test environments, test data, test scripts, testing schedules, and other documents that directly support the testing effort. The actual quantity of documentation varies widely with the size and duration of the testing project. Small, quick testing projects need only a few, concise premeditation documents. Large, extended duration testing projects can produce stacks of premeditation documents. One criticism publicly leveled at most commercial testing methods is that their required premeditation documentation is often overkill, wasting valuable tester resources and testing schedule to produce documentation that does not add commensurate value to the testing effort.

The message to the new software tester is clear. Too little premeditation places the testing project at risk to fail because of inadequate planning. Too much premeditation places the testing project at risk to fail because the extra time consumed in planning cannot be recovered during test execution.

3.3.3 Repeatability

This item arises from a software process dimension called "maturity." The Software Engineering Institute at Carnegie-Mellon has established an industry-wide yardstick for measuring the relative success that a company can expect when attempting software development. [19] This yardstick is called the Capability Maturity Model Integration (CMMi). Based on the CMMi, successful development and testing of software for wide ranges of applications requires the testing process to be institutionalized. In other words, once a test has been executed successfully, any member of the test team should be able to repeat all the tests and get the same results again. *Repeatability* of tests is a mature approach for test results confirmation. A testing technique called "regression test" described in a later chapter relies heavily on the repeatability of tests to succeed.

3.3.4 Accountability

Accountability is the third set of *written* documentation in SPRAE. This item discharges the tester's responsibility for proving he or she followed the test plan (premeditation) and executed all scheduled tests to validate the specifications.Contrary to many development managers' expectations, testing accountability does not include the correction of major defects discovered by testing. Defect correction lies squarely in development accountability. Supporting test completion documentation normally comes from two sources. The first source is the executed tests themselves in the form of execution logs. The more automated the testing process, the more voluminous the log files and reports tend to be. The second source is the tester's analysis and interpretation of the test results relative to the test plan objectives.

One significant implication of the accountability item is that the tester can determine when testing is complete. Although a clear understanding of test completion criteria appears to be a common sense milestone, you will be amazed by how many test teams simply plan to exhaust their available testing time and declare "testing is completed."

There exists a philosophy of software testing called "exploratory testing" that is emerging in the literature.[20] This philosophy advocates concurrent test design and test execution. Although some interesting results have been obtained by experienced testers using the "exploratory testing" approach, its premise seems to preclude accountability in the SPRAE context and appears to contradict prudent testing practices for the inexperienced tester.

3.3.5 Economy

The *economy* item is more representative of a kind of thinking and planning like repeatability than a kind of documentation like specifications and premeditation. The crux of the economy item is testing cost effectiveness, which can be measured in many ways. The introductory chapter examined some of the high-level cost issues around software testing, namely the total cost of testing compared to the total cost of the business risk reduced by testing. This SPRAE item requires the technical teams to develop a detailed testing budget from which the total cost of testing can be computed.

Because software testing is basically another kind of technology project, expected testing personnel and equipment costs are included in the testing budget. Budget items fairly unique to testing include test data preparation, testing environment setup and teardown (not just a desktop computer per tester), and possibly automated testing tools. These unique budget items will be examined in depth in a later chapter.

Finally, the testing schedule can be considered a contributor to the economy of a test project. Because testing is often considered (incorrectly) to be a necessary evil between development completion and deployment, the development manager may consider relegating the testing executions to the third shift where it can be done on schedule without interfering with daily development and routine business. This "night owl" approach to testing will actually increase the time necessary to complete testing, causing both testing and development schedule overruns.

To understand the reasons for this reverse economy, place yourself in a tester's shoes executing tests on schedule at 2 A.M. in the morning. One of your new test scripts blows up. Under daytime testing circumstances, you might contact one of the senior end users in your team to determine if the test script is attempting to validate the specifications incorrectly. Another possibility might be your contacting the developer to determine if the program code and application specifications are in conflict. A third possibility might be your contacting the system administrator to determine if there is a problem with the recent program build or data load for testing. None of these courses of action are available to help you resolve the test script problem. Everybody you need to contact is at home in bed fast asleep. The best you can do is leave notes around the office or on voice mail, close down your testing activity for the night (this problem is a testing showstopper), and go home to bed yourself. What could have been resolved in an hour or two during the day shift will now stretch over 8–10 hours while everybody finishes their night's sleep, find your notes, and begin to respond to your problem. Your testing schedule just went out the window with the first major testing problem encountered.

In summary, SPRAE gives the experienced software tester a simple and effective checklist of five items that can lead to successful testing. Subsequent chapters use SPRAE to examine and demonstrate the breadth of software testing techniques that represent foundation testing skills.

3.4 PUTTING THE OVERVIEW OF STRUCTURED TESTING IN PERSPECTIVE

The software testing profession has borrowed simple, proven approaches from other engineering disciplines to construct a reliable, consistently successful method for testing software. This successful software testing method relies heavily on a high-level checklist that ensures that the right questions are asked at each step of the testing process.

At first glance, each testing project is vastly different from the previous testing project due to the richness of software development. Taking the structured testing approach with checklists, you quickly realize that it is the answers to the checklist that are rich and varied, not the questions. This realization can give you a high degree of confidence in successfully validating any newly encountered software development.

KEY TERMS AND CONCEPTS

Checklist	Premeditation	Accountability
Specification	Repeatability	Economy

Chapter 4

Testing Strategy

LEARNING OBJECTIVES

- to examine the four basic testing approaches for software
- to illustrate single platform testing strategies for all involved levels of software across all development phases
- to illustrate multiplatform testing strategies for all involved levels of software across all development phases

4.1 INTRODUCTION

As with all technology projects, successful software testing starts with planning. We examined a number of reasons for doing software testing in Chapter 1. Planning is the process that we use to turn these reasons into achievable testing goals. SPRAE PRE-MEDITATION is the lens we will use to focus our attention on the test planning activity.

Test planning can be likened to a chess game. There are a number of pieces on your side of the board, each available to help you win the game. Your challenge is to develop a winning strategy and advance the specific chess pieces that will support your strategy. Similarly, you have a number of testing "pieces" on your side that you can choose to use at different times in the game to "win" the testing game.

4.2 THE CHESS PIECES FOR TESTING STRATEGIES

Over the last 25 years of software testing, four different test approaches have emerged as the approaches (chess pieces) of choice for successful testing. These four testing approaches include

static testing (pencil and paper—documents)

white box testing (you have the source code—logic paths)

Software Testing: Testing Across the Entire Software Development Life Cycle, by G. D. Everett and R. McLeod, Jr.
Copyright © 2007 John Wiley & Sons, Inc.

black box testing (you just have the executable code—behavior)

performance testing (Is the program somehow fast enough?)

Let us take a high-level look at the "moves" that these testing approaches provide. Once you understand the basic strategy of a testing plan, we will drill down into a more detailed discussion of each testing approach.

4.2.1 Static Testing

As we saw in Chapter 1, 85% of all software defects are introduced at the Design phase of development. The burning question is "What is there to test during the Design phase to reduce these defects?" The resounding answer is *not* "code!" The actual programming occurs in a later phase. If code is not available to test at the beginning of a development project, then what is? The answer *is* "documentation." Software development starts, continues, and ends with documentation. Early documentation is used to define the software to be built. Later documentation covers the software training, installation, and operation (user guides). There is plenty of documentation to test anytime in a software development project. Many developers view the writing of documentation as an afterthought. The truth is just the opposite. The more time and effort spent developing good documentation, especially requirements, design, and specifications, the better chance the developer has to write good code from that documentation. If you are now convinced that testing documentation is just as important as testing the code, then your next question will be "how do I test documentation ?" The short answer is by desk checking, inspections, walkthroughs, and presentations. All of these techniques are different ways of examining the correctness and completeness of the document being tested. Once discovered, document defects need to be diligently tracked to correction; otherwise, the document defect will remain in the document to cascade into many more defects in subsequent development phases.

Testers are the best group to static test development documents for two reasons. First, the testers are trained in appropriate document testing techniques seldom learned by the developer. Second, the testers represent an objective third party who is much more likely to identify document defects (especially what is missing) than the document author whose sense of ownership typically clouds the testing objectivity.

We will discuss some static testing techniques in Chapter 6. You just need an appreciation of static testing in order to do your test planning.

4.2.2 White Box Testing

White box testing is that kind of software testing you can do when you have both the source code and the executable code in hand. This situation is fairly common for in-house developers who are writing a new system or upgrading an existing system custom built for their company. Another group of developers who typically have access to the source code are developers of software for sale. If you purchase off-the-shelf software, the source code is not included because the source code represents the software vendor's trade secret.

Having the source code in hand, developers and their testing team mates have the opportunity to review and test every line of that code. Even with all the source code available, there is usually insufficient time or resources to test 100% of the source code. With all the pieces lying on the table, developers and testers still must create test plans that methodically test as much of the source code as practical (see the business cost/benefit discussion in Chapter 1).

A team of developers and testers is the best group to plan and execute white box test source code. The developer contributes knowledge of the program specifications, programming standards, and logic represented in the source code lines. It is the developer who knows what the code is supposed to do and how to prove that the code is doing it (positive testing). The developer is also the person who has access to the source code for testing execution. The tester contributes knowledge of white box testing techniques that will cause the developer to look beyond just proving that code works as specified to find out if the user can inadvertently "break" the code (negative testing). The combination of positive testing and negative testing are what make white box testing the most effective at finding defects.

There are several useful white box techniques for commercial software developers and testers. White box testing is also referred to as "logic path" testing because of the dominance of logic path analysis for this technique. We will examine these white box techniques in a subsequent chapter. You just need a general appreciation now for what white box testing is in order to do your test planning.

4.2.3 Black Box Testing

Black box testing is that kind of software testing you can do when you do not have the source code, just the executable code in hand. This situation occurs at some point in the development process regardless of the kind of development (custom software, software for sale) being done. As the programming becomes more complete, it is "packaged" as larger and larger components of code. This package is built by compiling, linking, or binding executable code modules to demonstrate the collective code's execution behavior with inputs and outputs.

Another way to get executable code for black box testing is to buy an off-the-shelf software product. You do test the software products you buy, don't you?

A group of testers, end users (business experts), and developers is the best team to do black box testing. The tester contributes substantial test planning and execution expertise in positive and negative black box testing. The end user contributes substantial knowledge of the proper business behavior to be expected of the software. The developer contributes substantial knowledge of the business behavior as implemented in the software (maybe different from what the user expects). The tester drives the black box testing with the end user and developer validating expected versus actual test results. The first question the tester must ask is "Do I know the correct expected results ?" When a black box test fails (actual results do not match expected results), the second question the tester must ask is "Did I run the test correctly to get the expected results ?" If the answer is "yes" to both questions, then it is the developer who must resolve the failed test as either a specification error or an implementation error.

Black box testing is also referred to as "behavior" testing because of the dominance of expected/actual results analysis for this technique. We will examine these black box techniques in a subsequent chapter. You just need a general appreciation now for what black box testing is in order to do your test planning.

4.2.4 Performance Testing

Performance testing is that kind of software testing you can do once the software has been shown to operate correctly. The testing emphasis changes from correctness to response time and throughput. This change in emphasis occurs at some point near the end of the development process regardless of the kind of development (custom, software for sale) being done. Off-the-shelf software products are certainly candidates for performance testing validation, especially because most software vendors advertise the performance you should expect from their software under various operating conditions. You do test the performance of software products you buy, don't you ?

A team of experienced testers is the best group to plan and execute performance tests. The tester is really the only development team member who understands and can execute performance tests correctly. Performance testing is complex and requires a number of testing skills that are usually found in a team of specialized testers rather than one individual. A testing environment with performance test tools must be created. The maximum mix (peak workload) of transactions (how many of which kind) for performance testing must be determined with the assistance of business experts. The system under test must be started empty and brought up to the maximum mix of transactions in some controlled way. Measurements are taken on the transaction responses individually and collectively during the maximum mix execution. The system under test is allowed to idle down gracefully. When a performance test fails, that is, transactions run too slow or not enough transactions completed per unit of time, the tester needs to provide the stakeholder and development team with the results so that corrective action can be determined and taken.

Here is another departure for performance testing. With white box and black box testing, the system behavior is tightly associated with particular business activities that, in turn, are dictated by that business (accounting principles, supply chain principles, sales principles, and so forth).

So a defect found by white box or black box testing strongly implies programming corrections. With performance testing, the system's response time and throughput are dictated more by the competition targeted by the system's business. Examples of competition targets would be cash register response times for a retail store, gas pump authorization response times for an auto gas station, or web page rendering response time for internet sales companies.

When performance tests indicate that the application will not be as fast as required, the first suggested solution from the development is usually a "quick fix" such as buying faster hardware, buying more memory (more cache for i/o), buying more network bandwidth, or buying more disk storage. Failing to find an adequate "quick fix," the developers are forced back to the drawing board for some expensive design changes and retesting.

Performance testing is also referred to as "load" testing because the best way to do performance testing is when you exert a load (many transactions) on the system like it will have in production. We will examine this black box technique in a subsequent chapter. You just need a general appreciation now for what performance testing is in order to do your test planning.

4.3   THE TWO-DIMENSIONAL TESTING STRATEGY CHESS BOARD

Now we have four chess pieces (static testing, white box testing, black box testing, and performance testing) that we can use to plan our winning moves. What does the chess board look like ? Figure 4.1 shows you the empty test planning "chess board" as a starting point. Figure 4.1 is Table 2.1 development stages for columns by software layers to be tested for rows.

The software testing techniques (chess board "pieces") we just discussed and their icons are shown in the upper right legend and are placed on appropriate squares in the chess board.

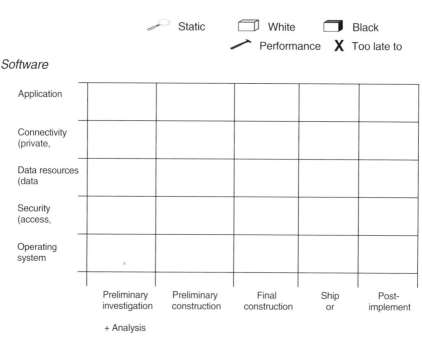

Figure 4.1   The testing strategy chess board

At the bottom along the horizontal axis, or *x*-axis, are the phases of the phased development methodology (PDM) discussed in Chapter 2. The PDM starts with the left-most column and proceeds left to right until implementation is complete. Each subsequent column to the right represents the next phase of development.

At the left side along the vertical axis, or *y*-axis, are the software platform layers necessary to operate a typical software application. The bottom-most row represents the most basic software, the operating system, the software that "talks" directly to the hardware. The next layer up is security software that restricts/allows access to all the layer activities above it. The next layer up is data resources that provides file or database management of data stored on fixed or removable media. The next layer up is connectivity that provides interchange of tasks and data among software components located on different computers via networks. These connected computers can be located physically in the same room, the next room, the next building, the next city, the next state, the next country, or the next continent. Finally, the topmost row represents the application under development that is the primary focus of the test plan. The existence of layers below the application under development gives us a strong indication that planning testing just for the application under development may be insufficient.

So far, software testing may appear to be a simple choice among a number of testing techniques whenever a tester sees the need. In fact, the strategy for using these techniques is much more complex. The key to successful testing is to develop the appropriate testing strategy for the application under development *and the*

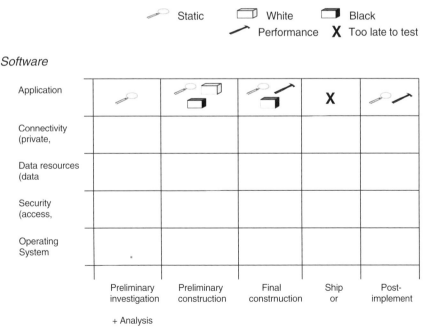

Figure 4.2   Testing strategy for the application under test

supporting layers beneath the application before any actual testing is begun. The testing strategy involves using an intelligent combination of testing techniques.

The testing strategy discussion will first focus on just the top row, the application under development. Assume for current discussion that the application under development will be custom written. Off-the-shelf software package testing will be discussed later in this chapter. Figure 4.2 shows you an optimal placing of chess pieces on the test planning "chess board for your custom-written application under development (top row).

For the Preliminary investigation, Analysis, and Design phases (leftmost column), there is only a magnifying glass strategy in the application under development (top row) indicating only static testing to be planned for these phases. At this stage in the life cycle, the application exists only as design documents: requirements, specifications, data structures, and so forth. No program code has been written yet. So the only development artifacts that can be tested are the documents. This kind of testing done at this stage in the life cycle is concerned with two issues:

1. identifying incomplete, incorrect, or conflicting information within each document and across all documents that describe all aspects of the application to be developed, and

2. confirming that the document objectives are testable when they have been translated into software.

For the Preliminary construction phase (second column from the left), there is a magnifying glass, a white box, and a black box strategy piece in the application under development row. At this phase in the life cycle, there is a rich set of artifacts to test: environment setup documentation, program source code, data, and program code that can be executed. Besides source code walkthroughs (magnifying glass), there is testing of the newly written code paths (white box) and code input/output behavior (black box) as the written code becomes complete.

For the Final construction phase (third column from the left), there is a magnifying glass, a black box, and a hammer strategy piece in the application under development row. Some of the later produced documentation like user's guides, training guides, installation guides, and operating manuals need to be tested here. Testing "inside" the code (white box) is no longer practical because all the code components have been "packaged" or integrated together via compilation, linking, or bindings. Testing of the packaged, more complex code component inputs and outputs (black box) is continued during this phase. The final testing that remains at the end of this phase is verification that the new application installs correctly and operates properly (both black box testing) in its documented production environment.

The hammer represents two different kinds of performance testing strategies: performance baseline and workload. In traditional performance baseline testing, response times for single transactions or activities in an empty system are verified against performance requirements as an extension of black box testing. This performance baseline testing is a wakeup call for the developers, knowing that a slow transaction in an empty system will get no faster as more transactions are added to the system. As the performance baseline results begin to fall in line with requirements, load testing of large numbers of transactions is planned and performed. The load testing decisions about the mix of transactions and how many of each transaction to test comes from a business workload analysis that will be discussed in Chapter 9.

For the Ship or Install phase (fourth column line from the left), we suggest that it is too late to test because the application is no longer available to the development team. Another way to say it is, "when the application is ready to ship, by definition the testing is done."

For the Post Implementation phase (last column to the right), there are magnifying glass and hammer strategies in the application under development row. The static testing (magnifying glass) of implementation checklists and first use of operational manuals are done after the new installation is verified correct. Lessons learned documents are also static tested for thoroughness, completeness, and accuracy. The first few days and weeks of new application operation are monitored to compare business workload and application performance test results with actual business workload and actual application performance under that workload in production. Comparison discrepancies found in either workload or performance testing become issues either for short-term solutions, for example, faster hardware, or longer term solutions, for example, redesign next release for better performance.

When a company purchases a software package, the development and testing situation is similar to the Final construction phase of custom-written software. The only application artifacts to test are the documentation and executable code. No requirements or specifications or source code are provided with purchased software. So you test what is available, namely the documentation (magnifying glass) and the input/output behavior (black box) against your company's purchase evaluation criteria. Performance (hammer) testing is done in the intended production environment with samples of real business data to validate the software package performance against your company's performance criteria. Companies that do not insist on testing a purchased package as a prerequisite to the purchase will always be disappointed with the products they buy.

Next release testing

Changes, corrections, and additional features are an inevitable part of the software development life cycle regardless of whether it is custom code or a purchased package. Just consider how many "versions" of your word processor you have installed in the last 5 years. For a next release, the development and testing activities typically follow an abbreviated version of the PDM. Many of the critical design decisions have already been made. The next release probably represents additional functionality within the context of the current design. So both the development and testing follow similar plans from the previous release and invest effort most heavily in the new or updated code required for the next release. If good test planning is done during the original development project, most of the black box test scripts are designed to be reusable in subsequent release tests. The reuse of these tests is called "regression testing." The primary purpose of regression testing is to verify that all the changes, corrections, and additional features included in the next release do not inadvertently introduce errors in the previously tested code. Regression testing will be discussed further in Chapter 7.

Figure 4.3 shows the updated testing strategy chess board. The top row representing the application under development test strategy is now complete and ready to drive the test plan. The remaining four rows representing the supporting software layers have their test strategies copied down from the first row as the first draft of their test strategy. The question mark to the right of each row indicates the need to validate or modify the draft test strategy at each subsequent layer.

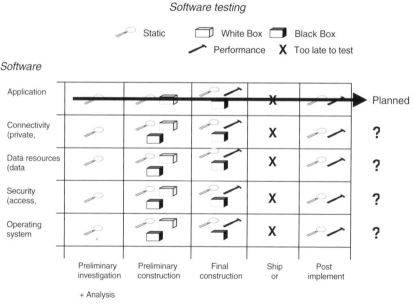

Figure 4.3   Testing strategy for the supporting software layers

If all of the support layers for the application under development have been used successfully many times by the developers, then the support layers are considered "trusted," and only cursory test planning is necessary to reverify their "trustedness."

If any of the support layers are new to development (and production by implication), then you need to seriously consider a full test plan for that support layer and all support layers above it. Strongly consider testing the support layers as far in advance of the application under development coding as possible. If the new support software layer does not pass all verification tests, the developers could be forced to redesign their application in mid-stream to use different support software ... that should likewise be tested before redevelopment is too far along.

Popular approaches for designing e-business software have presented the support layer testing strategist with a new dilemma. The design of the new e-business software may rely on trusted support layers, but the *combination* of trusted components is new to development and production. A cautious, conservative testing strategy is recommended. Consider testing the new support combinations more thoroughly than if they were truly trusted but less thoroughly than if they were completely new components. Test key features and functionality that the application under development must rely on. If no issues arise, complete the testing at a cursory level. If issues arise, deepen the testing effort to help the developers quickly formulate a go/no go decision with this support combination.

4.4   THE THREE-DIMENSIONAL TESTING STRATEGY CHESS BOARD

The internet has matured as a viable business marketplace. Part of that internet maturing process has been the implementation of successively larger, more complex e-business applications. At first blush, it would appear that you need a whole new set of testing skills and strategies to test these e-business applications. A closer examination of the situation reveals that over 95% of the testing skills and strategies used for traditional (non-e-business application) testing are still viable. The 5% new testing skills and strategies will be discussed in Chapter 14.

The best way to apply the 95% of testing strategies that you already know to e-business applications is to add a third dimension to the testing strategy chess board. This third dimension will represent the multiplicity of software platforms that e-business applications typically use.

4.4.1   Software Platforms—The Third Testing Strategy Dimension

Let us look at some examples of software platforms from a testing strategy perspective. Consider the grouping of all business computers into three categories: workstations, networks, and servers.

Workstations are those computers that end users and customers and employees use to accomplish work. These computers normally have some kind of human interface like a keyboard, touch pad, display screen, microphone, or speaker. Examples of workstation platforms are personal computers, palmpilots, cellphones and Blackberrys. New workstation devices are appearing in the market that combine features of existing workstations and add new features, like the cellphone that has a keyboard for e-mail and a display screen for streaming video.

Networks are those computers and connectivity equipment (wires and wireless broadcast) that permit the communication among workstations and servers and other workstations. Examples of network platforms are local area networks within one building or across a complex of adjacent buildings. Wide area networks connect computers in different geographies on the same continent and on different continents. Satellites are similar to wide area networks in geographical reach but do not require the physical cabling from point to point that wide area networks require; rather, they rely on a group of earth orbiting satellites to hop continents and oceans.

Servers are the business computer workhorses. Over time these workhorses have become specialized in the business services they provide. There are application servers that provide the daily business functionality like ordering, purchasing, fulfillment, billing, and accounting. There are database servers that organize, store, and, retrieve business records for customers, services, parts and supplies, equipment, music, or art. There are security servers that limit what an employee or a customer can do with company data, depending on that customer's contract status or that employee's job responsibilities. There are telephony servers that answer phones and with appropriate responses from the caller, can route calls to appropriate customer, service representatives. There are Web site servers that provide all the home page services necessary for a company to do business on the Internet. There are firewalls that protect company data from unauthorized access or updates from outside the company walls, usually via networks or the Internet.

IT professionals who remember working on the giant mainframe computers of the 1970s and 1980s often look for a fourth category called either "mainframes" or "host systems." The computers that would have been correctly placed in those categories in the 1980s are now being placed in the "servers" category. As companies have moved into the e-business arena, they have discovered that the ubiquitous mainframe is best utilized as an incredibly powerful and reliable multi-server, not a stand-alone monolith as in the past.

e-business requires many computers from all three categories of platforms. So, instead of requiring just one grid of testing decisions, the testing teams must consider three strategy grids, one for each platform involved. The expanded testing strategy chess board is shown in Figure 4.4.

The complex task of planning the testing strategy for these multiplatform applications can now be simplified to a familiar two-dimensional testing strategy

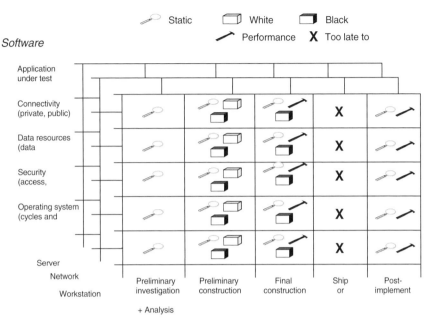

Figure 4.4   Testing strategy for multiple platforms

for each platform. Depending on the nature of the software components on each platform, the appropriate testing strategy questions can be asked and answered just for that platform. This allows clarity and independence of testing priorities across the platforms involved, yielding more thorough test planning for the entire development effort.

4.5 PUTTING THE TESTING STRATEGY INTO PERSPECTIVE

The rich repertoire of testing techniques can be grouped into four major approaches to simplify the understanding of when the approaches are appropriate during the software development life cycle. If these four major approaches are placed on a grid with the development phases and the different layers of software required to operate the application under test, useful patterns arise for test planning purposes. These patterns are further useful in determining what needs to be tested and what does *not* need to be tested at a fairly high level.

KEY TERMS AND CONCEPTS

Static testing

White box testing

Black box testing

Performance testing

Testing strategy chess board

Software platforms

Software platform layers

Application under test

Supporting software layers

Chapter 5

Test Planning

LEARNING OBJECTIVES

- to connect the test strategy to test plan development
- to connect a test plan to test writing and execution
- to synchronize test documentation writing with development phases

5.1 INTRODUCTION

The most effective and manageable way to develop and deliver your testing is to document the effort into two distinct parts. The first part contains the overall test plan description. The second part contains the detailed test execution instructions.

5.2 THE TEST PLAN

You will encounter different names in the literature for the first part: Master test plan, Comprehensive test plan, and High-level test plan, to name a few examples. For the purpose of discussion in this textbook, the overall test plan document will simply be called the Test Plan. The scope of the test plan is the whole testing strategy chess board: what application(s) will be tested and why, which support layers will be tested and why, and how much (if not all) of the development life cycle will require testing. A typical test plan should include the following:

1. application(s)/system(s) to be tested
2. testing objectives and their rationale (risk and requirements)
3. scope and limitations of the test plan
4. sources of business expertise for test planning and execution
5. source of development expertise for test planning and execution
6. sources of test data

Software Testing: Testing Across the Entire Software Development Life Cycle,   by G. D. Everett and R. McLeod, Jr. Copyright © 2007 John Wiley & Sons, Inc.

7. test environments and their management
8. testing strategy (chess board)
9. <Repeated> testing details for each development phase
   (a). development phase
   (b). how can you tell when you are ready to start testing?
   (c). how can you tell when you are finished testing?
   (d). <Draft> test cases list (ID, title, and brief description)
   (e). <Draft> test case writing schedule
   (f). <Draft> test case execution schedule
   (g). <Draft> test case execution results analysis and reporting schedule
10. <Draft> overall testing schedule

<Repeated>

This test plan table of contents has one item that begins with <Repeated>. This notation means that you should expect to repeat this item and all subitems for as many times as there are development phases.

<Draft>

This test plan table of contents has several items that begin with <Draft>. This notation means that at the time the test plan is first written, there is insufficient information from the development activities to fully document the <Draft> items. So the test manager and test team construct the test plan with the best answers they have at the time or leave a placeholder in the documentation for later entries. The test plans must be revisited regularly to update the <Draft> items with new information and revalidate the whole plan. All of the <Draft> items in the test plan should be finalized by the time the Preliminary construction development phase is started, usually one third the way through the development process.

Here is a brief description of each test plan item:

1. *Application(s)/systems(s) to be tested*—the application or group of applications that are included in the current testing effort.

2. *Testing objectives and their rationale*—the specific objectives that testing must achieve for the application(s)/system(s) named in item 1. Objectives must be focused on business needs and perceived business risk. Good objectives are measurable and achievable within the development project schedule. Testing objectives like "we'll test till we're tired" or 'we'll test till it is time to ship" are unacceptable.

3. *Scope and limitations of the test plan*—we need to state what will be tested and what will not be tested to more accurately forecast testing resource requirements and to set appropriate development project expectations.

Occasionally, a particular function or feature of an application is identified as being very expensive to test but poses only a low business risk to fail. So, that function or feature can be declared out of scope and not tested.

4. *Sources of business expertise for test planning and execution*—testers are usually not expected to be experts in the business to be supported by the application or system. So somebody in the "business side of the house" needs to be earmarked as a business expert who can assist the testing team with designing, executing, and interpreting tests in the correct business context.

5. *Sources of development expertise for test planning and execution*—the development team may design the new application or system with languages, databases, or support software unfamiliar to the testing team. So, somebody in the "technology side of the house" needs to be earmarked as a technology expert who can assist the testing team with building and executing tests correctly in the target technology environment.

6. *Sources of test data*—the testers will need test data as close to "real" data (production data) as possible. It is helpful from an overall project planning perspective to identify the sources and the amount of effort necessary to acquire data for the testing environment. Many times, it is both most effective from a testing perspective and easiest from a data preparation perspective to use copies of production files and databases.

7. *Test environments and their management*—after the code is written and tested by the developer (white box testing), that code needs to be migrated into a separate testing environment for independent testing by the test team (black box testing and performance testing). This separate testing environment needs to be a mirror image of the intended production environment for the test results to be credible. This separate testing environment also needs to be under the sole control and management of the test team so that tests can be run and rerun as needed without any restrictions or conflicts with development runs or production runs. One of the most challenging aspects of managing this testing environment is the coordination of multiple runs and reruns of test cases. Test cases that are successful must be rerun to prove repeatability of results. Test cases that are unsuccessful must be rerun to validate the subsequent software correction for the defect that caused the test case to be unsuccessful in the first place.

8. *Testing strategy (chess board)*—this is the testing strategy chess board defined for the application under test and all the software support layers as described in Chapter 4.

9. *<Repeated> Testing details for each development phase*—this list of items is repeated for each development phase. The content for each repeat is different because different kinds of testings are appropriate at each subsequent development phase. The intent is to tie each development phase's testing activities back to the overall test plan to ensure that the testing activities for each phase support the overall test plan objectives. It is so easy to become

curious about testing some aspect of an application and go off on a tangent, wasting both valuable time and resources on testing that is interesting but out of scope.

(a) *Development phase*—this is the name of the development phase for which these occurrences of the items (a) through (g) are planned.

(b) *How can you tell when you are ready to start testing in this phase?*—at first glance, this seems to be a trivial question, but on deeper examination, this may be a complex question based on the availability of only partially completed development.

(c) *How can you tell when you are finished testing in this phase?*—this is a complex question any way you wish to consider it. The crux of the matter is that all of the test cases may have been executed, but the backlog of software defects discovered by these test cases has not been resolved.

(d) *Test cases list (ID, title, and brief description) for this phase*—this is the summary list of test cases that you think are needed to adequately cover all the testing situations in this development phase. This list is refined a number of times as more details about the application design become available.

(e) *Test case writing schedule*—once the needed test cases are identified, somebody has to take the time to write out their details. This is a work-intensive activity with the testing expert doing the writing and with the assistance of the business expert and the development expert.

(f) *Test case execution schedule*—once the test case is written and validated, an execution schedule must be drafted that takes advantage of test case dependencies, precursors, and postcursors to provide the most expeditious test execution and results gathering possible.

(g) *Test case execution results analysis and reporting schedule*—this schedule extends the test execution schedule to include time to analyze and report test results. Usually, there is some analysis time and minimal report drafting time associated with each test execution so that the testers can begin to see the nature of the testing outcome early in the test execution schedule. Then, if adjustments need to be made in the test execution to accommodate surprises, there is test execution schedule remaining for the tactical adjustments. This first allotment of analysis and reporting time can range from a half day to a couple of days per test case. A second allotment of time is made for the analysis of results across multiple test case executions for more pervasive trends and completion of the drafted report. This second allotment of time can range from 2 to 4 weeks depending on the size and complexity of the testing project.

10. *<Draft>Overall testing schedule*—this schedule is the composite of all test case documentation, execution, and reporting schedules for all development phases. This schedule represents the master schedule of testing activity that the test team must manage.

Test plan items 1–8 describe the skills, process, and technology framework needed for the testing to be accomplished. Availability of all these items for the testing effort is prerequisite for successful testing of the application or system.

Items 9(a)–9(g) provide development phase-specific test planning activities that culminate in test results for that phase. The term "test case" is introduced here for the first time and is explained in the next section of this chapter.

One question that frequently arises about the test plan is the nature of the physical document. Some testing methodologies mandate that all the items must be written in a single, all-inclusive document. Other testing methodologies mandate that items 1–8 and 10 in the test plan be a stand-alone document and that each testing detail Section 9 be a stand-alone document. Both approaches represent extremes. The truth lies somewhere in between. Usually the size of the development project gives you an idea about the size of the test plan. If it is a small or medium size development project, say 1–15 developers, then perhaps the test plan can be written and updated conveniently as a single document. When the development project has more than 15 developers, then the complexity of each development phase may cause you to split out some or all of the test plan item 9 occurrences into separate documents for writing document management convenience.

By necessity, the first draft of the test plan will contain a testing schedule that closely follows the development schedule. As the development efforts proceed, more information is acquired and understood about the detailed nature of the testing to be done. The acquisition of additional testing detail will necessitate revisions to the test plan details and testing schedule to provide successively more accurate scheduling estimates. Expect the revised testing schedule in the test plan to become longer as testing concerns surface from the detailed development that were not apparent at the start of the development (the devil is in the details !). It is not unusual to find yourself one third of the way through the development phases and discover that testing completion will need 3 or 4 weeks more than the original development deadline.

5.3 TEST CASES

One outcome of preparing the test plan is a list of test cases needed for each development phase. Test cases are initially identified by the testing team as high-level testing requirements from the new application's business requirements, business risks, or software specifications. As the developers identify more and more details about the new application, the testers expand the description of the test case to include very detailed testing instructions and expected outcomes.

The test team manager might say, "at this phase of development, we need to test all the data entry screens." This would cause the test team to identify all the data entry screens to be developed and the general business functions these data entry screens will support. For example, if the application under test was a payroll system, then there might be six groups of data entry screens: employee personal information, employee benefits information, employee tax information, state tax information, and federal tax information. To keep testing execution management as simple as possible, the test team would define six test cases, one for each group of data entry screens—regardless of the actual number of data entry screens to be tested in each group. The writing schedule of these test cases then needs to be coordinated with the developer schedule for these data entry screens.

Another common example of test case planning is performance testing. Although we have not yet discussed the particulars of performance testing, hopefully the reader can identify at least four potential test cases for most applications: a baseline performance test case, a batch workload test case, an online workload test case, and an Internet workload test case.

5.3.1 Test Case Details

The purpose of the test plan is to collectively document the testing "what" and "why" for this application. We focus on the testing "how" for this application by drafting test cases. As we saw with the test plan terminology, you will find references to these "how" test documents as test scenarios, test cases, and test scripts elsewhere. As long as you understand the purpose of these test documents and confirm that you are collecting all the information necessary for successful testing, the terminology choice is arbitrary. For the purposes of discussion in this textbook, the detailed test execution document will simply be called the test case.

The contents of the test case take on the narrow focus of just one of many testing activities that collectively support the overall test plan. Defining the boundaries of a good testing case is still very much an art that is learned over a number of years of testing experience. A good starting place is to identify some of the smallest or simplest business activities that the new software needs to support and define test cases for each of these activities. Then, define test cases that portray either larger business activities or specific sequences of smaller business activities that tend to approximate useful business tasks. Check the software business requirements and confirm that you have accounted for all required business activities with your test cases and add test cases for the business activities that are not covered yet by testing. We will examine some test cases in Chapters 8 and 9 that cover other aspects of the software besides business activities, but business activities are the logical starting place for designing test cases. Test cases should include the following:

1. unique test case ID (from test plan)
2. unique title (from test plan)
3. brief description (from test plan)
4. development phase in which this test case is executed (from test plan)
5. specific testing goals and their achievement measures
6. suggested test data
7. suggested test tools
8. test startup procedure

9. test closedown procedure

10. test reset procedure for rerun

11. <Repeated> test execution steps

    (a). step number
    (b). step action
    (c). expected results
    (d). <Placeholder> actual results

12. <Placeholder> first attempt to execute this test case date: time

13. <Placeholder> number of attempts to successfully execute this test case

14. <Placeholder> list of software defects discovered by this test case

15. <Placeholder> is this test case executed successfully ? (yes/no)

<Placeholder>

Some of the items above are prefixed by <Placeholder>. This denotes the need for some type of tracking and reporting capability to provide that item from external sources. Some test teams opt to do this tracking and reporting with simple tools like spreadsheets or simple databases. Other test teams opt to do this tracking and reporting with more complex test management tools. At the end of the testing day, the approach you choose must tell you in detail what testing was attempted, what testing succeeded, and what testing failed.

Here is a brief description of each test case item:

1. *Unique test case ID*—a string of letters and numbers that uniquely identify this test case document. The ID is defined during test plan design and is entered on test plan item 9(d).

2. *Unique title*—a short descriptive label that clearly implies the purpose of this test case. The title is defined during test plan design and is entered on test plan item 9(d) beside the test case ID.

3. *Brief description*—a paragraph that expands on the title to give more details about the purpose of this test case. The description is defined during test plan design and is entered on test plan item 9(d) beside the test case ID and unique title.

4. *Development phase in which this test case is executed*—this is a cross-reference to the development phase section of the test plan that mentions this test case. It is meant to be a reminder of the development state of the code to be tested as a reality check against the kind of testing this test case is intended to accomplish.

5. *Specific testing goals and their achievement measures*—this item takes the purpose of the test case stated in the title and brief description and quantifies specific testing goals as well as how the test team can measure the achievement of these goals.

6. *Suggested test data*—this item identifies the minimal amount of data and most useful data sources for executing this test case in the test environment. For example, if the application under test is a payroll system, then a copy of the current employee master file would be one of the most useful data source for testing. The number of employee records needed for testing this test case would depend on the testing goals. Usually, a representative sample of employee records will be adequate for testing (see Generic black box testing techniques in Chapter 7). Sometimes it requires less effort to use a copy of the whole file rather than to carve out a representative sample.

7. *Suggested test tools*—if the tester is knowledgeable about automated test tools, this is where the tester suggests one or two that have capabilities particularly appropriate for executing this test case. A recap of all tool suggestions across all test cases in the test plan becomes the basis of the test manager's recommendation regarding the automated test tools in the testing environment. Not all test cases lend themselves to automated test tool usage. The cost of automated test tools makes them prohibitively expensive for a relatively small number of executions. Test tools will be examined further in Chapter 11.

8. *Test startup procedure*—this documents what hardware, software, and data must be available to start the test execution. It further identifies how the required software including the application under test must be launched or made active in order to allow the first execution step of this test case to be accomplished.

9. *Test closedown procedure*—this documents how to gracefully stop all the software launched or made active including the application under test. A graceful software stop allows the software activities to idle down and the software to terminate normally.

10. *Test reset procedure for rerun*—this documents what must be done between the most recent test execution closedown and the next test startup in order to allow this test case to be executed again. Most times, this section deals with restoring data to its previous state prior to adds, changes, and deletes caused by executing this test case after the startup.

11. *<Repeated> Test execution steps*—this list of items is repeated for each new step number. One execution attempt of this test case is achieved by performing all the steps once in step number order.

    (a). *Step number*—a unique number that sequences the test case steps for execution.

    (b). *Step action*—the specific, fully described action taken by a tester to evoke a desired software behavior. Examples of step actions include keystrokes, mouse movements, button clicks, drop-down list selections, and voice commands.

    (c). *Expected results*—the particular software behavior or response expected from the step action. Examples of expected results include screen responses, printer responses, file responses, and network responses.

(d). *<Placeholder> Actual results*—the particular software behavior or response actually observed from executing the step action. Examples of actual results include screen responses, printer responses, file responses, and network responses.

12. *<Placeholder> First attempt to execute this test case date: time*—this item documents the date and time when the steps of the test case are first attempted. This metric helps the test manager measure testing progress toward 100% test cases attempted.

13. *<Placeholder> Number of attempts to successfully execute this test case*—this item measures how many attempts become necessary to achieve a successful test case execution.

14. *<Placeholder> List of software defects discovered by this test case*—the log of genuine, correctable software defects discovered by this test case. If the software development process does not change significantly from project to project, then this log will begin to reveal defect patterns that may forecast the approximated number of defects to be discovered by the next development project. If the software development process does change significantly over time, then this log can demonstrate how much the new development process increases or decreases the software quality (fewer defects) by development phase. This kind of defect log interpretation is the subject of an entire section in Chapter 12.

15. *<Placeholder> Is this test case executed successfully? (yes/no)*—this item is answered only after the first test case attempt. The answer can subsequently be changed from "no" to "yes" after any number of attempts that achieve successful test case execution. Usually, some of these attempts occur after software correction in order to confirm the correction as well as achieve successful test case execution.

5.3.2 Step Action

Step actions are the documented keystrokes, mouse movements, and screen rendering for all of the end user steps to complete a business task. Using the data entry screen testing example, a sequence of step actions would describe the mouse or keyboard commands to move the cursor to the next data field to be tested. The next step actions would document the specific data entered by keyboard or selected by mouse from a dropdown menu. After a series of these keyboard entries and mouse movements on the screen, the next step actions might describe a "request completed" message that appears below the submit button or in a separate window. The overt intent of the step actions is to cause the system under test to behave as if the end users were performing routine business activities.

One of the major issues confronting the test case writer is the degree to which the test case is dependent on visual screen positioning of objects. Screen objects will change position (even by a pixel or two), change label, change label font, change color, or change some other property. If screen position validation *is not* a testing objective, then the test case author needs to avoid specifying the expected results based on absolute screen position. If screen position *is* part of the software requirement or specification, then be alert to how different kinds of screen monitors and screen display resolution will probably distort that positioning. This issue arises more when using automated testing tools than when using manual scripting due to the precision that the tools bring to the expected versus actual result comparisons.

5.3.2.1   Expected versus Actual Results in a "Failed" Execution Step

When the expected results match the actual results, the step is said to have "passed" the test. When the expected results do not match the actual results, the step is said to have "failed" the test and further diagnostic analysis is required. There are at least two possible causes of a "failed" step: the expected results are incorrect or the actual results are incorrect. Incorrect expected results can come from several sources starting with the tester's incorrect understanding of what the expected results should be and continuing to the developer's incorrect understanding of what the expected results should be to the business expert's incorrect understanding of what the expected results should be. If the tester, the developer, and the business expert all agree on the expected results, then the "failed" step has revealed a software defect. Who, when, and how the software defect is corrected is one of the topics in Chapter 12.

5.3.2.2   Validate Test Case Step Actions

Test case validation is a double check of the step actions and expected results with the software requirements, specifications, and business expert. The risk of not validating test cases is the increased likelihood that the test team will incorrectly report a number of "failed" step actions as software defects instead of step action design defects (testing defects). Put yourself in the shoes of a developer who is under much pressure to deliver a complex application on a tight deadline. Your work has just been interrupted a third time today to attend a meeting with the test team to discuss another suspected major software defect … and the last two meetings were halted 15 min into the discussion when you pointed out that the tester's expected results did not match the software specifications. How many more of these kinds of meetings will you attend before you tell your development manager that testing is a waste of time?

5.4   WRITING YOUR TEST PLAN AND TEST CASES IN THE REAL WORLD

It would be so nice for the test team to be able to walk into a development project and find all of the information needed on the first day to write all the test documents. As you have probably guessed, that is not how things happen. There definitely is enough information at the beginning of the development effort to draft the test plan, but the details sufficient to write test cases will not surface for a while. When they do, these surface details will arrive in reverse order relative to the execution of the. It is counter-intuitive to the way development planning occurs, but it works well for testing. You can find this relationship of development phases to test case writing, and execution will be referenced in the literature as either the "V-diagram" or the "bathtub diagram." Figure 5.1 shows the bathtub diagram.

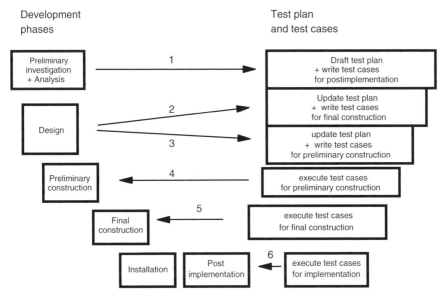

Figure 5.1   The bathtub diagram

The left-hand side of the bathtub diagram represents development phases. The right-hand side represents test planning, writing, and executing. The bathtub diagram is read from top to bottom to follow the development life cycle. Please refer to Chapter 4 to refresh your memory of the testing approaches expected for each development phase.

Here are the relationships that the arrows show:

- *Arrow 1* indicates that the development activities in Preliminary investigation and Analysis produce enough information about the new application that the test team can draft a test plan and write the test case for postimplementation.

- *Arrow 2* indicates that the development activities in design produce enough information about the new application that the test team can update the test plan and write the test case for final construction.

- *Arrow 3* indicates that later development activities in design also produce enough information about the new application that the test team can update the test plan and write the test case for preliminary construction.

- *Arrow 4* indicates that the development planning activities have been completed and the development programming activities in preliminary construction have begun, allowing the test team to follow the test plan and execute the test case for preliminary construction.

- *Arrow 5* indicates that the development programming activities in final construction have begun, allowing the test team to follow the test plan and execute the test case for final construction.

- *Arrow 6* indicates that the new application has been installed and made operational that is the starting point of post-implementation, allowing the test team to follow the test plan and execute the test case for postimplementation.

5.5   TEST DOCUMENT STANDARDS

Because software testing is a professional branch of software engineering, you expect to find standard software testing documentation templates. We introduce to two of the industry-recognized standards sources for testing documentation: the IEEE Computing Society and the Tigris Open Source SOFTWARE Community.

The IEEE Computing Society was founded in 1884 as a merger of the American Institute of Electrical Engineers (AIEE) and the Institute of Radio Engineers (IRE). The full name of the current organization is the Institute for Electrical and Electronics Engineers, Inc. Through its members, the IEEE is a leading authority in technical areas ranging from computer engineering, biomedical technology, and telecommunication to electric power, aerospace engineering, and consumer electronics. The IEEE currently has more than 3,65,000 members worldwide, over 68,000 student members, 39 societies, and 1.1 million documents in the IEEE/IEE Electronic Library. IEEE document templates are available on the IEEE Web site for subscribers only. [21]

The IEEE documentation standard #829-1998 for testing contains templates for

test plan

test design specification

test case specification

test procedure specification

test log specification

test incident report

test summary report

The test plan contents described in this textbook correspond somewhat to the IEEE test plan, test design specification, and test case specification. The test case contents described in this textbook correspond somewhat to the IEEE test design specification, test case specification, and test procedure specification. The textbook items in the test case marked <Placeholder>correspond somewhat to the test log specifications, test incident report, and test summary report.

The Tigris Open Source Software Community is a mid-size open source community focused on building better tools for collaborative software development. The Tigris Community is about 10 years old. The tool building activities are organized into projects. The Tigris project of most direct interest to this textbook's readers is the ReadySET project. ReadySET is an open source project to produce and maintain a library of reusable software engineering document templates. These templates provide a ready starting point for the documents used in software development projects.

The test plan contents described in this textbook correspond somewhat to the ReadySET QA plan template. The test case contents described in this textbook correspond somewhat to the ReadySET test case template. The ReadySET templates, being open source, are available on the Tigris Web site at no charge. [22]

What you should infer from this discussion is that nobody has found a single testing document adequate to cover all the test planning and execution requirements for all software development situations. The textbook examples, the ReadySET templates, and the IEEE templates are identified as starting points for your organization to develop and evolve your testing documentation. If the testing documentation has been done correctly, the testing execution results will be the same regardless of the documentation approach adopted. It is the thought behind the planning that makes the difference between a successful testing project and an unsuccessful one, not the documentation approach.

Knowing that there is no "one way" to document software testing, the obvious question is "how do I start." One rather low-risk, high-benefit way is to review a recent software development project and use its documentation to pilot a representative set of testing documentation described in this chapter. That representative set of documentation should include a test plan and test cases for a few test executions during each development phase. Conduct a pilot lessons-learned meeting where you discuss both the ease and difficulty of writing the test documentation with an eye toward minor document structure changes that would make the task easier next time or with a larger project. Consider also discussing which items included in the pilot documentation did not seem to be beneficial and could be dropped. Then, consider discussing any documentation gaps discovered by the pilot and which items might be added next time to fill those gaps.

Finally, consider doing a second pilot with a slightly larger software development project using the revised testing documentation from the first pilot lessons learned.

Because we do not have a subscription to the IEEE templates, we decided to use the ReadySET templates for all the case studies in this textbook.

5.6 PUTTING TEST PLANNING IN PERSPECTIVE

Inexperienced software testers tend to leap from the testing strategy directly into test cases much like inexperienced software developers tend to leap from application designs directly to coding. The outcome of such a leap is incomplete testing at best. The correct intermediate step for testers is a test plan.

It is the test plan perspective that helps the test team manager identify what will be tested and quickly assess if the planned testing will satisfy the testing goals. Test plan also guides the test team in the next test planning step of test cases development..

KEY TERMS AND CONCEPTS

Test plan
Test case
Test documentation standards

Chapter 6

Static Testing

LEARNING OBJECTIVES

- to examine the necessity of testing all documentation produced by a software development project
- to list the variety of software development documentation that should be tested
- to describe the techniques for testing software development documentation

6.1   INTRODUCTION

All good software development projects produce documentation as well as code. This documentation serves a wide variety of purposes from shaping the software itself to assisting the end user in successfully operating the software. Recalling Chapter 3, this documentation fulfills the specification item in the SPRAE checklist. The process of testing this documentation is called static testing. The term "static" in this context means "not while running" or "not while executing", and is used in contrast to testing software by running or executing it as described in Chapters 7–9. Recalling the testing strategy chess board in Chapter 4, static testing is considered a recommended strategy for all development phases except Installation.

6.2   GOAL OF STATIC TESTING

Static testing is the least expensive form of testing and, with Chapter 1 defect sources in mind, has the largest potential for reducing defects in software under development. The primary goal of static testing is defect reduction in the software by reducing defects in the documentation from which the software is developed. A secondary goal is correct operation of the software. This statement may seem like a statement of the obvious, but many software systems and products have been abandoned after

Software Testing: Testing Across the Entire Software Development Life Cycle,   by G. D. Everett and R. McLeod, Jr.
Copyright © 2007 John Wiley & Sons, Inc.

an investment of millions of dollars because the end users could not figure out how to properly operate the software to do their routine business. Human nature being what it is, the recipients of poor documentation and training do not say, "I will figure out how to operate this software"; rather, they say, "this software doesn't do what I need it to do, so I want the old system back."

6.3 CANDIDATE DOCUMENTS FOR STATIC TESTING

It is time to take a look at a reasonably representative list of software development document candidates for static testing.

1. Software development manager's documents
   (a) Software requirements
   (b) Software project plans
2. Software developers' documents
   (a) Use cases
   (b) Software designs
   (c) Software specifications
   (d) Data flow diagrams
   (e) Database and file designs
   (f) Online operating environment specifications
   (g) Batch operating environment specifications
   (h) Interfaces
   (i) Connectivity (network) specifications
   (j) Security specifications
   (k) Screen/window/page specifications
   (l) Report specifications
   (m) Code
3. Testers' documentation
   (a) Test plans
   (b) Test cases
   (c) Test environment specifications
   (d) Test data sources and preparation
   (e) Test tool installation and operation
4. Administrator's documentation
   (a) Installation guides
   (b) Operation/administration guides
5. End users' documentation
   (a) Users guides
   (b) Help screens
   (c) Training manuals

6.3.1   Software Development Manager's Documents

Software requirements are the foundation on which all subsequent documentation and code are written. If these critical documents are either missing (see Chapter 1's game of "Gossip") or incorrect, then no programming staff can deliver the correct software. The format for requirements varies widely from company to company. If your company is new to writing requirements for your software, consider starting with the software requirements templates found in the Rational Software Development Tool RequisitePro. [23] The templates in this tool enjoy a good industry reputation. So why not use recognized quality templates until your company has gained enough of its own experience to customize the requirements templates where appropriate … if you really find the need to customize.

Software project plans* contain the roadmap that the software development will follow for this particular system or product. If your software development projects always come in on time and under budget, then perhaps you do not need to static test this document. If your software development projects tend to be late or over budget, then perhaps a little static testing can help identify some of the planning gaps that contribute to those overruns.

6.3.2   Software Developers' Documents

Use cases are the formal documentation of the business processes that the new system must provide. This documentation identifies the actors (different roles the system users play) and activities (processes that are performed by specific actors). There is no industry consensus about who should write these use cases or how much process detail the use cases need to express. Because the development managers typically do not write use cases and the test teams typically base part of their test plans on use cases, it seems expedient to place the authorship of use cases somewhere in the development team's realm with or without business assistance.

Software designs contain the high-level technical solution (the *how*) for the business requirements (the *what*) that are expressed in part by use cases. It is the *what* to *how* linkage that is most often incomplete, leading to missed, or poorly understood features and capabilities. All the software developer's documents below *software designs*, that is, *software specifications, data flow diagrams, database and file designs, online operating environment specifications, batch operating environment specifications, interfaces, connectivity (network) specifications, security specifications, screen/window/page specifications, report specifications, and code* are successively deeper details of the technical implementation of the business requirements. Not all documents are needed for every system or application. Part of the software development manager's job is to identify which of these documents need to be written for the new project. There are two static testing concerns that run through this list of more detailed documents. The first static testing concern is completeness, that is, the more detailed documents must completely describe the next level of technology needed to fully respond to the higher level documents. The second static testing concern is that as the technical details are written, some of the details stray from or are not really a part of the original business requirements (out of scope).

6.3.3   Testers' Documentation

Tester's documentation (*test plans, test cases, test environment specifications, test data sources and preparation, and test tool installation and operation*) needs to be tested as thoroughly as other project documents. The sequence of development events that allow test plans to be developed were covered in the bathtub example in Chapter 5. The static testing concern is similar to the more detailed developer documentation: completeness of testing plans against the business requirements and intended development with no gratuitous testing.

6.3.4   Administrator's Documentation

Administrators' documentation (*installation guides* and *operation/administration guides*) documents the steps that must be taken by technical staff to install and support the new system or application. The static testing concern in these documents is double-sided. The first side is clear and unequivocal support of the business requirements. The second side is stepwise instructions that can be carried out successfully by the support staff at their expected administrative skill level.

6.3.5   End Users' Documentation

End users' documentation (*users guides, help screens, and training manuals*) documents the steps that must be taken by business end users to perform their routine daily activities on the new system or application. As with the administrative manuals, the static testing concern with these documents is the double-sided business requirements/operations within expected end user business skill level.

6.4   STATIC TESTING TECHNIQUES

Because static testing requires a high degree of interaction among software development team members, the most challenging aspect of static testing is to keep the testing activities objective and impersonal. The force working against you is the human tendency to take ownership of documents to the extent that a perceived attack on the document is a perceived personal attack on the owner-author. Document ownership is, in fact, a good thing. It causes the author to do his or her best job and gain a sense of pride in good-quality results. Static testing strives to help the owner-author produce the best possible (most correct) document by helping identify corrections and improvements to documents that might already be of good quality. This pride of ownership reaches its zenith with program code. Because no large software application is 100% defect free, all program code has room for improvement. Static testing is one of the more cost-effective ways to identify these improvements.

Consider using a two-step approach to static testing. For the first step, clean up the cosmetic appearance of the document: check spelling, check grammar, check punctuation, and check formatting. The benefit of doing the first step is that when the document is cosmetically clean, the readers can concentrate on the content. The liability of skipping the first step is that if the document is not cosmetically clean, the readers will surely stop reading the document for meaning and start proofreading—to the detriment of content review.

For the second step, use whatever techniques seem appropriate to focus expert review on document contents. Here are some of the more popular and effective techniques used for content review.

Static testing techniques for content review

- desk checking
- inspections
- walk-throughs

Desk checking is the least formal and least time-consuming static testing technique. Of all the techniques, desk checking is the only one whereby the author is encouraged to test his or her own document. The remaining techniques rely on independent eyes to provide a more thorough and objective review. Desk checking involves first running a spellchecker, grammar checker, syntax checker, or whatever tools are available to clean up the cosmetic appearance of the document. Then, the author slowly reviews the document trying to look for inconsistencies, incompleteness, and missing information. Problems detected in the contents should be corrected directly by the author with the possible advice of the project manager and other experts on the project. Once all corrections are made, the cosmetic testing is rerun to catch and correct all spelling, grammar, and punctuation errors introduced by the content corrections.

Inspections are a little more formal and a little more time consuming than desk checking. The technique also finds more document defects than desk checking. The intent of the technique is for an independent pair of eyes, usually a more senior member of the team, to read the document and discover content problems. As recommended with desk checking, the document to be inspected should be made as cosmetically clean as possible by the author so that the independent reader(s) can focus on the content. The independent reader then takes the document elsewhere and reviews it. Separating the document from the author allows the document to stand on its own merit. If the reviewer inspects the document in front of the author, the human tendency is for the author to kibitz the reviewer, which defeats the purpose of the independent reviewer. Suspected problems in the content should be documented by the independent reviewer and presented to the author in a subsequent meeting. The author then needs to provide suggested corrective action alongside the suspected problem. The project manager or someone senior on the project should then review the list of reviewer's suspected problems, and author's suggest corrective actions in order to negotiate an agreed corrective action.

Walk-throughs are the most formal and most time-consuming document testing techniques, but they are the most effective at identifying content problems. The walk-through is a scheduled meeting with a facilitator, the document author, and an audience of senior technical staff and possibly business staff. The author must scrub the document for cosmetic errors and send the document to all participants in advance of the meeting. The participants read the document and formulate questions about the document contents based on their own knowledge of the new system or application. At the appointed time, the author presents his or her document to the walk-through meeting. The facilitator becomes the clearinghouse for questions by the audience and answers by the author. The facilitator also ensures that the questions are posed in an objective, nonthreatening way. The walk-through facilitator documents all suspected content problems and author responses for later resolution by the project manager in a manner similar to the inspection resolutions.

6.5 TRACKING DEFECTS DETECTED BY STATIC TESTING

Each of the previously described static testing techniques involved writing down suspected or confirmed content problems, their suggested or negotiated corrective action, and a correction completion date. These lists can be managed using simple tools like spreadsheets or complex tools like databases. Either way, there are two compelling reasons for recording and tracking these defects to correction. The first reason is to enable the project management to verify the corrections are actually applied to the tested document in a timely manner. The second reason is to demonstrate the importance of current, correct documentation to the early success of the project. Without defect tracking as a reminder to get the documentation right, the attitude of "I'll document that after I've written the code" will rise up and make Capers Jones' gloomy prediction a reality for your project too.

6.6 PUTTING STATIC TESTING IN PERSPECTIVE

Static testing is one of the most frequently overlooked testing approaches. The mistaken impression of static testing is that it takes up time and effort that could be better spent on designing the system or writing the software. In fact, a few well spent hours static testing the development project documentation as it is written could save the project hundreds of hours correcting or redesigning the code caused by poor documentation in the first place.

KEY TERMS AND CONCEPTS

Static testing   Inspections
Desk checks   Presentations

Chapter 7

Functional Testing

LEARNING OBJECTIVES

- to examine the benefits of use case driven functional testing
- to extend the effectiveness of functional testing by regression testing
- to discover the depth of functional testing afforded by white box testing
- to discover the depth of functional testing afforded by black box testing and how it differs from white box testing

7.1 INTRODUCTION

Recalling our SPRAE testing approach in Chapter 3, the preparation for and execution of tests to validate software behavior are critical next steps in premeditation. The planning part of premeditation was accomplished in Chapters 4 and 5. Specification was accomplished in Chapter 6. The remainder of premeditation will be accomplished in Chapters 7–9.

Starting with this chapter, the next three chapters discuss testing techniques that validate the behavior of software as the software matures. Behavior in this context means that a tester provides an input to the software and observes the software's behavior (output). To make the software behave in an expected manner, the tester must execute the software code in a controlled testing environment. These execution testing techniques are fundamentally different in objective and approach from static testing where no code is executed.

The objective of functional testing is to validate the software behavior against the business functionality documented in the software requirements and specifications. Business functionality is generally defined as those activities that support routine daily business. Functional testing is achieved by a series of tests that exercise increasingly more of the software that directly enables users to accomplish this routine daily business.

Software Testing: Testing Across the Entire Software Development Life Cycle,   by G. D. Everett and R. McLeod, Jr. Copyright © 2007 John Wiley & Sons, Inc.

Chapter 5 described the desirable contents of a test plan and the associated test cases. The heart of the test plan is a series of test cases that detail the test execution steps needed to validate the software. The challenge for the tester is to progress from writing the test plan at a high level to writing the test cases at the test execution level. The experienced tester has discovered that the developer produced use cases provide a ready blueprint for test case authorship.

7.2 FUNCTIONAL TEST CASES FROM USE CASES

There is a relatively new scoping technique called use case that software developers employ to capture functional requirements of a system for the purpose of scoping the project. The technique became popular in the mid-1990s first as an object-oriented design technique and later broadened in appeal for other types of software development. If this topic sparks your interest, there are a number of recent textbooks that can give you more guidance about writing use cases. [23, 24]

The software development community has not yet standardized on the development team role that should write these use cases. Some organizations give this responsibility to the developers. Some organizations give this responsibility to the testers. Some organizations give this responsibility to a business analyst. As long as use cases are written by someone, testers can take advantage of these use cases when writing functional test cases.

The building blocks of this approach are actors, use cases, happy paths and alternate paths. Actors are those business roles who are going to directly use the software. The happy path is the sequence of actions that the actor must take in order to accomplish a specific use case. Alternative steps that could be used by an actor to complete the use case represent contingency use cases (customer not found, credit denied, accessories not available, and so forth.) to a happy path. A kind of node diagram of the software emerges that displays all the high-level tasks for a specific business role and the steps necessary to accomplish these tasks. This node diagram is translated into a text description. The combined node diagram and text description constitute the use case documentation.

For example, if a developer were to write a use case for an online purchasing system, the use case text might look like Figure 7.1.

As stated in the Use Case #001 title, this is a happy path, that is, all steps are expected to be completed by the customer in the sequence shown. An alternate path associated with this happy path would be dealing with rejection of the customer's attempted payment. The same products will ultimately be purchased as with the happy path, but there will be intervening action needed to solicit acceptable payment from the customer that the happy path does not encounter.

Use Case #001 provides a high-level description of the sequence of steps that the actor (customer) must take to complete an online purchase. Recall that in the test case content description in Chapter 5, there is a sequence of test steps. For functional testing, here is the helpful crossover. Consider drafting a test case for each use case

Actor	Action	Description
Customer	Log on	A homepage screen sets up the application, counts the user visits to the application, and starts the user at a main menu.
Customer	Browse catalog	The customer is able to search the product catalog by product category, manufacturer, and catalog number. Products of interest from the search can be selected for further consideration.
Customer	Browse product detail	The customer can display each selected product by product description, a product image, price, and the quantity in stock.
Customer	Update shopping cart	The customer can add, remove, or update products to be purchased in the shopping cart.
Customer	Purchase shopping cart products	The customer can review the products to be purchased, indicate customer delivery information, and collect customer billing/payment information.
Customer	Purchase order completion	This validates the customer's ability to pay for the products, provides a purchase order to the customer, and initiates product delivery.
Customer	Log off	This checks for completion of all customer actions during this session before disconnecting from the customer.

Figure 7.1 Example use case for an online purchasing application Use Case 001—product purchase (happy path)

happy path and each use case alternate path, bringing the use case sequence of actions into the test case steps almost one-for-one. Figure 7.2 shows what the steps of the Use Case #001 happy path test case might be.

Step no.	Step	Expected result
1.	Log on	Access the main menu
2.	Browse catalog	Find a blue widget
3.	Browse product detail	Display the blue widget descr.
4.	Update shopping cart	Add the blue widget
5.	Purchase shopping cart products	Buy the blue widget
6.	Purchase order completion	Get blue widget purchase confirm
7.	Log off	Exit the application successfully

Figure 7.2 A full business path test case from use case

The first draft of the use cases and the test cases have insufficient details to either write code or execute tests at this time. Both do represent a roadmap to the additional level of details needed for writing code and executing tests.

As the design phase of the software development project continues, details become available that spell out how each actor can accomplish the use case activities—menus, data entry web pages, data search web pages, report web pages, printouts, databases for purchases, and so forth. As these details emerge from the design work, the tester can identify the pieces that need testing individually before they can be tested together, possibly implying more test cases.

An example of this individual piece testing would be the purchase web page on which the customer indicates delivery information, billing information, and method of payment. For the purposes of discussion, one web page is assumed to collect all of this information. The purpose of the test case for the purchase page is to rigorously test all of the data entry fields (delivery street address), dropdown lists (state code and credit card), radio buttons (5-day ground, second day air, and so forth), and any other buttons on the page. The intent is to completely validate this web page before it is included in a happy path test case. Figure 7.3 shows what the steps of the more detailed purchase page test case might be.

Step no.	Step	Expected result
1.	Launch the purchase order screen	Screen appears
2.	Enter purchaser name	Accept valid names
3.	Enter purchaser address street	Accept multiple addresses
4.	Enter purchaser address state	Select multiple states
5.	Enter purchaser address zip	Select multiple zip areas
6.	Select method of payment	Select check/credit card
7.	Exit purchase order screen	Screen stops successfully

Figure 7.3   A full business path test case from use case

The more the individual web page validation that can be done before the happy path and alternate path validation, the more successful the first time path tests will be. The other way to look at it is that if all of the individual web pages work as advertised and one of the paths fails, then you can focus on the activity-to-activity interaction instead of asking which page might not be working correctly.

It is hopefully clear now that use cases are a powerful basis on which to develop business path test cases. Use cases contain the business functionality to be verified. As each use case is refined by additional requirements and design detail, the tester can leverage the more detailed use cases to develop detailed test cases for the individual application pieces. Execution of the test cases then proceeds in reverse order, that is, the test cases for the individual application pieces are executed first. When all of the pieces are validated, the test cases for the different business paths are executed. The next section gives you some approaches for designing both kinds of functional test cases.

There are some significant limitations to test case development from use cases. One significant limitation of use cases is the absence of structural (nonfunctional) software requirements like security, data management, and interfaces. Another significant limitation of use cases is the absence of performance requirements. We will explore alternative ways of developing structural test cases in Chapter 8 and alternative ways of developing performance test cases in Chapter 9.

7.3 AN APPROACH TO FUNCTIONAL TESTING

All functional testing uses business requirements and the associated software design specifications as the validation yardstick. If the business requirement says the software should do "x," then functional testing validates "x" as the expected result. If this topic sparks your interest, Whittaker's textbooks can give you more details and the results of current academic research. [25] The functional testing objectives typically include those described in the following subsections.

7.3.1 User Navigation Testing

If an application is strictly batch processing, then user navigation testing does not apply. Most software has a series of end user and administrator screens for directing the software's operation. The end user screens can be divided into two categories: navigation and transaction. Navigation screens are those log on and log off screens that control access to the software, all menus that provide alternate activity paths thru the software, and all screen-to-screen linkage that represents a continuum of some business activity. User navigation testing focuses on the user's ability to log on to the software with appropriate authority, traverse the application to the desired transaction screens, traverse the transaction screens correctly, and log off the software. This kind of testing is not concerned with what transaction activity is being performed on the transaction screens encountered, just that the screens can be encountered in the correct sequence. As the transaction screens themselves have become more complex, it takes fewer screen traversals to complete a business activity. The navigation becomes more intrascreen movement (tabbing) than interscreen movement.

It is the tester's job to design and execute tests that traverse all valid navigation paths and attempt to traverse as many invalid navigation paths as possible. The valid navigation paths are found primarily in the user guide. The input/expected result paradigm of black box testing becomes path taken/expected destination paradigm.

One of the more complex aspects of user navigation to both develop and test is the aspect of "stateless" user screens, that is, user screens that you can land on from a variety of other screens without a prerequisite screen sequence. Indeed, it is common for several "stateless" screens to be active at the same time.

7.3.2   Transaction Screen Testing

Once an end user or administrator has navigated to a transaction screen, he or she will perform some meaningful business activity on that transaction screen. The transaction screen normally has input data fields, lists of choices, options, and action buttons (Add, Change, Delete, Submit, Cancel, OK, and so forth). Some kind of results may be displayed on the transaction screen after appropriate action buttons are pressed.

It is the tester's job to design tests that validate the operation of every field, list, option, and action button on each transaction screen against the business requirements, the user guide, and the administrator guide. If results are also displayed on the transaction screen, then the black box inputs versus the expected result technique is used to validate the displayed results.

7.3.3   Transaction Flow Testing

Transaction flow testing takes the transaction screens that have been validated by testing and determines if their combined results of correct navigation completes the intended business activity in some specified way. An example of transaction flow testing is to validate customer profile updates as

transaction screen 1 for customer name, address, and contact person

transaction screen 2 for customer line of credit approval

transaction screen 3 for customer payment terms and discounts

transaction screen 4 for profile summary and update action

transaction screen 5 for viewing updated customer profile

The result of the sequence of five screens being completed is expected to be a master file or database file update with all the information collected on these transaction screens. Another example of transaction flow is when you purchase something online. The expected result is a purchase order for the product(s) you want to order and pay for. A third example of transaction flow is when you pay a bill online. The expected result is a transfer of funds from your bank account or posting against your credit card to the company you are paying.

It is the tester's job to validate that correctly completing the sequence of transaction screens does provide a correct result. The tester also validates that if any of the system's business rules are violated, the system does not provide any result (all results under the circumstances are normally not valid). Although the tester's task for transaction flow testing is more complex than the transaction screen testing, the efficient tester will use sequences of successful transaction screen test actions to drive more complex transaction flow testing. There is no need to reinvent transaction screen test actions just for flow testing.

7.3.4   Report Screen Testing

Report screen testing is similar to transaction screen testing. The difference is that you are attempting to retrieve and display data from the system using the report screens instead of entering data using the transaction screens. The difficulty in report screen testing usually lies in the variety of ways an end user can specify which data are retrieved (search criteria) and how these data are displayed (sorting and formatting options).

The tester's job is to pay particular attention to the data retrieved and displayed because the wrong data may have been selected or, worse yet, not all data requested were displayed.

7.3.5   Report Flow Testing

Report flow testing becomes different from report screen testing when the report results are provided in other modalities besides on-screen display. For example, hardcopy output would be one of the more popular alternate report modalities. The tester must ask the question, "Does the software send *exactly* the same results to the printer that it displays on the report screen?" Having a printer option implies the possibility of the report screen offering a selection of print fonts, another fertile area for testing. Another rseport modality might be a print file to disk (floppy, hard disk, CD, or e-mail).

It is the tester's job to validate the report results on all the alternative report modalities supported by the software. Similar to our suggestion with transaction flow testing, use successful report screen tests to drive the report flow testing.

7.3.6   Database Create/Retrieve/Update/Delete Testing

Many applications use databases behind their transaction and report screens to manage the application's data. Database functional testing is normally done in two steps. The first step is to test the database design viability by successfully performing the application data manipulations outside of the application.

A brief word of explanation might be needed at this juncture. Databases are managed by database management systems or DBMSs. Examples of DBMSs are DB2, Oracle, Sybase, and MicroSoft Access. Each DBMS has a language for describing data structures (DDLs) and manipulating data within these structures (DML). Typically, a database administrator is well versed in both languages and sets up the databases for the application development team. Once the databases are set up, programmers can create new records, retrieve records, update records, and delete records using the DBMS language totally independent of any application.

Back to the first database testing, the tester needs to see if the data in the databases can be managed per the application requirements. Using our previous transaction flow example, the tester must be able to successfully add a new user profile, updating an existing user profile, and deleting a user profile just using the DBMS commands. What this kind of testing validates is the viability of the database design for the intended application. If the database design is not viable, then the application can never maintain its data correctly regardless of the expertise of the application programmers.

The second step is to test the application software's use of the validated database design. This testing amounts to looking at the "back side" of the application after successful flow testing has been completed. The test results may look good on the screen; however, the testing question is "have those same results been correctly managed in the database by the application?" This kind of testing is easiest done by pairing up validated transaction flow screens with validated report flow screens. If what is seen going into the transaction screens appears on the report screens, chances are good (not 100%) that the underlying database structure that supports these screens is being manipulated correctly.

Testing application databases requires cooperation and collaboration between the tester and the database administrator due to the complexity of DBMS languages, design, and operations.

7.4 AN APPROACH TO REGRESSION TESTING

The easiest way to describe regression testing is to quote the famous Humphrey Bogart line in the movie Casablanca, "play it again, Sam." The term itself means to regress or go back to a less mature or less stable state. Applied to software, regression testing means to search for software corrections that make the current version less stable by unintentionally affecting code not directly related to the corrections. If this topic sparks your interest, there are a number of good textbooks that can give you more details and the results of current academic research. [26–28]

Regression testing is normally started while new code is being written and existing code is being corrected. The addition of new code or corrections to existing code always raises the possibility that the new or changed code may accidentally "break" the already tested code. The testing response to this possibility is to rerun all successful test cases to date on a new build of the software. If the previously tested code is not affected by the new or changed code, the previously tested code will again pass all tests and the testing can go forward. If the regression testing discovers defects, then the nature and location of the new or changed code is used to help diagnose the defect because the new or changed code is the number one suspect. Planning for regression testing includes standard approaches to writing test actions and scripts so that they are rerunable and maintained in some kind of library to facilitate many reruns after many builds. Regression testing is also done from version to version. The intent is to rerun the prior version suite of test cases on the next version build to verify that the new version has not interfered with any prior functionality. The next version will usually have additional functionality, one of the primary reasons for a new release. Once the new version has been tested and verified ready to ship or place in production, the new functionality test activities and scripts need to be added to the prior version regression suite.

Notice that if any of the functionality of the prior version is either changed or removed, the prior version suite of test cases will predictably fail for those changes or removals. The response to these test failures is not the usual attempt to try to fix the code; rather, the response is to retire the obsolete test activities and scripts from the next version regression suite. Therefore, the regression suite will not be cast in concrete per the first version. Rather, it will evolve with functional additions and changes introduced in each subsequent release.

7.5 DETAILED WHITE BOX TESTING TECHNIQUES

The objective of white box testing is to verify the correctness of the software's statements, code paths, conditions, loops, and data flow. This objective is often referred to as logic coverage. The prerequisites for white box testing include the software requirements, use cases, the executable program, its data, *and its source code*. If this topic sparks your interest, there are a number of good textbooks that can give you more details and the results of current academic research.[29–33]

The software developer normally does white box testing as an extension of code debugging activity early in the development cycle. Software developers usually focus on "making the code work" according to use case activities, which gives them the tendency to debug only the code they know works (selective logic test coverage). Testers add value to developer debugging activity by helping the developer plan and debug more of the code than usual (more thorough logic test coverage). The more the logic test coverage you attain while debugging, the fewer the defects will be discovered later by other kinds of testing.

As Capers Jones concludes, the earlier these defects can be discovered, the less expensive they are to correct. The business motivation behind white box testing is expected economies of testing. Much of the research you will find in white box testing will relate to hypotheses, algorithms, and procedures that attempt to achieve 100% logic test coverage under certain, very controlled circumstances. Research has not yet produced a white box approach that guarantees 100% logic test coverage for all situations.

We will briefly discuss six generic white box testing techniques.

7.5.1 Statement Coverage Technique

Statement coverage techniques focus on determining what percentage of the source code lines in a program has been executed. If there are 5,000 lines of source code in a program and you can determine manually or with a tool that you have executed 4,537 lines of source code, then you have achieved a 90.7% statement coverage (exceptionally high for complex programs). The underlying hypothesis is that the higher the source code test coverage, the fewer will be the defects found later. The practical conclusion is that new, unexecuted code lines are just a software time bomb waiting to explode at the most inopportune moment in production. The question is not "if" they will explode, only a question of "when."

7.5.2 Branch (Simple Condition) Coverage Technique

Branch coverage techniques focus on determining what percentage of the source code branch (true/false) logic in a program has been executed. If there are 1,500 source code branch points in a program and you can determine manually or with a tool that you have executed 1,145 branches (count true and false branch executions separately), then you have achieved a 76.3% branch point coverage (exceptionally high for complex programs). The underlying hypothesis is that the higher the branch point test coverage, the fewer will be the defects found later. The practical conclusion is that unexecuted branches, true or false, are just a software time bomb waiting to explode just like unexecuted statements. The co-occurrence of unexecuted branches with unexecuted statements is found most often in untested error recovery logic.

Because all computer logic conditions resolve to either true or false, you may wonder about the stipulation of simple conditions in this technique. Choosing to test the simple condition branches before the compound condition branches requires fewer initial test actions. All the developer needs to do is choose any test value that will force a true branch and any test value that will force a false branch, just two test values per branch.

7.5.3 Compound Condition Coverage Technique

The compound condition coverage technique extends the branch coverage technique to branches with compound conditions, ones that contain combinations of Boolean operators AND, OR, and NOT along with pairs of parentheses, possibly nested. The challenge is to identify all the test value combinations that will evaluate to true and false for every simple condition and every Boolean combination of simple conditions. Truth tables are normally employed at this point in the white box test planning to enumerate all the possible condition permutations. Here is a compound condition containing two simple conditions.

(AGE > 18 AND SEX = M)

In order to identify the test data for 100% compound condition coverage, the following truth table is constructed.

AGE	SEX	ANDed condition
=18 False	=F False	=F False
=18 False	=M True	=F False
=19 True	=F False	=F False
=19 True	=M True	=T True

From this truth table, you can see that a simple branch test that evaluated to the only true condition and one false condition would miss the two additional test data input combinations that would evaluate to false ... and possibly discovering a logic error.

The truth table becomes larger and more complex with additional Boolean conditions, allowing more opportunity for missing logic coverage when using only simple branching coverage. Here is a compound condition with three simple conditions.

((AGE > 18 AND SEX = M) OR HEIGHT > 6 ft)

There are standard programming language rules for the order of evaluating complex expressions such as this example. In order to identify the test data for 100% compound condition coverage, the previous example would expand in the following way using standard Boolean evaluation rules.

AGE	SEX	ANDed Condition	HEIGHT	ORed Condition
=18 False	= F False	= F False	=16 False	= F False
=18 False	= M True	= F False	=16 False	= F False
=19 True	= F False	= F False	=16 False	= F False
=19 True	= M True	= T True	=16 False	= T True
=18 False	= F False	= F False	=17 True	= T True
=18 False	= M True	= F False	=17 True	= T True
=19 True	= F False	= F False	=17 True	= T True
=19 True	= M True	= T True	=17 True	= T True

From this truth table, you can see that a simple branch test that evaluated to one true condition and one false condition would miss the six additional test data input combinations that would evaluate to both true and false ... and possibly discovering a logic error.

7.5.4   Path Coverage Technique

Path coverage techniques focus on determining what percentage of the source code paths in a program have been traversed completely. There are a number of definitions of source code paths in the literature. In its simplest form, a source code path is the sequence of program statements from the first executable statement through a series of arithmetic, replacement, input/output, branching, and looping statements to a return/stop/end/exit statement. If there are 943 different paths through a program and you can determine manually or with a tool that you have executed 766 of them, then you have achieved an 81.2% path coverage (exceptionally high for complex programs). The underlying hypothesis is that the higher the path test coverage, the fewer will be the defects found later. The practical conclusion is that unexecuted paths are just a time bomb waiting to explode at the most inopportune moment in production, even though all of the statements and branch points in the path have been individually tested.

7.5.5   Loop Coverage Technique

Loop coverage techniques focus on determining what percentage of the source code loops in a program has been cycled completely. There are several loop constructs in programming languages like DO, FOR, WHILE, and UNTIL. Some loops are a clever construct of IF statements and subsequent returns to these IF statements. Regardless of the loop construct, the objective of loop testing is to force the program through the loop zero times, one time, $n/2$ times (where n is the terminal loop value), n times, and $n + 1$ times. The one-time loop, the $n/2$-time loop, and n-time loop validate expected loop response at the beginning, middle, and end of the longest loop. The zero-time and $n + 1$-time loop test for unexpected and inappropriate looping conditions. We will see this end-point/mid-point testing tactic again in black box boundary value testing. If there are 732 loops in a program and you can determine manually or with a tool that you have executed 312, then you have achieved a 42.6% loop coverage (about average for complex programs). The underlying hypothesis is that the higher the loop test coverage, the fewer will be the defects found later. The practical conclusion is that unexecuted loops and loops execute only within expected loop limits are just a time bomb waiting to explode at the most inopportune moment in production.

7.5.6   Intuition and Experience

This section is devoted to those software aspects that experienced testers have found to be troublesome areas of coding that the more formal debugging and testing techniques tend to miss. Here is a summary of those troublesome aspects.

7.5.6.1   Dates

Dates present three unique data challenges to the developer: valid formats, sort sequence, and calculations. The original mm/dd/yyyy format of dates remains problematic because for each mm (month) there is a specific range of values for dd (day) depending on yyyy (years like leap years). The validation of mm versus dd versus yyyy remains complex and grows more because we crossed the century boundary with computer systems (the infamous Y2K problem). The global nature of the Internet has caused software to support a variety of date input formats. For example, the U.S. date standard is mm/dd/yyyy, whereas the British date standard is dd/mm/yyyy. Throw in the spelling or abbreviation of the month represented by mm, and the date input formats become a sizeable format coding challenge.

Date sort sequencing can also be a significant application problem. If the application wishes to maintain its records in date order (either ascending or descending), the application must convert the input date to a yyyy/mm/dd sort format in order for the year to be the primary sort key, the month to be the secondary sort key, and the day to be the tertiary sort key.

An alternative approach to converting dates back and forth between sort and report formats is to calculate the number of days elapsed since some "anchor date" in the past. If the data are really historical, then systems choose a very old anchor date like October 15, 1582, the advent of the Gregorian calendar and leap year. If the data just span a century or two, then January 1, 1800 might be an appropriate anchor date. Then, every date is sorted in two formats, a display format and number of days elapsed since the anchor date. The number of days elapsed then becomes a much simpler sort key to manage, just a positive integer. A secondary advantage of this calculation and storage of days elapsed is that you have the data structure sufficient to readily calculate "date + x days" or "date − y days" or day of the week (Monday, Tuesday, and so forth).

All of these date calculations are possible sources of date processing error or failure. The tester can plan and execute most of the date testing by collaborating with the developers to identify and understand where dates and date calculations are imbedded in the software input/output design, file designs, and database designs.

7.5.6.2   Zero Length Anything

There are a number of programming situations that can produce zero data or counts or process steps. Here is a partial list.

arrays

blank inputs

divide by zero

loops

pointers

record lengths

records (empty files)

sorts

As with the dates, many of these zero items can be forced by pressing the "send" key when you have supplied no data. Also, where calculations are known to exist, entering blank or zero for some or all of the input values also force these behaviors. More specific testing might require collaboration with the developer to identify other potential zero-causing areas of the software.

This is one of the areas in which your background and experience as a software developer will tend to guide you toward zero-causing areas of the software because that is where you would place it if you were coding it.

7.5.6.3 Buffer Overflow

Buffer overflow is a particularly insidious programming problem because it does not manifest itself until the software is relatively busy. The problem arises when an area in memory called a buffer is set aside to manage transient data like user input or report output or database records or internet packets. When that buffer area becomes full of data, something must happen to empty part of the buffer and accommodate more data. Some refill strategies dictate that a full buffer must be completely emptied before more data can be accommodated. Other refill strategies wrap the data around the buffer, accommodating more data while emptying what it has. So, you can be filling and emptying a buffer a number of different ways when the buffer overflows its area. This can make buffer overflow errors exceptionally challenging to repeat.

The symptoms of buffer overflow are as insidious as the event itself because when a buffer overflows, it overwrites adjacent areas in the computer's memory. If that adjacent area also holds data, then the data become corrupt for no apparent reason. If that adjacent area holds instructions, then the software begins bizarre behavior that might implicate perfectly correct code under normal conditions.

The buffer overflow problem takes on a higher level of testing criticality when you realize that many computer viruses are introduced by forcing buffer overflow into the software's instructions.

One of the most effective ways to test for buffer overflow is to drive the software with a large volume of input data, force a large volume of internal file processing or database processing, and force a large volume of output for specific buffer areas. As with the date calculation situation, the tester must collaborate with the developer to identify the specific inputs, outputs, file processing, and database processing that rely on specific buffers that need to be tested. It may make sense to combine some of the buffer overflow white box testing with later performance black box testing described in Chapter 9 to get the volume of buffer traffic necessary to cause overflow.

All of the white box testing techniques presented here attempt to increase the logical coverage of source code debugging/testing. The underlying premise is that unexecuted source code is one of the most frequent and predictable sources of defects.

7.6 DETAILED BLACK BOX TESTING TECHNIQUES

The objective of black box testing is to verify the correctness of the software's behavior that directly supports daily business activity. This objective is often referred to as behavior coverage. The requirements for black box testing are the software requirements, use cases, only the executable program, and its data. These requirements are usually met during the middle phases of the development life cycle when large pieces of code begin to operate together or when software is purchased from a vendor. If this topic sparks your interest, there are a number of good textbooks that can give you more details and the results of current academic research. [34–36]

It is reasonable for anyone (developer or tester) to do the black box testing as long as the person doing the testing is not the person who authored the code. Software developers usually focus their black box testing on validating expected behavior of the code (positive testing) against use cases, which gives them the tendency to ignore unexpected behavior (negative testing). Testers add value to black box testing by planning and executing both positive and negative behavior testing because the tester knows that the majority of user-detected defects arise from unexpected behavior. Much of the research you will find in black box testing will relate to structured approaches that attempt to provide 100% positive and negative behavior coverage under certain controlled circumstances. The best reference for these structured approaches in detail is Whittaker's textbook.

We will briefly discuss four generic black box testing techniques.

7.6.1 Equivalence Classes Technique

Equivalence class techniques focus on identifying groups of input data that tend to cause the application under test to behave the same way for all values in the group. The rationale behind this search for input data test groups is to substantially reduce the volume of test data needed to verify a specific behavior. Two simple examples will help you understand this rationale better.

The first example is a data field with data values grouped by other characteristics. Consider the application under test to be a security system with a logon ID requirement. Furthermore, consider that the security system must validate over 5,000 log on IDs when in production.

The tester might decide to validate every one of the 5,000 logon IDs. Alternatively, if the tester knows that there are only three categories (clerks, supervisors, and managers) of logon IDs, then perhaps a sampling from each category will provide sufficient validation. Consider testing 50 logon IDs from each category. If any of the 50 logon IDs for a given category is not correctly accepted, consider increasing the sample size of logon IDs for that category and continue testing. If the initial sample of 150 logon IDs for all three categories are correctly accepted, then the tester has achieved the desired test results using only 3% of the possible test data.

The second example is a data field with a range of possible numerical values. Consider the application under test to be a hospital admission system, and it is required to admit patients ranging in age from 1 year old to 99 years old, inclusively. The tester might decide to test all 99 possible age values. Alternatively, the tester could select the equivalence class of ages 1, 50, and 99 and test the same behavior using 97% fewer test values. The set of values (1, 50, and 99) is said to be an equivalence class of the set of all possible values (1, 2, 3, …, 97, 98, 99).

The example becomes more dramatic if real number values are to be tested. Consider the same hospital admission system to require a co-pay before admission (money the patient must pay first before his or her insurance will pay the rest of the bill). If the co-pay input field allowed from $0.00 (no co-pay) to $1000.00, then the tester might decide to test all 1,00,001 possible co-pay values. Alternatively, the tester could select the equivalence class of co-pay amounts $0.00, $0.99, $1.00, $1.99, $10.00, $10.99, $100.00, $100.99, $999.00, $999.99, and $1000.00 and test the same behavior using 99.992% fewer test values.

Please notice that in both examples, test values at the beginning, in the middle, and end of the data range were chosen as the equivalence class. Correct middle range value behavior by the software does not necessarily guarantee correct beginning or end value behavior by the software. Conversely, correct beginning and end value behavior by the software do not necessarily guarantee correct middle range value behavior by the software. So, the recommended black box technique for selecting equivalence class values includes values at the beginning, in the middle, and at the end of the range. Please notice that the second equivalence class example, co-pay, also had values for the different possible value lengths (numbers of significant digits).

7.6.2 Boundary Value Analysis Technique

The boundary value analysis technique extends the analysis of beginning and ending input value possibilities for an equivalence class. Boundary values are of interest to testers because a large percentage of functional errors from input and output data occur on or around these boundaries.

The traditional boundary value analysis begins by identifying the smallest value increment in a specific equivalence class. This smallest value increment is called the *boundary value epsilon*. The epsilon is used to calculate $+/-$ values around the beginning and ending values in an equivalence class. In the previous example, the admission age boundary value epsilon is 1 because the input field allows for no age increment less than a whole year. The admission co-pay boundary value epsilon is $0.01 because the input field allows for no payment increment smaller than a penny.

In the case of admission age, the beginning boundary test ages would be -1, 0, and $+1$, which are $+/-$ epsilon around the beginning value 0. The ending boundary test ages would be 98, 99, and 100, which are $+/-$ epsilon around the ending value 99. Good boundary value testing technique suggests that you also test epsilon values around the equivalence class midpoint like 49, 50, and 51 for the admission age midpoint of 50. The resulting equivalence class with boundary value analysis results would then be the set of values (-1, 0, 1, 49, 50, 51, 98, 99, and 100).

In the case of admission co-pay, the beginning boundary test co-pay would be $-\$0.01$, \$0.00, and $+\$0.01$, which are $+/-$ epsilon around the beginning value \$0.00. The ending boundary test co-pay would be \$999.99, \$1000.00, and \$1,000.01, which are $+/-$ epsilon around the ending value \$1000.00. The midvalue epsilon test values would be \$499.99, \$500.00, and \$500.01. The resulting equivalence class with boundary value analysis results would then be the set of values ($-\$0.01$, \$0.00, \$0.01, 0.99, \$1.00, \$1.99, \$10.00, \$10.99, \$100.00, \$100.99, \$499.99, \$500.00, \$500.01, \$999.00, \$999.99, \$1000.00, and \$1000.01).

The result of a boundary value analysis is additional input test values to the equivalence class of values to specifically exercise the application's behavior where that behavior tends to fail most often. Even with the additional boundary test values, the equivalence classes remain significantly smaller than the set of all possible values for the input under consideration.

Equivalence classes of inputs with boundary values are executed as one of the first step in black box testing. Once correct input value acceptance has be verified, you can begin to verify correct output results.

7.6.3 Expected Results Coverage Technique

While equivalence classes and boundary value analysis focus on input test values, expected results coverage focuses on output test values for associated input values. The first step is to find the business rules in the application requirements that define the expected results. We will use our hospital admission example to demonstrate what kind of business rules might be found in the requirements documentation. Presented with an admission age and a co-pay, the application under test must determine the maximum daily hospital room rate for hospital room assignment. The maximum room rate insurance coverage business rules might look like the table below.

Business rules for maximum room rate insurance coverage

Input	Input	Output/result
Age on admission	Co-pay	Maximum room rate
0–6 years	\$50.00	\$50.00
7–17 years	\$75.00	\$100.00
18–35 years	\$100.00	\$150.00
36–49 years	\$125.00	\$300.00
50–74 years	\$200.00	\$350.00
75–99 years	\$250.00	\$400.00

The next step is to develop a table of valid combinations of equivalence class inputs with boundary values per the business rules that are expected to give the business rule results. Below is the start of the table of valid combinations for the hospital admission business rules.

Table of valid combinations—maximum room rate (partial table)

Input	Input	Output/result
Age on admission	Co-pay	Maximum room rate
0–6 years	*$50.00*	*$50.00*
0	$50.00	$50.00
1	$50.00	$50.00
3	$50.00	$50.00
5	$50.00	$50.00
6	$50.00	$50.00
6–17 years	*$75.00*	*$100.00*
7	$75.00	$100.00

The next step is to extend the table of combinations to disallowed combinations by the business rules. For these disallowed combinations, some kind of error message should be found in the corresponding expected results column rather than a maximum room rate. The programming specifications should be the source of these expected error messages in lieu of maximum room rates. Below is the extension of the table of combinations to account for disallowed combinations.

Table of valid and disallowed combinations—maximum room rate (partial table)

Input	Input	Output/result
Age on admission	Co-pay	Maximum room rate
0–6 years	*$50.00*	*$50.00*
−1	$50.00	error—age not in range
0	$50.00	$50.00
1	$50.00	$50.00
3	$50.00	$50.00
5	$50.00	$50.00
6	$50.00	$50.00
7	$50.00	error—co-pay not valid for age
3	$49.99	error—co-pay not valid for age
3	$50.01	error—co-pay not valid for age
6–17 years	*$75.00*	*$100.00*
5	$75.00	error—co-pay not valid for age
6	$75.00	$100.00
7	$75.00	$100.00

The final step is to add a column on the right side of the combinations table for actual test results. The resulting table is called an expected value coverage matrix. The partial matrix for this example is given below.

Expected results matrix—maximum room rate (partial table)

Input	Input	Expected results	Actual results
Age	Co-pay	Maximum room rate	Maximum room rate
0–6 years	*$50.00*	*$50.00*	
−1	$50.00	error—age not in range	
0	$50.00	$50.00	
1	$50.00	$50.00	
3	$50.00	$50.00	
5	$50.00	$50.00	
6	$50.00	$50.00	
7	$50.00	error—co-pay not valid for age	
3	$49.99	error—co-pay not valid for age	
3	$50.01	error—co-pay not valid for age	
6–17 years	*$75.00*	*$100.00*	
5	$75.00	error—co-pay not valid for age	
6	$75.00	$100.00	
7	$75.00	$100.00	

The actual test results are posted in the matrix as the black box test execution is performed. Differences between expected results and actual results for any combination of inputs should cause further analysis to determine if the difference is (a) faulty test design, (b) unclear ambiguous business rules, or (c) program error.

7.6.4   Intuition and Experience

This section is devoted to those software aspects that testers have found by repeated experience to be troublesome areas in an application under development that the more formal behavioral testing tends to miss. Here is a summary of these troublesome aspects.

7.6.4.1   Error Handling

Error handling is by far the most complex and most onerous programming to develop. By its very nature, error handling is supposed to expect the unexpected and gracefully recover to the pre-error operation state. It is not surprising that error handling represents the greatest risk of behavior failure. Error handling challenges the programmer first to detect that an error in data or processing has occurred. Then, error handling challenges the programmer to correctly alert the end user to the situation. Finally, error handling challenges the programmer to correctly recover both data and processing from the error and allow the end user to continue error-free operation.

The richness of the error recovery code is limited in part to the programmer's exposure to end users of similar kinds of applications or support technologies. The richness of error recovery testing is also limited in part to the tester's exposure to error recovery techniques that do not work well regardless of the business application or support technologies.

In an ideal development project, the programmers maintain a single list of errors that end users can encounter. This list would contain items like

Application X—message list contents

unique error code/ID

error message text

error description

code module that detects the error condition

severity of the error encountered

    I = Informational
    W = Warning
    A = Abort current activity and attempt to recover to preerror operation

user action required

application action required

likelihood of data loss

Such a list becomes the basis for planning 100% error handling validation. The testing challenge is to repeatably (remember SPRAE) cause the errors on demand.

The sad truth is that many development projects let their programmers imbed most of this error message information in the source code. The practice of scattering error handling information throughout the source code is so prevalent in Internet applications that software vendors have found a thriving niche market in providing reverse engineering tools that find and list out all error messages in an application. The testing challenge is to determine what circumstances can cause each reverse engineered error message to appear.

7.6.4.2 Data Type Conversions

Any time user inputs are converted from one data type to another, for example, alphabetic to numeric, there is the possibility of an incorrect or failed conversion. Depending on the programming language(s) used to develop the new application, this failed conversion can cause a range of execution responses from benign return codes that the application can intercept and interpret to malignant execution halts. The corollary to failed conversion is the application's ability to identify incorrect conversions (alphas in a strictly numeric field) before they are attempted.

The tester has the challenge of identifying input and output fields that are data type sensitive and design execution tests to validate their correctness and robustness (will not fail). The primary source for this test planning is the user guide that is supposed to spell out all input field data type restrictions.

7.6.4.3 Dates

We discussed the complexities of date formats and date calculations in white box testing. Dates reappear in the black box discussion because there is date behavior that a user can observe and a tester can test without having the code available. These dates typically appear on data entry screens, in information search criteria, and on reports. The user guide is the best source of expected behavior for dates that the user directly controls and sees. This is also the situation in which the tester discovers date formatting choices in some kind of user profile, for example, the formats mm/dd/yyyy or dd/mm/yyyy or Month, yyyyy. So, the tester is challenged to test the default date format wherever it is used in the software, as well as all the other formatting choices in the same software locations.

7.7 SUMMARY

The objective of functional testing is to validate the software behavior against the business functionality documented in the software requirements and specifications. Business functionality is generally defined as those activities that support routine daily business. Functional testing is achieved by a series of tests that exercise increasingly more of the software that directly enables users to accomplish this routine daily business.

There is a relatively new development scoping technique called a use case that software developers employ to capture user-functional requirements of a system for the purpose of scoping the project. The technique became popular in the mid-1990s first as an object-oriented design technique and later broadened in appeal for other types of software development. Consider drafting a test case for each use case happy path and each use case alternate path, bringing the use case sequence of actions into the test case steps almost one-for-one.

As the design phase of the software development project continues, details become available that spell out how each actor can accomplish the use case activities—menus, data entry web pages, data search web pages, report web pages, printouts, databases for purchases, and so forth. As these details emerge from the design work, the tester can identify the pieces that need testing individually before they can be tested together, implying more test cases. Use cases are a powerful basis to develop business path test cases. Use cases contain the business functionality to be verified. As each use case is refined by additional requirements and design detail, the tester can leverage the more detailed use cases to develop detailed test cases for the individual application pieces. Execution of the test cases then proceeds in reverse order, that is, the test cases for the individual application pieces are executed first. When all of the pieces are validated, the test cases for the different business paths are executed.

All functional testing uses business requirements and the associated software design specifications as the validation yardstick. If the business requirement says the software should do "*x*," then functional testing validates "*x*" as the expected result. The functional testing objectives typically include

1. user navigation testing
2. transaction screen testing
3. transaction flow testing
4. report screen testing
5. report flow testing
6. database create/retrieve/update/delete testing

The term "regression testing" means to regress or go back to a less mature or less stable state. Applied to software, regression testing means to search for software corrections that make the current version less stable by unintentionally affecting code not directly related to the corrections. Regression testing is normally started while new code is being written and existing code is being corrected. The addition of new code or corrections to existing code always raises the possibility that the new or changed code may accidentally "break" the already tested code. The testing response to this possibility is to rerun all successful test actions and scripts to date on a new build of the software.

The objective of white box testing is to verify the correctness of the software's statements, code paths, conditions, loops, and data flow. This objective is often referred to as logic coverage. The prerequisites for white box testing include the software requirements, use cases, the executable program, its data, *and its source code.* Six generic white box testing techniques are as follows:

1. statement coverage technique
2. branch (single condition) coverage technique
3. compound condition coverage technique
4. path coverage technique
5. loop coverage technique
6. intuition and experience

The objective of black box testing is to verify the correctness of the software's behavior that directly supports daily business activity. This objective is often referred to as behavior coverage. The requirements for black box testing are the software requirements, use cases, only the executable program, and its data. These requirements are usually met during the middle phases of the development life cycle when large pieces of code begin to operate together or when software is purchased from a vendor. Four generic black box testing techniques are

1. equivalence classes technique
2. boundary value analysis technique

3. expected results coverage technique

4. intuition and experience

7.8 PUTTING FUNCTIONAL TESTING IN PERSPECTIVE

The most visible and well understood kind of testing is functional testing. Both the need for functional testing and the best description of functional testing goals come from the business requirements. The most common test shortcomings in functional testing tend to arise from the alternate paths, the exceptions, and the negative situations. Much of this chapter is devoted to a variety of general and detailed functional testing techniques that when conscientiously applied in a comprehensive test plan tend to reduce these shortcomings.

KEY TERMS AND CONCEPTS

White box testing	Black box testing	Functional testing
Logic coverage	Behavior coverage	Use case testing
Anchor date	Boundary value epsilon	Regression testing

Chapter 8

Structural (Non-functional) Testing

LEARNING OBJECTIVES

- to examine structural testing approaches
- to assess the potential business liabilities of ignoring structural testing

8.1 INTRODUCTION

This section continues the discussion of software testing that validates the behavior of software. The objective of structural testing is to validate the behavior of software that supports the software the user touches. Said another way, the business application software must operate on a hardware platform with an operating system and one or more software support components such as security, connectivity, and some kind of data management. This collective support software is often called the software platform. The software platform purpose is basically different from the application software. The software platform is not written for one specific business application. Conversely, a software platform is written as a generic capability that can support many different kinds of business applications at the same time. Therefore, software platforms are a possible point of failure when newly developed software is run. The risk of software platform failure is reduced by structural testing techniques.

The term non-functional testing is used parenthetically in the chapter title because it is a popular synonym for structural testing in much of the testing literature. The authors choose to use the term structural instead of non-functional in this textbook to avoid the common rejoinder, "if the code we are testing is non-functional, doesn't that mean we already know it does not work ??!" The structural testing techniques in this section should be viewed more as a buffet rather than a strict diet plan. Apply these techniques only to the software platform components necessary to support your new application.

Software Testing: Testing Across the Entire Software Development Life Cycle, by G. D. Everett and R. McLeod, Jr.
Copyright © 2007 John Wiley & Sons, Inc.

Because most software platform components come prepackaged (no source code available), the white box techniques cannot be applied to the software platform. Because the software platform behavior is seldom observed directly by the end user, most of the black box testing techniques except intuition and experience cannot be applied to the software platform as well. This is an area of testing that relies on the tester's own experience of some kind as a system administrator role or the tester's collaboration with system administrators. Several structural testing techniques have been described here.

8.2 INTERFACE TESTING

Interface testing focuses on data transferred between the application under test and different software platform components. Examples of data transfer mechanisms that need testing include data files, application program interfaces (APIs), database requests, and network data transfers. One helpful way to develop interface testing is to consider a four-step approach.

First, write tests that cause the application to produce data for transfer but have the transfer itself inhibited. That will allow the tester to validate that the application is producing the correct data in the correct format for use by the receiving software platform components.

Second, remove the data transfer inhibitors and observe if the receiving software platform component deals with the incoming data from the application correctly. This will allow the tester to validate that the software platform is correctly processing the already validated application data. If problems are found with this data transfer, then you have isolated the problem to the vendor's interface component or its data specification.

Third, write tests that cause the application to request data from other software platform components, but manually substitute the requested data in lieu of a "live" data feed from the involved software platform. This technique is referred to as "stubbing" the inputs. You will need to create and validate the manual data using the software platform component vendor interface specifications. This will allow testers to validate that the application is correctly accepting the data from the software platform.

Fourth, connect the application to the software platform components and rerun the data requests with "live" data feeds. This will allow the tester to validate that the software platform is producing data per its data specifications. If the problems are found with these data, you have isolated the problem to the vendor's interface component (does not work as advertised) or its data specifications.

Here is a pictorial view of these four steps.

1st: Application under test → Data (validate)
2nd: Application under test → Data → Support platform (validate)
3rd: Application under test (validate) ← Data ← Manual substitution
4th: Application under test ← Data (validate) ← Support platform

8.3 SECURITY TESTING

Consider leveraging equivalence classes for security behavior testing. Most security systems have different types or levels of security relating to end user processing restrictions based on job roles. For example, a typical three-level security system would define (1) clerks and other employees who just need to view data at security level 1, (2) clerk managers who need to view and update at security level 2, and (3) security administrators at security level 3 to grant and deny permissions to clerks at security level 1 and clerk managers at security level 2.

A brute force approach to testing these security behaviors would be to collect all of the user ID/password pairs in the company (very sensitive corporate information) and test each user ID/password pair to verify that the user ID under test is authorized and has the appropriate security access. In smaller companies, this could require testing hundreds of ID/password pairs. In larger companies, this could require testing thousands of pairs. Applying equivalence class analysis to the situation would allow you to choose may be 20–50 ID/password pairs for each level of security. Remember that in each equivalence class of ID/passwords by security level, you want to choose some valid ID/password pairs for the level (positive testing) and some invalid ID/password pairs for the level (negative testing).

Security for the new application may include encryption of passwords, as well as data that may be sent or received by the application. Testing techniques for encryption are beyond the scope of this textbook; however, we have provided a starting point for further reading. [37–41]

Once ID/password combinations, ID/password pair security levels, and data encryption have been tested, there is one remaining area of security concern. As with all software capabilities, security comes with a performance price tag. It takes a finite amount of time (greater than zero) to complete a security activity every time it is needed. Some software designers prefer to do security checking only at the start of a user session. Other software designers prefer to do security checking before each activity a user invokes. Still other software designers use a combination of initial checking and ongoing checking during end-user sessions. Regardless of the approach that the software designer takes to implementing security, the tester needs to measure the application's performance degradation specifically due to security. We have seen companies decide not to test security performance but to "turn on" security just before the system goes "live" because security was not expected to add noticeable processing overhead. These companies then faced the following question midday the first day the new application is live, "How can we disable security until we find out what is making the application run so slow in production?"

Although performance testing is the subject of the next chapter, it is reasonable to raise the security testing concern here and encourage the software development team to turn on full security as early in the application as practical both from a regression standpoint and a performance standpoint.

8.4 INSTALLATION TESTING

Installation testing focuses on the way the new application or system is placed into its production environment. The installation process itself can vary from a simple startup. exe that copies all application files to their proper place to a complex set of files and an instruction manual for an experienced system installer. Regardless of the simplicity or complexity of the installation process, it needs to be tested to ensure that the recipients of the new application or system can be successful at making it ready for use.

The recommended approach is to have a test environment with the hardware platform(s) and software platform set up to look exactly like the intended production environment. Then the test is to execute the installation procedure as written with the files provided to validate successful installation.

During the last 10 years, installation processes were weak in helping the end-user installer determine if the installation was successful. There has been a resurgence of vendors that include installation verification aids, both manual and automatic, with the installation packages. Do not forget to test the verification aids too!

8.5 THE SMOKE TEST

With the new, complex software applications, verification of a successful installation is not sufficient to allow the end user to start using the software for routine business. Two more tasks must be completed first: configuration and administration. This section deals with configuration verification. The next section deals with administration verification.

Configuring an installed application means selecting among a list of optional ways the software can be operated to make the software operate more closely to the specific organization's requirements. Typical configuration tasks include setting startup parameters and choosing process rules. Examples of startup parameters are the location of data files, maximum number of user sessions, maximum user session duration before automatic timeout, ID/password of the system administrator, default date formats, and geography-specific settings for language and culture. Examples of process rules are definitions of security classes, startup/shutdown schedules, backup schedules and destination files, accounting rules, and travel reservation rules.

The smoke test is used to verify that a successfully installed software application can be subsequently configured properly. As you can see by the variety of configuration examples, there are a large number of configuration combinations possible for most applications. The challenge of the smoke test planner is to identify the most likely configuration combination for the 10 most important customer installations.

The tester starts with a successfully installed copy of the software and proceeds to configure/reconfigure the software per the 10 combinations. Each time a different configuration combination is established, the tester executes minimal steps that demonstrate the software is correctly honoring the new configuration.

The term "smoke test" comes from the hardware engineering practice of plugging a new piece of equipment into an electrical outlet and looking for smoke. If there is no sign of smoke, the engineer starts using the equipment. The software smoke test is not exhaustive like regression testing. Rather, it is an attempt to verify the usability of the most likely first production configurations independent of the configuration test cases that were executed during software development.

8.6 ADMINISTRATION TESTING

Administration of a new application or system is the next operational step after successful installation and smoke test. Administration can include such technically complex activities as applying updates and fixes to the software. Administration can also include organization-specific activities such as adding users to the system, adding user security to the system, and building master files (customer lists, product lists, sales history, and so forth).

Administration testing is an extension of functional testing of business activities to functional testing of business *support* activities. If the administrative software components are developed first, then the results of successful administrative tests can be saved as the starting point for business function testing that relies on correct administrative setup. If the administrative components are developed second to business functions, then the manually built system setup files used to successfully test the business functions can be used as the expected results of the administrative component tests.

8.7 BACKUP AND RECOVERY TESTING

Sooner or later, all business software applications fail. The extent of financial damage that occurs with this failure is directly proportional to the software developer's effort to minimize that financial damage. If little thought is given to recovery after failure, the business will not be able to recover. A surprising number of commercial software packages simply instruct you to "start over" when a failure occurs.

If serious thought is given to recovery after failure, a backup strategy emerges that enables that recovery to occur. The accepted approach is that you start your failure defense by periodically making backup copies of critical business files such as master files, transaction files, and before/after update images. Then, when (not if) the software fails, the backup files are used to restore the software close to its pre-failure state.

Depending on what resources you are willing to spend on routine backup activities, the recovery pre-failure state can range from last weekend's backups (fairly inexpensive) to last night's backups (more expensive) to *all* backed up transactions except the one that caused the failure (very expensive but guarantees minimum loss of business). To test backup and recovery processes, you must perform a number of backups, interrupt the application abnormally, and restore the application using just the backups. Recovery data are then validated against the expected pre-failure state.

This testing approach seems relatively straightforward and somewhat intuitive. Be aware that the authors have seen more companies skip restore testing than perform restore testing. For some unexplained reason, these companies concentrate on validating the backup schedule and procedures, never trying to restore business from those backups. More often than not, when the untested but now business-critical restore process is used for the first time on real data, the attempt will fail for a variety of preventable reasons. For example, the backup files are empty or the backup file rotation is erroneous, causing you to write over the backup files last weekend that you so desperately need now. It is truly a career-altering experience.

8.8   PUTTING STRUCTURAL TESTING IN PERSPECTIVE

The obvious focus of test planning for software is the application or system under development. A less obvious but just as important focus is the software that supports the new application. Although the support software cannot compensate for a poor application implementation, it can detract from a good application implementation. The motivation to plan and execute structural tests is to validate this software application enabler.

8.9   SUMMARY

The objective of structural testing is to validate the behavior of software that supports the software the user touches. This collective support software is often called the software platform. The software platform purpose is basically different from the application software. The software platform is not written for one specific business application. Conversely, a software platform is written as a generic capability that can support many different kinds of business applications at the same time. Therefore, software platforms are a possible point of failure when a newly developed software is run. The risk of software platform failure is reduced by structural testing techniques.

Because most software platform components come prepackaged (no source code available), the white box techniques cannot be applied to the software platform. Because the software platform behavior is seldom observed directly by the end user, most of the black box testing techniques except intuition and experience cannot be applied to the software platform as well. This is an area of testing that relies on the tester's own experience of some kind as a system administrator role or the tester's collaboration with system administrators. Structural testing techniques include the following:

1. interface testing
2. security testing

3. installation testing
4. the smoke test
5. administration testing
6. backup and recovery testing

KEY TERMS

Software platform
Interface testing
Security testing

Installation testing
Smoke test

Administration testing
Backup and recovery
 testing

Chapter 9

Performance Testing

LEARNING OBJECTIVES

- to define the kind of testing that measures the speed of software
- to analyze techniques that simplify the intrinsically complex performance testing of software transaction mixes
- to assess the potential business liabilities of ignoring performance testing

9.1 INTRODUCTION

We advance from testing techniques that validate the software behavior to testing techniques that validate the software "speed." Speed in this context means that a tester measures aspects of software response time while the software is laboring under a controlled amount of work, called a "workload." To make the software reveal its true production speed, the tester must execute the performance tests in a testing environment that approximates the intended production environment as closely as possible. These execution testing techniques are fundamentally different in objective and approach from functional testing where the objective is validating correct code behavior regardless of speed.

Performance testing occurs after the functional testing is mostly completed and the software has become quite stable (fewer and fewer changes or corrections). Functional defects in the software may be revealed during performance testing, but this is not the testing objective.

The objective of performance testing is to validate the software "speed" against the business need for "speed" as documented in the software requirements. Software "speed" is generally defined as some combination of response time and workload during peak load times. These peak load times may occur during lunch time, at the opening of the stock market day, or after midnight when all online customers are in bed (overnight batch workload). Performance testing is achieved by a series of tests

Software Testing: Testing Across the Entire Software Development Life Cycle, by G. D. Everett and R. McLeod, Jr.
Copyright © 2007 John Wiley & Sons, Inc.

that introduces increasingly more workload of increasingly more complex business transaction mixes.

9.2 WORKLOAD PLANNING TECHNIQUES

Your first thoughts about performance testing may revolve around timing measurement precision. If the workload is incorrectly planned or executed, the most precise timing measurements will not bear any resemblance to the timing exhibited by the software in production. So we need to consider workload planning as the first step in performance testing.

The performance tester's first workload challenge is to identify which business transactions and activities need to be measured for performance. In all but the simplest software applications, it is difficult to identify the most important transaction and activity candidates for performance testing. The difficulty lies partly with the software end user's typical reaction, "everything must respond in less than 3 seconds." Somehow the tester must convince the end-user that different groups of transactions and activities will have different performance requirements based on different business priorities.

For example, customer purchase transactions may need to be completed in less than 3 seconds in order to keep the customer interested in buying more merchandise. By contrast, the transactions like credit card validation or warehouse ship ordering that occur to complete the purchase can be done 3 hours later and the customer will still get his or her merchandise delivered on the same date next week. This slow response time grouping may not thrill the employees, but as long as they can get their job done in time, the business investment required to speed up the employee transaction grouping response time faster than 3 hours has a very low return on investment.

Another example would be bank customer online requests for fund transfers. Because it is the policy of most banks to make the fund transfer available no sooner than overnight, the online customer request confirmation for fund transfer may have a 5 seconds response time requirement whereas the transfer transaction itself has a 12 hours response time (batch, overnight).

Lurking in the background of all online transaction rate discussions is the "Rule of 8." The Rule of 8 is a human behavior discovered in the 1970s by measuring the productivity of computer users as their system response time slows from subseconds to 20 seconds. The conclusion back in the 1970s and reconfirmed in the 1990s is that when the system response slows down beyond 8 seconds per transaction, human productivity falls off dramatically. The popularly accepted explanation for this phenomenon is that when the system responds in 8 seconds or less, the computer user can retain his or her train of thought about intended next actions. Response times longer than 8 seconds cause the computer user to forget what he or she was doing or intended to do next. For this reason, there was much emphasis placed on response times of 8 seconds or less for mainframe and client/server applications during the 1980s and 1990s.

Here is an interesting side note to the Rule of 8. Computer center staff continually need to manage the expectations of their users. If something does not work correctly, the users get upset. If something does not work fast enough, the users get upset. By the late 1970s, large mainframe computers had the capacity for delivering subsecond response times over a wide range of software activities for a large number of users. Computer center managers opted to "tune" these mainframes to a 4–5 seconds (intentionally slowed down) response time. Users became accustomed to the 4–5 seconds response time as the norm and certainly satisfactory with respect to the Rule of 8. Then, as new software was added to the mainframe, there was reserve capacity that the computer center managers could "tune" back in so that the response time never slowed down beyond the 4–5 seconds range. The users came to expect that adding software to the mainframe's workload would not slow down the response time as they had experienced in the 1960s and early 1970s. The computer center managers found a way to manage performance expectations of their users without giving the users the absolute best performance that the technology could provide.

The emergence of Internet applications has caused great consternation among end users. Internet application response times often range in the 10 seconds–3 min range with little hope for improvement using the current technology. Knowing that the Rule of 8 is still alive and well, the tester must team with the developer in setting realistic end-user expectations about performance capabilities and limitations of a new Internet system.

9.2.1 Documenting the Performance Workload Requirements

The outcome of this workload analysis for a purchasing application might be the following groups of transactions and their performance requirements. Notice that the performance requirement is stated as a maximum response time (no slower than) rather than an average response time.

Draft 1   Performance workload plan

Transaction group	Response time requirement
Menu navigation	Max 3 seconds
Log on/Log off	Max 3 seconds
Product detail display	Max 4 seconds
Purchase steps	Max 7 seconds
Catalog search	Max 10 seconds
Credit card payment	Max 30 seconds
Product ship	Max 24 hours

9.2.2 Documenting the Performance Workload Peaks

The performance tester's second workload challenge is to determine peak usage of each group of transactions and the timeframes in which the peak usage occurs.

Peak usage is normally measured in terms of active users. For example, if 500 users normally log on to the purchasing system over the lunch hour and 2,000 users normally log on around 7P.M. in the evening, then the peak expected workload for all log on/log off is 2,000 users. Notice also that the peak expected workload is 2,000 users whether the user base is 2,000 users or 2,000,000 users.

When researching the peak workload of users for a particular group of transactions, specify that you are interested in numbers of *active* users at peak workload time rather than the number of *concurrent* users. Concurrent user workloads are of interest for specific tests such as database record lock contention, deadly embraces, or network packet collisions. The actual occurrence of truly concurrent activity is rare. For example, if the peak workload is 2,000 active users, then it will be most unusual to observe more than five truly concurrent users at any time. Truly, concurrent users press the Enter key on the same transaction at precisely the same time causing the same transaction to launch in the application and follow exactly the same execution path.

Active users access the system during the same timeframe, have been allocated system resources for a work session, and are launching a variety of activities or transactions based on their job role or customer needs. It is this allocation/reallocation of system resources during the active work sessions that will affect the vast majority of transactions being launched. Each launched transaction will compete with every other launched transaction for these finite system resources. It will be the objective of the performance instrumentation to measure how well the transactions compete for these resources under different workload situations.

The peak usage of each transaction group is now added to the workload plan:

Draft 2   Performance workload plan

Transaction group	Response time requirement	Peak active users/ customers	Day/time of peak activity
Menu navigation	Max 3 seconds	2,000	Mon–Fri 12–1 P.M.
Log on/Log off	Max 3 seconds	2,000	Mon–Fri 12–1 P.M.
Product detail display	Max 4 seconds	2,000	Mon–Fri 12–1 P.M.
Purchase steps	Max 7 seconds	500	Sat 9–11 A.M.
Catalog search	Max 10 seconds	2,000	Mon–Fri 12–1 P.M.
Credit card payment	Max 30 seconds	500	Sat 9–11 A.M.

The Mon–Fri 12–1 P.M. peak activity entry means that a peak of 2,000 customers use the system during lunchtime at least one workday of the week. From a performance testing perspective, it does not matter which specific day it occurs or if it occurs during several weekdays. The peak is the peak from a performance testing perspective. Later in the development process, the production staff will want very much to know which day(s) of the week the peak occurs for production schedule perspective.

The third performance tester's challenge is to clarify just how many different workload peaks need to be tested. Looking down the Draft 2 plan, you will notice that not all of the transaction groups peak Mon–Fri noon. Some of the groups peak during Sat A.M. Looking a little closer, you will realize that the weekday noon transaction groups are predominantly browsing activities in contrast to the Saturday transaction groups that are predominantly purchasing activities. This weekly workload has more than one peak. To complete the workload plan, you will need to revisit each of the two peaks and develop separate workload plans, now designated weekday browsing and Saturday purchasing.

Look for the peak active users for each transaction group in all workload plans. Failure to revisit each transaction group for all plans may cause performance test underreporting. For example, if you test the weekday browse peak workload without any purchases because purchases peak on Saturday, you may miss the fact that a few purchase transactions during the weekday could noticeably slow down a browse response. Although the number of customers making purchases during the week does not reach the Saturday 500 peak, you should strongly suspect that there may be at least 50 purchases (10% of Saturday peak) during the weekday browse workload peak. Similarly, the number of customers doing catalog searches on Saturday does not reach the 2,000 weekday peak; however, you should suspect that there may be at least 200 catalog browses (10% of the weekday peak) during the purchase Saturday workload peak.

Here is the revised workload plan split out to represent the two workload peaks discovered so far.

Draft 3   Performance workload plan for weekday browsing

Transaction group	Response time requirement	Peak active users/Customers	day/time of peak activity
Menu navigation	Max 3 seconds	2,000	Mon–Fri 12–1 P.M.
Log on/Log off	Max 3 seconds	2,000	Mon–Fri 12–1 P.M.
Product detail display	Max 4 seconds	2,000	Mon–Fri 12–1 P.M.
Purchase steps	Max 7 seconds	50	Mon–Fri 12–1 P.M.
Catalog search	Max 10 seconds	2,000	Mon–Fri 12–1 P.M.
Credit card payment	Max 30 seconds	50	Mon–Fri 12–1 P.M.

Draft 3   Performance workload plan for saturday purchases

Transaction group	Response time requirement	Peak active users/ customers	Day/time of peak activity
Menu navigation	Max 3 seconds	500	Sat 9 A.M.–11
Log on/Log off	Max 3 seconds	500	Sat 9 A.M.–11
Product detail display	Max 4 seconds	200	Sat 9 A.M.–11
Purchase steps	Max 7 seconds	500	Sat 9 A.M.–11
Catalog search	Max 10 seconds	200	Sat 9 A.M.–11
Credit card payment	Max 30 seconds	500	Sat 9 A.M.–11

9.3 WORKLOAD EXECUTION TECHNIQUES

Once you have identified the groups and volumes of transactions for each peak workload test, you need to develop the steps to create that peak in a test environment so that performance measurements can be taken. There are three traditional steps for executing performance test workload.

9.3.1 Workload Ramp-up to Peak

Workload ramp-up is the process of initiating enough user sessions to drive the peak workload. If the peak is 2,000 users, then 2,000 users must be logged on to the system in the test environment during the first part of the peak workload window. In real life, 2,000 users would not simultaneously log on within the first seconds of the lunch hour. The log ons would be staggered over a period of 5–10 min (more workload analysis information is needed here) as users put away their daily business and prepare to browse during their lunchtimes.

Successful ramp-up without any user transaction activity is the testing objective of the first step. Said another way, if the peak workload of users cannot even log on, then workload transaction response time is moot. The log on or launch or startup user activity may appear simple on the screen; however, this is normally the time when the largest number of processing resources (memory, files, and process threads) are allocated to the user. Complete resource depletion of the application's test operating environment occurs frequently during initial attempts to ramp up active users to peak.

The first time you attempt to ramp up any large number (hundreds) of users, the application is expected to fail before half of the intended users have been initiated. Try the ramp-up in small increments of 5 or 10 users to better isolate the ramp-up failure point. At this time in the development and testing cycle, only a small number (less than five) of users have ever been launched at any time by either the developers or testers. The ramp-up will reveal all kinds of resource problems such as not enough memory, not enough processing threads, or not enough file space.

Once the application has been able to successfully ramp up the peak workload log on without any user activity, the application is tested for successful ramp-up within a peak time window, say 10 min in our example. Again, expect the application to fail several ramp-up attempts within the required time interval. The resource starvation issues will shift from memory, files, and process units to raw CPU speed and communication bandwidth that really have not been taxed fully by slow ramp-up testing at this point. Expect some software under development to never achieve the required peak workload ramp-up in the required time interval due to inadequate performance design. If the peak workload within the time interval is a contractual requirement, then the developers are faced with either a major redesign effort and associated contract penalties or abandonment of the software and loss of the software development contract.

9.3.2   Workload Ramp-down From Peak

Workload ramp-down is the process of gracefully ending all the active user sessions that drove the peak workload. At the end of lunchtime, users log off the system, maybe over a 2–3 min period (more workload analysis information is needed here too).

With peak workload ramp-up successfully achieved, ramp-down testing commences in a similar way. During ramp-up testing, the ramp-down is not an issue. You close down the active users in the test environment any way you can as quickly as you can to clean up and get ready for the next ramp-up test. Now we need to focus on achieving successful ramp-down. As with the ramp-up, a successful ramp-down should be attempted first in increments of 5 or 10. While releasing resources should be faster and less error-prone than acquiring resources, ramp-down errors will be encountered. Continue to ramp up/ramp down in additional user increments. Once gentle ramp-down has been achieved from peak workload, perform the ramp-down again within a required ramp-down time interval if such a requirement exists. Expect more errors to be encountered during the timed ramp-downs.

9.3.3   Performance Measurement at the Peak

Having successfully achieved ramp-up and ramp-down for the peak workload, you are now ready to consider the timing aspects of performance measurement at peak workload. We are going to set aside the workload plans for a moment and gain a perspective on measuring the responsiveness of software. Then, we will marry that measurement perspective with the workload ramp-up/ramp-down testing that we have just completed.

9.4   COMPONENT PERFORMANCE TESTING

The term "performance testing" has come to mean a variety of different software testing techniques where the common characteristic is the measurement of some kind of response time from the software. Performance testing can mean that you measure the response time of some component of the software that is suspected of contributing a large delay in completing a task. An example of performance testing at the component level would be database searches on various criteria in database files of various sizes regardless of what is done with the search results. Another example of performance testing at the component level would be rendering (painting) a screen with results from some processing such as a name search or a product search. To do this kind of performance testing, the software development need not necessarily be finished, but the candidate components must have already passed the tests for functional correctness. A really fast search that provides an incorrect result is not a good performance.

The purpose of doing performance testing on components is to get an early idea of whether the sum of the individual component response times can be expected to come anywhere close to the performance response time maximum we have recorded in our peak workload plans. If, for example, the worst database search response time for our invoice item display is 6 seconds and the worst screen rendering for that item's description is 5 seconds, then you can alert the developer that the current version of the Invoice Item Detail Display code has an 11 seconds total response time. If the business performance requirement for this display is 7 seconds, you have just given the developer an early warning that his or her code as is will not meet the performance requirements.

9.5   ROUND TRIP PERFORMANCE

Other meanings of the term "performance testing" tend to encompass more and more of the application activities to be included in response time measurement. At the far end of the performance testing definition spectrum is the measurement of the application's response time from when the "enter" key or "submit" button is pressed until the results have been fully rendered on the screen or until the report has been printed out or when the product is delivered to your door. Although there are several terms in the literature for this kind of performance testing, we will use the term "round trip performance testing." When we use this term, we will explicitly mean the time that it takes for one transaction or activity to be initiated by the user pressing Enter or Submit until the complete result such as a screen, report, or file is returned to the user. This overall timing will include all intervening processing done on the user's computer, all necessary communications with other support computers via networks, and all secondary processing done on other support computers for a given transaction.

To demonstrate what round trip performance testing might look like, consider putting timing points at various strategic points in the test environment platform of the application such as on the client computer, on the network, and on the server computer. Then, consider running just one purchase step transaction in the empty test environment. For the purposes of discussion, say the completed round trip took a total of 5.8 seconds and was comprised of the following individual timings:

Purchase step transaction round trip performance instrumentation

0.5 seconds client—purchase screen data input record generation

0.2 seconds network—transmission of new purchase record to server

2.4 seconds server—new database purchase record insert into database

1.3 seconds server—generate warehouse order record

0.7 seconds server—generate purchase order confirmation record

0.1 seconds network – transmission of confirmation record to client

0.6 seconds client – display confirmation record / successful completion

=====

5.8 seconds total round trip performance response time in an empty test system

This is less than the 7 seconds maximum in our peak workload plans. The conclusion is that this transaction is ready for workload testing where we know the round trip performance will get slower as the transaction competes for resources in a busier system. Maybe it will stay below the 7 seconds maximum when the peak workload number of purchase steps are executed together, maybe not.

Carrying the thought one step further, it has been found to be very beneficial from a test management perspective to plan for the round trip performance testing of all transactions or representative transactions of all groups individually in an empty system. After recording the results on the peak workload plans, you should alert the developers as to which transactions did not perform under the maximum response time allowed by the software requirements. There is no need to start workload testing of these transactions yet because they already exceed their performance boundaries. In contrast, the transactions that did perform under the maximum response time allowed by the software requirements are ready for workload testing. Draft 4 shows what the extended workload plans might look like with the round trip performance results in an empty system. Round trip performance numbers with a (green) notation indicate that the transaction group on that row is ready for peak workload testing. Round trip performance numbers with a (red) notation indicate that the transaction group on that row is not ready for peak workload testing.

Draft 4   Performance workload plan for weekday browsing

Transaction group	Response time requirement	Round trip performance (red/green)	Peak active users/ customers	Day/time of peak activity
Menu navigation	Max 3 seconds	4.5 seconds (red)	2,000	Mon–Fri 12–1 P.M.
Log on/Log off	Max 3 seconds	2.0 seconds (green)	2,000	Mon–Fri 12–1 P.M.
Product detail display	Max 4 seconds	15.3 seconds (red)	2,000	Mon–Fri 12–1 P.M.
Purchase steps	Max 7 seconds	3.0 seconds (green)	50	Mon–Fri 12–1 P.M.
Catalog search	Max 10 seconds	1.6 seconds (green)	2,000	Mon–Fri 12–1 P.M.
Credit card payment	Max 30 seconds	103 seconds (red)	50	Mon–Fri 12–1 P.M.

Draft 4   Performance workload plan for saturday purchases

Transaction group	response time requirement	Round trip performance (red/green)	Peak active users/ customers	Day/time of peak activity
Menu navigation	Max 3 seconds	4.5 seconds (red)	500	Sat 9 A.M.–11
Log on/Log off	Max 3 seconds	2.0 seconds (green)	500	Sat 9 A.M.–11
Product detail display	Max 4 seconds	15.3 seconds (red)	200	Sat 9 A.M.–11
Purchase steps	Max 7 seconds	3.0 seconds (green)	500	Sat 9 A.M.–11
Catalog search	Max 10 seconds	1.6 seconds (green)	200	Sat 9 A.M.–11
Credit card payment	Max 30 seconds	103 seconds (red)	500	Sat 9 A.M.–11

9.5.1 A Typical Performance Response Curve

Starting with an empty test environment, you should launch more and more copies of the same transaction and watch a predictable pattern of round trip performance emerge under increasingly higher workload conditions. Figure 9.1 illustrates what the plot will look like if you keep adding more transactions.

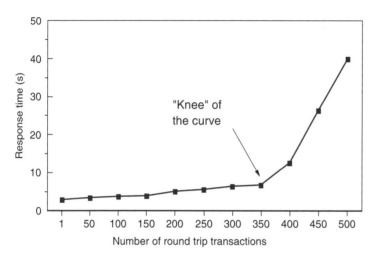

Figure 9.1 Round trip performance for catalog browse transactions

The *x*-axis is the number of transactions active at the same time. The *y*-axis is the slowest response time measured for any of the active transactions. Using either the average response time or the fastest response time for comparison with the performance requirement will, in effect, mask the worst response times. A reasonably well-designed transaction process will exhibit linear performance up to a point, in this case 350 transactions. More than 350 transactions exhibit an exponential response time. The point at which the trend changes from linear to exponential is traditionally called the "knee" of the curve. This curve inflection represents some kind of bottleneck arising in the transaction process path. The plot does not tell you the nature of the bottleneck, just the circumstances. Currently, the only way to discover the location of the knee is to execute the workload and plot the results.

Your first impression of using the performance curve might be that you must push your workload till you encounter the knee of the curve, but that may not be necessary. Consider the plot in Figure 9.2 and our business performance requirement of 10 seconds maximum per catalog browse for a peak workload of 250 active transactions.

Box A represents the peak workload round trip response time of 250 active transactions. At 250 transactions, the worst transaction response time was about

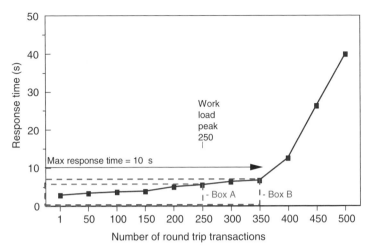

Figure 9.2   Round trip performance for catalog browse transactions

5.6 seconds, well below the 10 seconds maximum response time (arrow). Knowing that the knee of the curve is lurking somewhere out there, you extend your peak workload test to 350 transactions per Box B and see that the plot is still linear and still below the 10 seconds maximum. So you have just discovered that you have at least a 40% margin of safety with the performance requirement without seeing the knee of the curve.

Consider the plot in Figure 9.3 with the same 10 seconds response time requirement maximum for a peak workload of 350 active transactions.

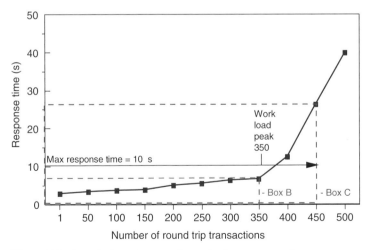

Figure 9.3   Round trip performance for catalog browse transactions

Box B still represents the peak workload response time for 350 active transactions. At the new 350 transaction peak, the worst transaction response time is about 6.8 seconds, still well below the 10 seconds maximum response time (arrow). Knowing the knee of the curve is lurking somewhere out there, you extend your peak workload test to 450 transactions as illustrated with Box C and, in fact, see the knee of the curve push your transaction response time to 26.4 seconds, well above the 10 seconds maximum response. So you have just discovered that there is no margin of safety in the 350 peak workload. As soon as something in the business forces more than 350 transactions active at the same time, the transaction will begin to slow down unacceptably.

What do you do with this information ? You should discuss your findings with the development team. They may want to analyze the code for the apparent response bottleneck, make some programming changes, and attempt to push the knee well to the right by some agreed safety margin. They may want to cap the system just to the left of the knee. Because the knee is 350 transactions in this case, the developer might put a governor on the transaction with a 10% safety margin so that when 315 transactions have become active, the user attempting to submit the 316th transaction will get a message like "The system is responding to the maximum number of catalog browse requests. Please wait a moment and try your request again." Regardless of which alternative the developers choose to implement, you will need to retest their solution to confirm that the changes keep the system off the knee of the performance curve.

Recapping your performance testing activities so far, you have developed the needed peak workload plans; you have successfully ramped your workloads up and down, and you have run your round trip performance tests for each transaction that will be in the peak workload mix. The next step is to run the round trip performance tests with the peak workload mix.

9.5.2 Saturday Peak Workload in an Empty Test System

We return to our performance workload Draft 4 plans to demonstrate what can happen when you test a workload mix. We will focus first on the workload mix for Saturday purchasing. For simplicity of discussion, we will place just three transaction groups in our demonstration: log on/log off, purchase steps, and catalog search. We choose the Saturday workload to mix first because, of the two workload plans, the Saturday plan requires fewer transactions at the testing peak. This is what we know about these three transaction groups for the Saturday workload:

Transaction group	Response time max	Peak workload
Log on/log off	3 seconds	500
Purchase steps	7 seconds	500
Catalog search	10 seconds	200

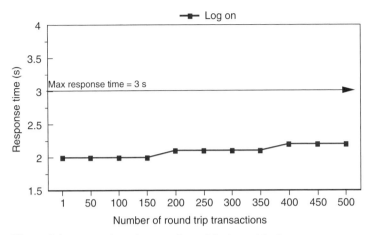

Figure 9.4   Round trip performance for peak logon workload

Next we test each transaction group with its Saturday workload volume. Figure 9.4 shows the first results of testing those transactions individually at peak workload before we mix them into one workload. First we test and confirm that the log on/log off response times are well below the requirement maximum for the Saturday peak workload for that transaction.

Next, in Figure 9.5 we test and confirm that the purchase steps response times are well below the requirement maximum for the Saturday peak workload for that transaction.

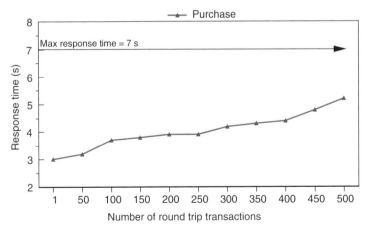

Figure 9.5   Round trip performance for peak purchase workload

Last, in Figure 9.6 we test and confirm that the catalog browse response times are well below the requirement maximum for the Saturday peak workload for that transaction.

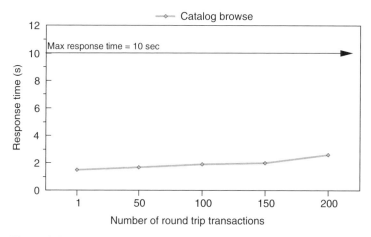

Figure 9.6 Round trip performance for peak catalog workload

9.5.3 Saturday Peak Workload Mix

Because all three transaction groups perform below (faster than) their required response times at peak workload, it is appropriate to attempt a workload mix of the same volume of transactions. Your first thought might be to throw all three transaction groups into the same performance measurement window and see if they continue to demonstrate performance below their requirements. The problem with this approach is that if one or more of the transaction groups' response times go above the requirement maximum, you do not have many clues as to what in the mix changed the performance.

Consider a deliberate ramp-up of each transaction group into the mix in an order that reflects the business priority of the workload. For example, the business priority of the Saturday workload is purchasing. So the suggested transaction group mix sequence for the Saturday workload is (1) log on/log off, (2) purchase steps, and (3) catalog search.

Figure 9.7 shows the results of ramping up the log on/log off to peak workload, then launching purchase steps to peak workload.

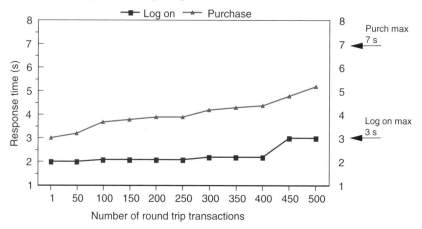

Figure 9.7 Round trip performance for peak logon + purchase workload mix

The purchase step transaction group is behaving well (not slowing down much) throughout the workload. The log on/log off transaction group behaved well until the workload reached 400 users. At that point, the log on/log off performance jumped to the requirement maximum. The performance tester should use this information to alert the developer that the log on performance becomes marginal when the purchase step workload exceeds 400 active transactions.

Figure 9.8 shows the results of ramping up the log on/log off along with launching purchase steps *and* catalog browser transactions to peak workload.

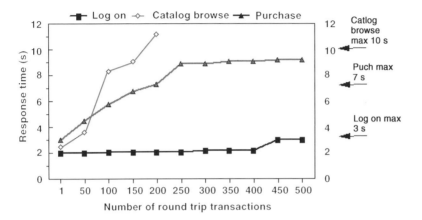

Figure 9.8   Round trip performance for peak logon + purchase + catalog browse workload mix

9.5.4   Saturday Workload Showstoppers

Clearly, there is some kind of resource conflict between the purchase steps and the catalog browse. The performance requirement max for the catalog browse was exceeded when the ramp-up achieved only 100 active users. These results are sufficiently severe as to halt further performance testing of the Saturday workload until the development team diagnoses and implements some performance solutions. This kind of testing discovery is referred to as a "showstopper" from the testing perspective. Furthermore, because we chose the lower volume workload peak to test first, we know that there is no benefit to starting the weekday workload testing that demands an even higher volume of the same poorly performing transactions.

While the performance testers await development solutions to these response time problems, other types of testing such as functional and structural testing can continue. Notice that testers doing the other types of testing will be affected when the developers do find solutions to the response time problems. Specifically, the development solutions to the performance problems will need to be retested (regression testing) to verify that the performance solutions affect only the performance aspect of the software and not inadvertently impair any functional aspects of the software. Regression testing here will add time and effort to the test schedule that may not have been anticipated in the original test execution schedule.

9.5.5 Saturday Workload Showstopper Corrections, We Think

At this point in our discussion, we receive the corrected, functionally regressed software ready for performance workload retesting. We learn from the code correction log and discussions with the developers that the logon code modules experienced interference from the purchase steps at 400 active users because the memory area allocated for user IDs and passwords began to "leak" into the purchase step execution area. We also learn from the same sources that the purchase steps and catalog browse code modules shared a set of utility routines in a common dynamic library that began to degrade the performance of both modules by the way the utility routines were loaded for execution.

Our next step is to rerun the individual transaction groups in an empty test system to verify that the performance fixes did not, in fact, slow down the code. Figures 9.9–9.11 show the results of our empty system ramp-up performance measurements in an empty test system.

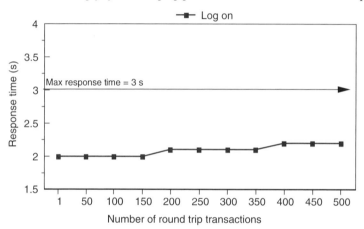

Figure 9.9 Round trip performance for peak logon workload after performance corrections have been applied

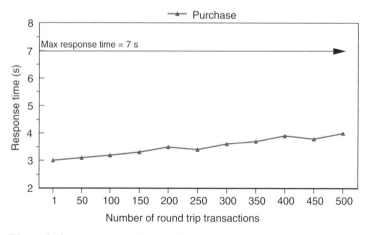

Figure 9.10 Round trip performance for peak purchase workload after performance corrections have been applied

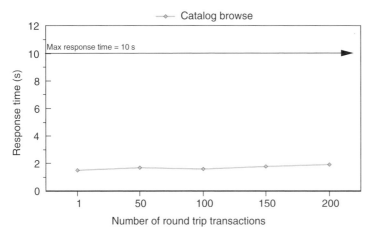

Figure 9.11   Round trip performance for peak catalog browse workload after performance corrections have been applied

The empty system performance of the log on/log off code has not been affected by the code changes. This response pattern is expected because the correction is supposed to make a difference only when other transaction groups are added to the workload mix. The purchase steps code and catalog browse code both show slightly improved performance in empty system workloads. This is a pleasant surprise because the code corrections were focused on cross-transaction performance degradation due to a poor common utility-routine-sharing strategy. The improved sharing strategy also helped each transaction group independently of the workload mix.

Because the individual transaction group workload rerun responses stay well below the requirement maximums, our final step for this workload plan is to rerun the transaction group mixes to verify that the performance fixes did speed up the transactions in competition for computing resources. In Figure 9.12 we see the first results of our transaction mix performance test reruns.

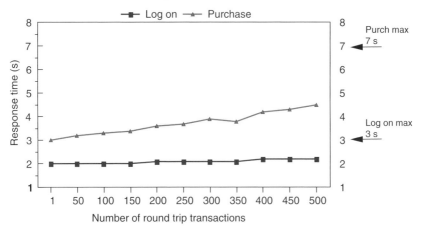

Figure 9.12   Round trip performance for peak logon + purchase workload mix after performance corrections have been applied

We can see that the log on/log off code performance correction did solve the problem. Now log on/log off response is not adversely affected after 400 purchase steps have been launched. Both transaction groups remain well below their requirement maximums.

Because the rerun of the first mix of transaction groups stay well below requirement maximums, we are ready to add catalog browse transaction groups to the mix to verify that the crosstransaction performance fixes did speed up the transactions in competition for computing resources. Figure 9.13 illustrates the results of our second transaction mix performance test rerun.

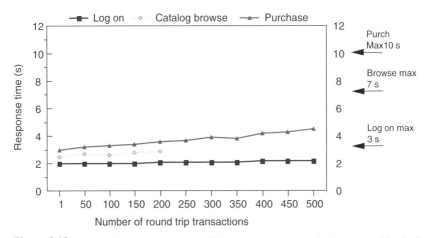

Figure 9.13   Round trip performance for peak logon + purchase + catalog browse workload mix after performance corrections have been applied

With these results, the performance corrections are now verified as lowering all mixed performance response times below the requirement maximums without adversely affecting functionality. The application under test passes the Saturday workload performance test. As more of the application is completed, the performance tests become a part of the regression test to prove that newly added functionality does not inadvertently degrade performance beyond the requirement maximums.

9.5.6 Weekday Workload Performance Plan Execution

You will approach the weekday workload testing in the same way that we performed the Saturday workload testing. Ramp up each transaction group in the workload to confirm that the transaction group response times are below the required maximums before any transaction mixing is attempted. If all transactions pass this first hurdle, then systematic mixing of workloads is attempted until all mixes are successful or until the testing hits a showstopper. The showstopper/correction/regression/retest cycle is repeated until the required performance is achieved. Rather than using more charts to demonstrate what might happen with the weekday workload testing, we will discuss the outcomes you might expect and why you might expect them. The associated charts should leap to mind.

The most noticeable difference between the Saturday and weekday workloads is the volume of work, almost four times more transactions. This would lead you to expect new volume-related issues to be revealed by the weekday performance testing. For example, we learned that the logon/logoff code was designed to operate primarily from lists (active user ID and password) in memory as opposed to lists on disk files. While it is true that everything runs faster in memory than from disk, it is also true that memory usually has a much smaller storage capacity. One possible outcome of this design strategy tradeoff is that the logon/logoff transaction group could become a memory exhaustion showstopper before the 2,000 weekday log on workload is achieved. Buying 2,000 memory chips costing $100 each may be a less desirable solution than revising the logon/logoff performance maximums to a slower response and revising the logon/logoff code to maintain some of its user ID/password information on disk files. The tradeoff faced by the application owner is the cost of additional hardware versus the cost of revising the logon/logoff code and attendant slower disk access performance expectation.

Because we will test fewer purchase step transaction groups during the weekday workload tests than we did during the Saturday workload tests, the purchase steps should rightfully be expected to stay below the performance maximums or at least not exceed them. The catalog browse transaction group is just the opposite situation from the purchase steps. The weekday workload will require many more catalog browse transaction groups than the Saturday workload tests. There is a distinct possibility that the catalog browse plot will reveal a curve knee before its workload peak is achieved. Aided by performance test results, the developers should be able to make the corrections that will ultimately allow the software to pass the weekday workload performance tests as well.

9.6 PUTTING PERFORMANCE TESTING IN PERSPECTIVE

Software performance is the ugly stepchild of software functionality. Both developers and testers spend significant time and effort to ensure that the required software functionality is delivered. Many development teams have discovered that if the software delivers correct functionality too slowly, the end-user is just as dissatisfied with the software as if the functionality were incorrect in the first place. The reason for this end-user attitude is because correct answers delivered too late lose business opportunity just as surely as if the correct answers were never delivered at all.

This chapter describes an approach to performance testing that will alert the development team about software performance shortfalls before the software is delivered to end-users. Although software delivery of business functionality has advanced significantly in the past 30 years, performance delivery continues to be problematic. Expect the first performance tests from any new software to reveal not "if" the software is performing to requirements but "how much" the software is missing the performance requirements.

9.7 SUMMARY

The objective of performance testing is to validate the software "speed" against the business need for "speed" as documented in the software requirements. Software "speed" is generally defined as some combination of response time and workload during peak load times. These peak load times may occur during lunchtime, at the opening of the stock market day, or after midnight when all online customers are in bed (overnight batch workload). Performance testing is achieved by a series of tests that introduces increasingly more workload of increasingly more complex business transaction mixes.

Performance testing occurs after the functional testing is mostly completed and the software has become quite stable (fewer and fewer changes or corrections). Functional defects in the software may be revealed during performance testing, but this is not the testing objective.

The performance tester's first workload challenge is to identify which business transactions and activities need to be measured for performance. In all but the simplest software applications, it is difficult to identify the most important transaction and activity candidates for performance testing. The difficulty lies partly with the software end-user's typical reaction, "everything must respond in less than 3 seconds." Somehow the tester must convince the end user that different groups of transactions and activities will have different performance requirements based on different business priorities.

The performance tester's second workload challenge is to determine peak usage of each group of transactions and the timeframes in which the peak usage occurs. Peak usage is normally measured in terms of active users. The third performance tester's challenge is to clarify just how many different workload peaks need to be tested.

Once you have identified the groups and volumes of transactions for each peak workload test, you need to develop the steps to create this peak in a test environment so that performance measurements can be taken. There are three traditional steps for executing performance test workload. First, you execute workload ramp-up to peak load. Then, you execute performance measurements at the peak. Finally, you execute workload ramp-down from the peak.

KEY TERMS

Response time
Response time requirement
Workload
Workload peak
Peak workload in an
   empty test system

Peak workload mix
Rule of 8
Ramp up to peak
Ramp down from peak
Performance
   measurement at the peak

Round trip performance
Response curve
Knee of the curve
Margin of safety
Testing showstopper

Chapter 10

The Testing Environment

LEARNING OBJECTIVES

- to know what constitutes a testing environment
- to know why testing environments are the most effective approach to measure the behavior of software before it goes into production
- to understand when a testing environment is normally set up and torn down
- to know what testing environment setup issues challenge the test team
- to know what testing environment control issues challenge the test team

10.1 INTRODUCTION

Thus far, we have discussed test planning and a variety of ways to accomplish test execution. The implicit assumption is that we know how to set up and tear down the test execution environment(s) that are needed to carry out that test planning and execution. The objective of this chapter is to examine the testing environment as a legitimate and important testing topic itself.

A testing environment allows the testers to observe execution results that the customer or user will actually experience in production before the software is deployed into production. This testing environment approach should be compared critically with similar sounding approaches that do not give equivalent results or anything close. The two similar sounding approaches that you will hear proposed most often in lieu of a good testing environment are simulations and benchmarks. Both of these approaches provide valuable information to the software development team, but that information is not as relevant as test execution results in a good testing environment. Let us examine these similar sounding approaches briefly and determine why they do not give results comparable to test environment execution.

Software Testing: Testing Across the Entire Software Development Life Cycle, by G. D. Everett and R. McLeod, Jr.
Copyright © 2007 John Wiley & Sons, Inc.

10.2 SIMULATIONS

Simulations have been used in development shops for at least 40 years. The idea is simple but the activity is complex and work intensive. Simulations are based on the correct assumption that the behavior of hardware is measurable and predictable. Simulations are mathematical models of hardware behavior that can be linked together to approximate the production environment of a new application or system *under ideal conditions.* The argument for using simulation predictions is that they are much less expensive than acquiring the hardware just for testing purposes. This assertion tends to discount the enormous effort necessary to collect the detailed data needed to make the simulation results better than an experienced systems programmer's best guess. How many corporate executives would be willing to risk a $100 million revenue forecast based on a programmer's best guess? If you hear someone behind you in class mumble "none," then you have just experienced why simulation as a testing technique fell into disfavor with corporate IT departments.

In the last 5 years, simulations have experienced resurgence in popularity in the role of design validation. Simulations are now used to identify and discard designs that truly will not meet the design goals, allowing designers to focus on the designs that have the best prospects (not guarantees) of meeting the design goals.

10.3 BENCHMARKING

Benchmarking techniques have existed about as long as simulations. Like simulations, they became very popular in the 1960s. Also like simulations, they fell into disuse. Unlike simulations, they have not experienced a real resurgence. A benchmark is the execution of a specific application or system under very controlled circumstances that are thoroughly measured and well documented.

The original impetus behind benchmarks was to have a public comparison of products for prospective buyers. For example, if you are interested in buying an industrial strength database management system, you might shop DB2, Oracle, and Sybase. If the brochure features of all three database management systems meet your purchase criteria, then you look for benchmark results from each vendor that reflect circumstances closest to the way you intend to use the product. The more dissimilar the benchmark circumstances are from your needs, the less valuable the benchmark results are in comparison shopping.

The benchmark owes its popularity in part to the fact that the benchmark cost is not born by the prospective customer. It is part of the vendor's marketing cost. Unfortunately, public benchmarks are seldom run exactly as the customer intends to use the product; furthermore, if the new application or system is not off-the-shelf software, then its benchmark is probably not cost justified.

10.4   TESTING ENVIRONMENTS

The third approach to testing is to set up a separate computing environment very similar to the target or production computing environment for testing the new software. Then, testers plan and execute tests against the software in operation to validate the software's behavior by direct observation and measurement in a copy of its intended operating environment. This special computing environment is called the "testing environment."

Questions about the composition of the testing environment should arise very early in the development project. The documentation during the developers' Preliminary investigation and Analysis lifecycle stages should contain a moderately detailed description of the target production environment for the new software application or system. Referring to the bathtub diagram in Figure 5.1, the draft test plan developed from Preliminary investigation and Analysis should adopt the targeted production environment as its first draft testing environment. This will enable the test team to narrow its strategic plan questions to just those platforms and software layers in Figure 4.4 that are actually needed to support the new application or system in production.

10.5   THE GOAL OF A TESTING ENVIRONMENT

The goal of a testing environment is to cause the application under test to exhibit true production behavior while being observed and measured outside of its production environment. Achieving this goal can be just as challenging as designing and executing the tests themselves.

As previously stated, the test team becomes aware of the application's target production environment very early in the software development lifecycle. Because it takes time to design and code software to be tested, the test team has a built-in window of opportunity to plan the test environment, acquire the needed hardware and software, and set up the test environment well in advance of the first scheduled test executions. This test environment setup should include activities that validate the viability and correctness of the test environment for running tests. If the decision is made to use automated test tools, then the test environment setup must include installing the test tool in the testing environment, validating that the test tool is operational and, if necessary, calibrating the tool. We will examine automated test tools in the next chapter.

You may need to enlist the help of several different kinds of systems experts to acquire and set up the test environment components. Out-of-the-box default operating system installations rarely reflect the way they are used in business. If the test environment operating system is very complex, you will need to find an operating systems expert to set it up correctly in the testing environment. Here is a more complete list of test environment components for which you may need to seek expert systems assistance for testing setup.

- Operating systems
- Security

- File systems
- Databases
- Connectivity (LANs, WANs, Satellite, Wireless, and Internet)

Finally, you will need to seek test data experts for three reasons. The first reason is that you will need to find the best possible test data sources to represent expected production data. The second reason is that you will need to determine how best to load that test data into the test environment as a testing starting point. The third reason is that you will need to determine how best to reload that test data for reruns once a series of tests has been executed, regardless of whether the tests were successful. Examples of groups that you might contact for test data help include experienced end-users, senior developers, database administrators, and operations management.

The way you load and reload test data in the test environment seldom reflects the production backup and recovery strategy for the application under test. Production backup and recovery serve an entirely different purpose for the application in production, namely business continuity. Recall from Chapter 8 that there are testing techniques specifically for backup and recovery.

It is common to find multiple testing environments in many development shops. The first and most common testing environment you will find is the developer environment itself that may not be considered a true testing environment. Recall the white box testing discussion in Chapter 7. This kind of testing must be performed by the developer because the tester rarely has access to the source code under construction. Quite naturally, the developer completes white box testing in the same environment in which he or she does development. The observation is made to differentiate code debugging from testing but does not add any further value to the discussion of test environments.

The next kind of testing environment you may find is called a "staging" environment or a "migration" environment or a "deployment" environment. The developers see this environment as the next place their programs go prior to "going live." It represents the collection point over time of all finished programming. It also represents an excellent testing environment for the finished programming both as the finished components become available and as the application itself becomes complete. Figure 10.1 illustrates what a simple computing environment strategy such as this might look like.

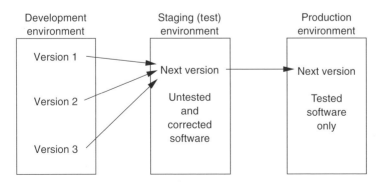

Figure 10.1   Simple computing environment strategy

Depending on the size and complexity of the application being developed, there may be multiple smaller staging environments for major subcomponents of the application. For example, an enterprise-wide application may have separate staging environments for the accounting subcomponent, the marketing subcomponent, the manufacturing component, and the warehousing component. All of these subcomponent staging environments represent excellent testing environments prior to the complete enterprise-wide application availability for testing. Figure 10.2 shows what a complex computing environment strategy like this might look like.

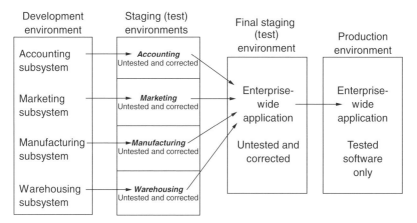

Figure 10.2   Complex computing environment strategy

It is important for the test team to control the test environment from a test schedule perspective and from a data reload and rerun perspective. Control of the testing environment needs to encompass the additional dimension of controlled staging or "builds." A "build" is the collection of specific versions of application components for executing specific test cases. When software is ready to be tested, that software must be moved somehow from the development environment to the testing environment. Staging of software from development to test is typically accomplished either by manual procedures or by automated staging tools.

The lifetime of a test environment is determined by several factors. If the software being developed is expected to have multiple versions over a number of months or years, then it makes good sense to establish and maintain a reusable test environment for the duration of the software development schedule. The economy of scale is derived from the increasing number of subsequent versions tested in the same test environment because the cost of personnel to set up and tear down a testing environment will exceed the cost of the test hardware over time.

When it is clear that the testing environment is needed for just a small number of versions to be tested or the time in between version tests is months or years, then a short-term testing environment might make more economic sense. The largest cost of setting up a short-term testing environment is usually the hardware cost. It is very difficult to justify the outright purchase of hardware for one or two tests. Often, it is significantly less expensive to rent or lease computer equipment for a short time (1–3 months) than it is to purchase the equipment. The cost of setting up and tearing down the test environment becomes a standard line item of the testing project budget.

What about testing environments whose lifetime falls somewhere in between the two extremes? The recommendation is to start with pricing research for the needed testing equipment both as a short-term rental and as a long-term purchase. Then, determine from previous testing projects the estimated effort in setting up and tearing down the testing environment. Finally, estimate the number of times the test environment will be used over a 1-year period starting as soon as the software development project begins. Do the math and determine which approach is most cost-effective for your software development projects.

10.6 GOOD TESTING ENVIRONMENTS AND WHY THEY SHOULD BE USED

A good testing environment is one that very closely operates like the intended or existing production environment and is totally controlled by the test team.

The closer the testing environment resembles the production environment, the more valid the test results become. In many cases, the testing environment can be set up truly identical to the production environment. Testing in this kind of duplicate environment gives the developer and the end user an exceptionally accurate view of how the new software will behave in production.

Test team control of the testing environment has two major benefits. The first benefit relates to the controlled repeatability of all testing. When the test team does control the testing environment, then the team knows exactly what versions of software components are in the testing environment at all times, as well as the state of all test data files. As defects are detected in the software, the tester can repeat the test and confirm the defect discovery for anybody who needs to see the defect demonstrated … like the developers. The second benefit of a tester-controlled environment is the testers' ability to plan and execute tests without being interfered by or interfering with development activity. The testers drive the test schedule, whether it is to complete a certain set of tests by a certain date or to rerun a set of tests to validate correction of previously detected defects. A final implication of tester control of the testing environment is that testers can ensure that no software corrections are made directly in the testing environment. Modify a previously tested piece of code, and the previous test results are null and void. Corrections and modifications must be made in the developer's environment and be re-staged into the testing environment using the same staging process as first introduced.

Staging procedures also represent a level of testing environment control. Good staging procedures take advantage of automated staging tools. The primary intent of staging tools is to *guarantee* that the software that arrives in the testing environment is the *same* as the software that departed from the development environment ready for testing. The secondary intent is to guarantee that each staging is repeatable, that is, rerunning the staging tool for the same versions provides the tester with *exactly* the same software to test. Very often, the migration tool used to move software from development to testing is also the tool used to move software from testing to production. This approach guarantees that the software verified as behaving correctly in the test environment is *guaranteed* to be *the* correctly behaving software placed in production.

10.7   BAD TESTING ENVIRONMENTS AND WHY THEY SHOULD BE AVOIDED

A bad testing environment is one that is only similar to the intended or existing production environment and is shared by other groups such as the developers or the training staff.

The more dissimilar the testing environment is from the production environment, the less valid the test results become. For example, suppose your application uses a number of disk files to maintain application data. Further suppose the development and test teams get the fastest computers available to speed up the development and testing schedules. Your test computers then use a larger, faster disk drive than the production computers, resulting in performance tests that will mislead the end-users to believe the application will run faster in production. The corollary situation (more common) is that the test team is given older, hand-me-down computers that have slower, lower capacity disk drives than in production. In this situation, the performance tests will under-report the application's response times ... if the application runs in the test environment at all. Extend the disk drive example to CPU speed, resident memory capacity, network topology, network speed, network capacity, printer speed, monitor screen refresh rate and you will quickly realize how many ways the testing environment execution dimensions can miss the mark.

When the test team shares any of the testing environments with other teams, the loss of control can be disastrous for the test effort. The most obvious downside of not controlling the testing environment is that the test team will be forced occasionally to pause and possibly reschedule tests because the test environment is "busy."

Another example of a busy test environment that impacts the test team schedule is when testing is relegated to the third shift (11 P.M.–7 A.M.) of a computing environment not used at night. Working at night does eliminate testing conflicts with development. The real issue that arises is that when a tester finds a possible defect in the middle of the night, there is nobody around at 3 A.M. from either development or end-user groups to help confirm the defect discovery. Everybody the tester needs to contact is at home in bed. In this situation, the testing may need to be halted until the next morning when everybody the tester wants to contact comes to work. Of course, the tester will not be at the office to greet them. The tester will come to work late because he or she has been up all night. The result is the very delay hoped to be avoided by third shift testing in the first place.

Without clear management and coordination of the testing environment, it is also possible that multiple test teams needing to reset the environment data in conflicting ways cannot get their conflict resolved in a timely and supportive way.

A less obvious downside of not controlling the testing environment is that someone other than the testers may place rogue software in the testing environment that affects the test runs unknowingly and undetected. The first clue that there is rogue software in the test environment arises when test execution results cannot be repeated.

Decisions to reject automated staging tools in favor of manual procedures also impact the testing validity. The primary intent of manual staging is usually to circumvent the staging rules and be able to easily introduce alternate versions of the software components to be tested. Although this approach seems to offer more flexibility than staging tools on the surface, the fact is that circumventing the staging rules diminishes the veracity of subsequent test results. Furthermore, circumventing the staging rules is the quickest way to *guarantee* that the software test results are *not* repeatable.

The other way to look at the staging alternatives is to conclude that "quick fixes" via manual staging are neither quick nor helpful. If manual staging is problematic for testing, then it is a disaster for production. Too many companies still allow their software developers to place untested fixes directly into production and are amazed when the application crashes. [42] The irony of the decision is that it takes more time and resources to correct and test the quick fix than it would have taken to correct the original problem the right way in the first place.

10.8 PUTTING THE TESTING ENVIRONMENT IN PERSPECTIVE

All too often, the testing environment is an afterthought of the development project that is already tight on budget and computing resources. The first reaction is to give the test team "orphan" equipment that nobody else wants or uses. The consequence is test failures on the tester computers that cannot be recreated on the developer computers because of the disparity in computing resources. It does not take many of these false test failures for all testing results to be completely dismissed by the project. Of course the true test failures also become dismissed.

The "pay me now or pay me later" axiom certainly applies to this situation. The development project really has two choices:

1. Plan to provide an appropriate testing environment separate from all other project environments to get the best possible test results throughout the project
2. Plan to scrimp on the testing environment and likely experience end user discovered defects that cost much more to diagnose and fix than an appropriate testing environment would have in the first place.

10.9 SUMMARY

A testing environment allows the testers to observe the execution results that the customer or user will actually experience in production before the software is deployed into production. Questions about the composition of the testing environment should arise very early in the development project. The documentation during the developers' Preliminary investigation and Analysis lifecycle stages should contain a moderately detailed description of the target production environment for the new software application or system. This will enable the test team to narrow its strategic plan questions to just those platforms and software layers in Figure 4.4 that are actually needed to support the new application or system in production.

The goal of a testing environment is to cause the application under test to exhibit true production behavior while being observed and measured outside of its production environment. Achieving this goal can be just as challenging as designing and executing the tests themselves.

The closer the operation of the testing environment to the production environment, the more valid the test results become. In many cases, the testing environment can be set up truly identical to the production environment. Testing in this kind of duplicate environment gives the developer and the end user an exceptionally accurate view of how the new software will behave in production. The more dissimilar the testing environment is from the production environment, the less valid the test results become.

KEY TERMS

Simulations	Testing environment	Staging
Benchmarks	Testing environment	Test repeatability
Test execution	control	
Production behavior	Test data	

Chapter 11

Automated Testing Tools

LEARNING OBJECTIVES

- to compare the small number of tool paradigms used for automated testing
- to describe the large number of automated testing tools available
- to identify the considerations for choosing manual testing versus tool testing

11.1 INTRODUCTION

The dominant role that automated testing tools play in the successful development of business software compels a software tester to learn something about them. Automated testing tools are a collection of software products designed specifically to assist software testers and software testing managers with different aspects of a testing project. The current commercial tool market has over 300 products. Each of these tools offers to assist the tester with one or more of the tester's activities. So far, no one tool has been proven to offer assistance with *all* tester activities.

It may sound like heresy to some testing professionals, but this chapter will teach you that automated testing tools are *not* always required for successful software testing. There are testing situations in which the use of automated testing tools is inappropriate, disadvantageous, and expensive. There are also testing situations in which the use of automated testing tools is appropriate, advantageous, and cost-effective. We will examine both kinds of situations in this chapter.

The first time a tester has experienced success with a testing tool, a kind of technical euphoria sets in that tends to cloud decisions about future tool use. The effect is best described by the old saying: "when you first learn how to use a hammer, everything looks like a nail." Part of the purpose of this chapter is to burst the tool euphoria bubble and bring the tester back to a rational level of decisions about appropriate tool choices and use. It is not the purpose of this chapter to tell you which test tool to buy.

Software Testing: Testing Across the Entire Software Development Life Cycle,   by G. D. Everett and R. McLeod, Jr.
Copyright © 2007 John Wiley & Sons, Inc.

159

11.2   BRIEF HISTORY OF AUTOMATED TESTING TOOLS FOR SOFTWARE

Three hundred test tools sound like a lot of tools. Where did they come from? Is the market expanding? Will there be 500 tools next year? A brief history of automated testing tools may lower your anxiety level with so many alternatives.

Robust, industrial strength testing tools began to appear in the software marketplace around 1980. The tools were simple, single-purpose products focused primarily on functional testing activities. Many of these activities were a useful extension of program code debugging. As these functional testing tools gained popularity, management tools to organize and maintain tool data, command sets, execution schedule, results, and reports began to appear in the market.

The combined use of a test management tool and a functional test tool proved to be much more effective than either tool used separately. The main drawback to such combined tool use was the awkwardness of the interfaces between the tools. Around 1990, test tool vendors addressed this combined tool awkwardness by marketing tool suites that offered tightly interfaced test management tools with functional test tools. Half of these tool suite offerings were written from scratch, leveraging prior user experience with the individual tools. Half of these tool suite offerings were company acquisitions with focused integration of tools that already worked pretty well together.

Around 1995, a new type of automated test tool began to emerge in the marketplace. This new tool was designed to measure software performance as we defined it in Chapter 9: response time and throughput. As with the functional test tools, the first performance test tools provided only basic performance measurements on a few computing platforms for simple workloads. As the tools matured, their capabilities expanded to provide a variety of performance measurements on a variety of computing platforms for complex workloads. Unlike the functional test tool evolution, performance test tools appeared with management and reporting capabilities from the beginning. At a cursory level, one would expect the new performance tools to leverage the management and reporting tool designs already field proven for the functional test tools; however, performance test tool execution and results are not based on pass/fail like functional test tools. With functional test tools, there is an automated comparison of expected versus actual data or screen contents or report contents. Either the results compare exactly (pass) or they do not (fail). Performance test tools simply report the speed with which the instrumented code responds. The goal of performance testing is usually expressed in a slowest response time or a response time range that must be manually compared with the tool-reported response times. The results can either be clear-cut such as "the software function responds within the response time limit by 2 seconds or not so clear-cut as "the software function responds just 0.2 seconds slower than the limit that is still acceptable."

Around 2000, tool vendors began aggregating their tools into more comprehensive tool suites, providing test management, functional testing, and performance testing in the same tool suite. The indisputable advantages of one-stop shopping for an integrated tool suite caused the automated test tool market to become dominated by only a dozen tool vendors who could provide these tool suites. With sophisticated tool suites available, the user demand for more powerful, easier to use, fully integrated tools was replaced by a user demand from a surprising new direction. As with all software product designs, each tool suite had limitations. Some of these limitations were apparent during tool feature shopping. Other limitations surfaced with hands-on tool experience. As companies began to have second thoughts about the tool suites they purchased and started shopping for new tool suites, they discovered that they could not easily leverage their sizeable investment in the current tool's training, scripting, data, results, and reporting when migrating to a different vendor's tool suite.

This tool suite migration roadblock presented the tool vendors with an interesting dilemma: eliminate the migration roadblock and customers can abandon a product too easily; provide no migration assistance to other tool suites and risk losing initial sales due to customer-perceived "bundled" products that were so despised in the 1960s and 1970s. Some amount of migration assistance is the desirable compromise, but how much is "some?"

In the middle of the 2002–2003 timeframe, major tool suite vendors chose a professionally creative and potentially durable long-term solution to the migration challenge. By the time this textbook is published, their solution will be either accepted by the tool customer community as the norm or rejected by the tool customer community causing vendors to seek a different solution. The chosen solution is for all test tool vendors to adopt a standard product architecture using standard architecture components. The standard architecture and components afford a moderately difficult but achievable suite-to-suite migration while allowing each vendor to retain the majority of its unique capabilities.

The new architecture and component standard chosen by the automation tool industry is Eclipse/Hyades.[43, 44] The Eclipse Foundation describes itself as an independent, open ecosystem around royalty-free technology and a universal platform for tools integration. Eclipse is a nonprofit corporation that was established in November 2001 and is comprised of many of the computer industry leaders. The Eclipse web site documents the current corporate membership.

As described on the Eclipse web site, the Eclipse Platform is an integrated development environment that can be used to create a diverse collection of applications based on Java and C++. Eclipse provides a plug-in-based framework that makes it easier to create, integrate, and utilize software tools, saving time and money.

Hyades is the name of an Eclipse project to provide an open-source platform for automated software quality tools. Hyades delivers an extensible infrastructure for automated testing, tracing, profiling, monitoring, and asset management. Finally, Hyades is designed to support a full range of testing methodologies via an open-source infrastructure layer and Eclipse plug-ins.

Concluding the tool background discussion, it can be seen that a corporate software tester will normally encounter, use, and become proficient in maybe a dozen different tool suites. This number is impressive but it is nothing approaching the 300 individual tools in the market.

11.3 TEST TOOL RECORD/PLAYBACK PARADIGM

Automated test tools that execute the application under test (AUT) are designed to be used in a unique way. This unique way is referred to as "record/playback." The term is shorthand for the following repeatable three-step process.

Step 1.   An end-user operates the AUT to accomplish some useful business task.

Step 2.   The test tool "watches" the end-user operations and records/saves the actions in a file of reusable commands called a script file.

Step 3.   The test tool plays the script file back in order to precisely recreate the end-user operations in the application without human intervention.

Figure 11.1 illustrates this unique record/playback paradigm.

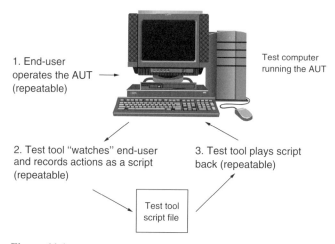

Figure 11.1   Tets tool record/playback paradigm

The end-user provides the application intelligence to the test tool by operating the AUT in a presumably correct manner. The test tool "looks over the end-user's shoulder" and writes down what the end-user does. The test tool's recording of the end-user operations is saved as some kind of command file, called a script file, for later playback. At a later time, the tool can be directed to use this script file to cause the AUT to operate exactly as if the end-user was sitting in the chair and operating it.

All three steps are designed to be repeatable and in fact are repeated many times during the course of correct test tool usage. The end-user can operate the AUT for many different business activities or for the same business activity many times as the activity becomes more refined during the development process.

The test tool can be used to record and rerecord any end-user session. Rerecording might be necessary because the end-user made a mistake in operation and needs to repeat the operation. Rerecording might also be necessary because the previously recorded operation has been changed during software development.

The test tool will be used to play back a script several times. If the AUT operates perfectly the first time the script is played back; a recommended tester practice is to play back the script at least one more time to prove repeatability of these perfect results. If the (AUT) does not operate perfectly, then the script is played back again after developers make the necessary code corrections to verify that the corrections solved the problem. The more defects that a test tool script reveals in the AUT, the more times the test script will be replayed to verify code corrections.

11.3.1   Test Script Command Language

There is no standard or universal script command language for all test tools. Because all script languages have a common purpose within the same record/play-back paradigm, the language skill a tester acquires using one vendor's tool script transfers substantially intact to a different vendor's tool script. Tool vendors have typically chosen one of two approaches to designing their test tool's script language. The first approach is to invent a scripting language from scratch that addressed the unique kinds of activities that operate a computer without end-user intervention. The vendors who started their scripting languages from scratch quickly recognized the need to add flow of control constructs to their scripting languages like those found in such standard programming languages as COBOL, FORTRAN, PL/1, and BASIC. The second approach was to adopt one of the standard programming languages for flow of control and extend that language with commands that are uniquely needed for robot control of a computer. The four standard programming languages most often extended for test tool scripting are PASCAL, C, Visual Basic, and most recently Java.

Because the tool scripting languages follow standard programming language conventions, timing point information from the operating system clock is readily available. The implication for performance testing is that specific application actions can be timed very accurately. For example, if an application lets the end user search a catalog for products, the test script language allows timing points to be placed just before and just after the search button is clicked. The difference between these two timing points tells the tester and the developer precisely how long the search took. These timing points are used both to find bottlenecks in the application (places where the application transaction takes the most time to complete) and to establish the performance baseline described in Chapter 9. The performance baseline is measured by adding timing points at the very beginning and very end of a script that has already verified the correct behavior of a particular business transaction. Re-executing the script with these two added timing points provides the precise total processing time necessary to complete the verified business transaction in an empty system.

A time-saving feature called data-driven execution has emerged in most script-ing languages. This feature allows the tester to record a simple end-user activity such as logging into the AUT with one user ID. Then, by using data-driven execution features, the tester can make the same simple recorded script execute with hundreds or thousands of additional user IDs. The key to the data-driven execution approach is for the tester to replace the end-user typed values such as user ID "JONES" with a reference to a data file containing 350 user IDs, for example. When the tester replays the script, each of the 350 user IDs (perhaps including "JONES") on the data file are attempted for log-in.

The time-saving nature of data-driven execution becomes more profound as more recorded script values are replaced by data file references, enabling large numbers of permutations to be tested just as easily as the original set of values. For example, a test tool records an end user placing an order for one office supply item. Three end-user data fields are subsequently identified for a large number of permutation tests. The first permutation data field is the customer's shipping address zip-code (say 2,000 different zip-codes) that signifies the customer's delivery geography. The application must identify which office supply items are available for purchase in which geography. The second permutation data field is customer type which can be one of the four values: 1 = small retail customer, 2 = large retail customer, 3 = small wholesale customer and 4 = large wholesale customer. Different standard discounts are offered on different office supplies depending on customer type. The third and final permutation data field is the office supply item code (say 5,000 different item codes). So the test script recorded for a purchase in just one zip code, one customer type, and one office supply item can have these end-user supplied values substituted for data files with all possible values to produce a simple test script capable of verifying $2,000 \times 4 \times 5,000 = 40,000,000$ permutations.

One last set of features resulting from the record/playback paradigm needs to be acknowledged here and described in more detail later in this chapter. About midway through the test tool maturity cycle, maybe the early 1990s, test tools began providing some means of test tool management: capturing results of an end-user recording session, scheduling tool playback sessions, and capturing results of playback sessions for reporting. These results could range from a message on the screen to the appearance of new screens to the hidden update of particular database records. These test tool management features will be discussed in the Test Management Paradigm section of this chapter. Examples of all of these features can be found in the current major test tool vendors' products. [45–47]

11.4 TEST TOOL TOUCHPOINT PARADIGMS

There are only two touchpoint paradigms that underlie the large number of available test tool products. A test tool touchpoint is the location of a test tool probe, either hardware or software, in the computer under test in order to measure some specific operational aspect of this test computer. The situation is similar to the small number of software development paradigms we found in Chapter 2 for a large number of software development methods. If we understand these two touchpoint paradigms, we can quickly understand and anticipate how a particular test tool will be used.

11.4.1   Touchpoint Paradigm for Functional Test Tools

The first touchpoint paradigm is used by functional testing tools. The goal of this paradigm is to directly operate a computer as if the end-user was performing the actions from his or her chair. Terms frequently used to describe this operation are "autopilot" and "robot mode." It is a little strange for a programmer or end-user to observe this tool paradigm in action for the first time: the screen is changing, the cursor is moving, menu entries are selected, data fields are being typed in … with nobody sitting in front of the computer. In order to succeed at this autopilot operation, the test tool must be able to record and play back actions from the keyboard, the mouse, and the computer monitor. These touchpoints are collectively referred to as "foreground" touchpoints because their actions are observable by the end-user. Figure 11.2 illustrates the location of the touchpoints for functional test tools.

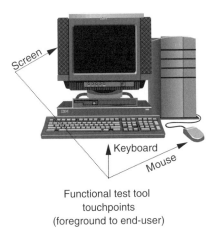

Functional test tool
touchpoints
(foreground to end-user)

Figure 11.2   Touchpoint paradigam for functional test tools

The functional touchpoint paradigm is implemented by tool software that runs on the same computer as the AUT. This one-to-one relationship between the tool computer and the test computer is necessary because the tool software must directly "observe" the interactions on the keyboard, mouse, and screen. This also represents a computer resource testing constraint. If you want to do functional testing for one business transaction at a time, you need one computer. If you want to do functional testing for two business transactions at the same time, you need two computers. If you want to do functional testing for 20 business transactions at the same time, you need 20 computers. There are no economies of scale. Figure 11.3 illustrates this AUT–test tool computer relationship for functional testing.

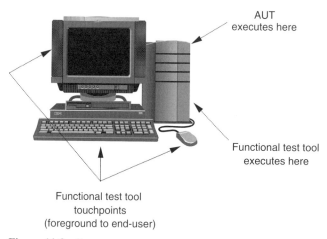

Functional test tool
touchpoints
(foreground to end-user)

Figure 11.3 Computer necessary to execute functional tests

11.4.2 Touchpoint Paradigm for Performance Test Tools

The second touchpoint paradigm is used by performance testing tools. The goal of this paradigm is to capture the messages and message timing passed between client computers and server computers that are all contributors to the AUT. The basis of this paradigm is the client/server computing architecture popularized in the early 1980s and made pervasive by the Internet. The client/server computing architecture distributes the computing workload from the end-user's computer to one or more specialized server computers. As an end-user operates the AUT, messages are periodically sent back and forth between the end-user's client computer and one or more server computers elsewhere in a network. The nature of the messages is determined by the communication protocol. The total response time of an application is the sum of the processing times on all involved computers plus the sum of all communication times.

The performance touchpoint is referred to as a "background" touchpoint because its action is not observable by the end-user. Figure 11.4 illustrates the location of the touchpoint for performance test tools.

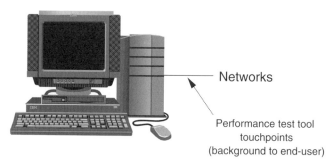

Networks

Performance test tool
touchpoints
(background to end-user)

Figure 11.4 Touchpoint paradigm for performance test tools

The performance touchpoint paradigm is implemented by tool software that runs on a different computer than the one used to run the AUT. This makes the tool computer independent of the number of network-connected computers running the AUT. In this case, the tool software "observes" the interactions among the application computers by watching the network traffic. Theoretically, one performance tool computer could record and play back an infinite number of client computer sessions to a very large number of servers. In reality, each client computer playback tool session requires a small but measurable amount of tool computer memory. So the practical upper limit of the number of client computer sessions that one performance tool computer can support is in the range of 500 to a few thousand, depending on the tool vendor's design and available tool server memory. This paradigm becomes even more attractive when you realize that once the recording session has been completed, zero client computers are required for the performance tool to play back the script and measure the workload on the server(s). There are definitely testing resource economies of scale here. Figure 11.5 illustrates this AUT–test tool computer relationship for performance testing.

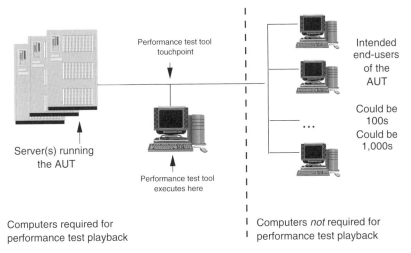

Figure 11.5 Computer(s) necessary to execute performance tests

The really good news for testers is that the two touchpoint paradigms do not conflict. Both touchpoint paradigms can be invoked by using functional test tools and performance test tools at the same testing time in the same testing environment. Figure 11.6 illustrates how this dual paradigm can work.

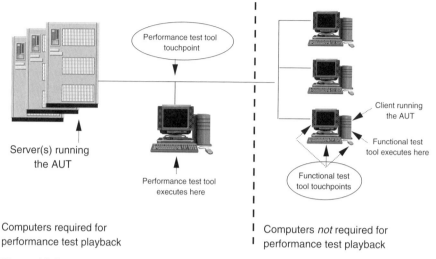

Figure 11.6   Test computer environment using both touchpoint paradigms

11.5   TEST TOOL EXECUTION PARADIGM

As test tools became more complex in the ways they were used and what they measured, there arose a need for the tester to be able to manage the test tools better. Tool vendors addressed this tester need by developing a test tool that manages test tools. Examples of the capabilities designed into these test management tools include

- test script library management
- test execution harness management
- expected values capture from script recordings
- actual values capture from script executions

Test script library management is the capability to store and retrieve test script files by some kind of naming convention and disk file structure. The source of the test scripts can be an automated test execution tool record session or a manually prepared script using some kind of text editor. If the test execution tool supports data-driven testing, then the test script library management capability will also provide naming conventions and disk file structures to store and retrieve the execution-time data files. Designs used to accomplish test script library management vary from vendor to vendor.

Test execution harness management is the capability to launch the test execution tools selectively for record and playback. Depending on the tool vendor's design, this capability can be simple or elaborate. Simple test execution management is performed by a sequential list that causes test script A to be executed, then test script B to be executed, then test script C to be executed, and so on. The tester clicks some kind of "start the test executions" button, and the harness dutifully performs the list of test executions. Complex test execution management adds alarm clocks and dependency flow to the simple execution list. Alarm clocks allow the tester to indicate that the next test execution sequence will start at 2 A.M. on Sunday so that the results can be reviewed first thing Monday morning. Dependency flow allows the tester to indicate that "if script A completes successfully, then start script B, otherwise skip script B and start script C." Dependency in this context means that the execution of a subsequent test script is dependent on the success or failure of an earlier test script in the list.

The last two capabilities of a test management tool address a concept that was not introduced in the prior test tool discussions. The concept is that behavior validation requires the comparison of two kinds of information: expected results and actual results. Expected results are defined to be the documented correct behavior or response to a specific set of conditions and inputs. Actual results are defined to be the behavior or experienced response exhibited to a specific set of conditions and inputs. Actual results may or may not match expected results. If actual results *do match* the expected results, the test is normally considered *successful (pass)*. If actual results *do not match* the expected results, the test is normally considered *unsuccessful (fail)*.

In order for a test management tool to be capable of capturing expected values from initial test script recordings, there needs to be some kind of complex tool-to-tool communication in which values captured during recording will be the expected value set. Sometimes the expected values are the keyboard entries that an end user types during script recording. Sometimes the expected values appear on the test computer screen after the end user has completed a particular action. Sometimes the expected values are hidden from the end user in some kind of data file or database. Sometimes the expected values have been predetermined and, in a manner similar to data-driven test preparation, the expected values are made available to the test management tool independent of the script recording activity.

In order for a test management tool to be capable of capturing actual values from subsequent test script playback, there needs to be some kind of complex tool-to-tool communication. This communication enables predetermined variables, screen areas, and data files or databases to be interrogated during test script playback for actual values to compare with the expected values. Once the actual values are collected from a test execution, the actual values are automatically compared with the expected values, and the success or failure of the comparison is indicated for the test execution just completed. Many test management tools that provide this expected values/actual values comparison also allow for the collection and comparison of actual values from multiple playback sessions with the same expected values.

The complexity and intimacy with which the test management tool must interact with function test execution tools and performance execution test tools has caused tool vendors to redesign their separate tool products into tool suites. These tool suites provide better intertool communication and operability while presenting the tester with a consistent look-and-feel of the tools individually. One of the welcomed byproducts of such a tool suite design is a lower tool training threshold before the tester becomes proficient in the tool suite.

11.6   THE BENEFITS THAT TESTING TOOLS CAN PROVIDE

Based on the previous sections in this chapter, you may conclude incorrectly that it is a good idea for a tester to *always* use automated testing tools. This would cause the tester to worry first about *which* test tool to use. Quite the contrary, one of the early-development lifecycle decisions a test team leader must make is *whether* to include automated testing tools in the test environment plans. Only after the appropriateness of test tool usage has been determined does the question of tool choice arise. The remainder of this chapter deals only with identifying development project circumstances that determine the appropriateness or inappropriateness of automated test tool use.

11.6.1   Repeatability—a Return on Investment Issue

If a particular test script will be executed three or more times, a test tool can begin to provide an economy of scale. The effort, resources, and cost to build the automated test script the first time are substantially higher than a single manual test that performs the same script steps. The second time the automated script is executed, none of the build costs are incurred. The second manual test of the same test script costs as much as the first manual test to perform.

After three or more test executions of the same script, the accumulated cost of performing these executions using a test tool is less than the accumulated cost of performing these same executions manually. The more times the automated test script is repeated beyond three times, the less expensive the total execution effort becomes relative to the same manual testing activity. Because manual testing offers no economies of scale, the total cost of manual testing continues to grow linearly by the same incremental cost for each subsequent test execution.

11.6.2   Repeatability Precision—a Technology Issue

One of the most frustrating and time-consuming situations for a software developer is for a tester to report a suspected defect that the developer cannot recreate. This situation can arise from a number of different causes, the most common of which is incomplete manual test case execution script documentation. In other words, the tester cannot tell the developer the *exact* sequence of actions and events that led to the defect discovery. The developer must use trial and error to fill in the tester's information gaps and try the most likely actions and events to recreate the suspected defect.

Another possible cause of defect recreation difficulty for the developer lies with the tester's ability to follow directions. The manual test execution script may be very crisp and clear about the steps to be completed and the expected results. Testers, being human, may inadvertently skip a step or complete only part of the step action because the instruction continued on the next page. The likelihood of this human element creeping into test execution increases with the number of times the tester must repeat the test due to a false sense of familiarity with the steps.

Automated testing tools directly address both of these repeatability precision issues. Every action to be taken by a testing tool is included in the tool's test script. The state of test data prior to script execution is defined in the test case. The testing tool executes its script with well-defined test data without human intervention. The combination of explicit script, explicit data state, and human non-intervention guarantees repeatable test results with very high precision. This precision translates into more expedient developer diagnosis of discovered defects.

11.6.3   Hidden Action and Results Verification—a Technology Issue

Although many application responses are revealed directly to the end-user, there may be many application responses that are hidden from the end user's view. Examples of revealed responses are new screen messages indicating "successful submission," new screens indicating successful submission with processing details, or new screens with requested search results. An example of hidden responses is a control item in a screen object like a "submit" button that becomes hidden from the end user afterwards to inhibit duplicated submissions.

Another example of hidden responses is database changes resulting from the end user submitting some kind of response (search request, purchase order, and so on). The revealed response is "successful submission." The hidden response is a set of database updates that may not be directly displayed to the end user or viewable by the end user. Developers go to great lengths to keep these actions and results hidden from the end user, either because revealing them will not help the end user do a better job or because revealing them will allow the end user to put the application in unexpected states of processing with potentially disastrous results to the business.

Testing tool designers are aware of this duality: end user versus developer view of the application responses. Knowing that both views are necessary for complete testing results, the testing tool designers have produced testing tools that can observe and act on both views of the AUT.

11.6.4   Timing Point Precision and Distribution—a Technology Issue

One of the test tool capabilities arguably most beneficial for software development in the 21st century is precision timing points. Prior to having this capability, testers were relegated to using a stopwatch, a wall clock, or a sweep second hand on their wristwatch. If the application activity took 15 or 20 min to complete as was common in the 1970s, then chronometers provided sufficient timing point precision.

As application response speeds became much faster, the Rule of 8 (see Chapter 9) reflected new sub-minute response time measurement needs. The tester needed and was provided with tool timing point precision to the millisecond. This leap in precision afforded the tester extremely precise response time measurements for both the total application process and subprocesses previously unattainable from stopwatch accuracy. The testing benefit of subprocess timing point precision is the ability to identify bottlenecks in the response path as illustrated in the Round Trip Performance Testing section of Chapter 9.

The trend toward distributed computing in the 1980s led to an additional challenge for performance testers. The application was no longer spending time just on the end-user computer and a large host computer. The application time was distributed across a number of specialized midsize computers called servers. Even if application response times had remained in the multiple-minute range, the tester would have been challenged to apply a stopwatch to several servers that would most likely be dispersed geographically, one of the primary advantages of distributed computing. The advent of viable Internet business applications has caused the span of these geographically distributed computing environments to stretch around the world. Test tools can and do provide millisecond response time measurements across these widely distributed computing environments without the tester leaving his chair.

11.6.5 Achievement of Impossible Manual Tests—a Return on Investment Issue

Choosing to do manual performance testing in preference to tool testing is likened to going hunting for elephants with a rock instead of a rifle. Although stopwatch timing may not be the most precise way to measure an application's response times, stopwatch timing can still get the job done if no testing tools are available. The true limitation of this approach resides in the size and complexity of the workload to be tested as described in Chapter 9.

Consider the situation of a workload to be tested in the range of 10–100 active business transactions and no test tools available. This situation can be tested manually by calling in the entire office staff on a Saturday, give them manual scripts to run, feed them pizza and beer, and have them pound on the system all day. The results are not particularly precise or repeatable, but the job does get done. The authors know of large companies who still do "Saturday Special" timing of their applications.

Any performance workload requirement beyond 100 active business transactions cannot be tested manually. The good news is that performance test tools have matured to the point that they can test workloads well beyond the 100 transaction breakpoint for manual testing. It is commonplace to achieve performance tool testing of workloads in the thousands of transactions. Some of the more specialized Internet performance testing tools can drive workloads of 500,000 transactions or more.

11.6.6 Reusability (Regression Testing)—a Return on Investment Issue

Test tools have been designed from the beginning to easily and reliably reuse test scripts. As testing processes have matured, this reusability feature has greatly enabled the concept and practice of regression testing described in Chapters 7 and 8.

If the tester manages and maintains all test scripts produced for the first version of an application, then this set of test scripts for Version 1 can be applied to an early copy of Version 2. Code untouched by Version 2 should pass the Version 1 script tests. Code touched to accommodate Version 2 changes should also pass the Version 1 script tests. New code for Version 2 will require test script additions or modifications for whatever new functionality that Version 2 provides. Functionality in Version 1 no longer supported in Version 2 will require test script retirement.

11.7 THE LIABILITIES THAT TESTING TOOLS CAN IMPOSE

Before the test manager can calculate a prospective test tool's return on investment, he or she needs to be aware of all the costs that should be included in the calculation denominator. Some of the costs are obvious. Some of the costs are hidden.

11.7.1 Testing Tool Costs—a Financial, Resources, and Skills Issue

The most obvious cost of a testing tool is its price tag. This price tag can range from several thousand dollars to almost a million dollars. Many tools have a base price and some form of usage price. The usage price can be expressed in terms of licenses by (1) the number of computers that will run the test tool, (2) the number of testers who will use the tool, or (3) the peak number of sessions to be run at any given time. To determine the total price tag of the test tool for your project, you will need fairly detailed test plans that can be used to predict the number of licenses to buy. Buy too few licenses and you impact your testing schedule. Buy too many licenses and you have spent too much money on tools.

A less obvious cost of test tools is the computer equipment that they may require. Many of the functional test tools run on the same hardware as the application. Additional equipment purchases for these tools are not automatically required. The combination of computing resources for both the application and the test tool may cause the test team to need larger capacity computers after all. All of the performance test tools require additional hardware at least for the tool server. Because performance tool server resources are not infinite, the workloads you plan to test may require two or more performance tool servers and ancillary network equipment.

A scheduling cost often overlooked is the test tool installation in the testing environment. Normally, the testing environment is being set up while the testers are deep into planning. The decision to use a testing tool will add tool installation time to the testing environment setup schedule. The result is that when the testers expect the testing environment to be available for test execution, the testing environment may still be busy with test tool installation.

A resource cost often overlooked is the skill set for the chosen testing tool. The testing environment setup activities will require a tool expert to install the chosen tool and verify its correct operation. Later in the testing execution activities, the same kind of tool expert will have to be consulted to determine whether the source of a possible defect is really incorrect tool usage by testers. Once the testing tool is available in the testing environment, there is a skill set issue for the test team. The testers who will use the testing tool must have either prior experience with that tool or be sent to training specific for that tool.

11.7.2 One-off Testing Setup Costs

We previously stated that the return on investment from testing tools occurs after three or more repeat uses of the same test scripts. This saving is mostly due to economies of scale (repetition). The first time a test tool test script is written and validated, it is an expensive proposition in both time and resources. The only successful argument for using a testing tool in a one-off situation is that the test results are critical to the success of the software or that the testing cannot be accomplished manually.

11.7.3 Boundaries of Testing Tool Capabilities

There is a dimension of tool capabilities often missed during tool evaluation and selection. This dimension is flexibility with respect to application changes. Some of the most powerful tool capabilities are viable only if the software does not change from build to build or release to release. In these cases when the software changes, many if not all of the test scripts must be recorded again!

Here is an example of both sides of this capability-with-change issue. Classically, functional test tools for Windows record what is happening on the screen in one of the two ways. The first way is by the pixel coordinates of the objects of interest (data field, button, and text message) on the screen. The object coordinates are very precise and allow some amazing scripting capabilities; however, if the programmer moves a scripted object one pixel in any direction, the script will no longer execute correctly.

The second way is by standard properties of the objects of interest on the screen. This method of object recording is independent of the object's screen coordinates. This means that the programmer can move a scripted object from one side of the screen to another and the script will execute correctly. This second way of recording objects loses its flexibility in the long run when the object properties change in subsequent release modifications. In either event, test tool scripts require a level of ongoing maintenance not usually required by manual test scripts.

11.8 PUTTING AUTOMATED TESTING TOOLS IN PERSPECTIVE

Anybody who has attempted do-it-yourself projects around home comes to appreciate the value of the right tool for the right job. Similarly, with the plethora of automated test tools in the marketplace, it becomes important to know the right test tool for the right test case.

Rather than trying to gain experience in all the available tools, the suggestion is to understand the touchpoint paradigms of the different groups of tools. As soon as a tester identifies the tool paradigm most appropriate for the test situation, the number of tool choices shrink dramatically. As new tools emerge in the marketplace, testers can use touchpoint paradigm understanding to place the new tool in a group of comparable, familiar tools for further feature comparison.

11.9   SUMMARY

Automated testing tools are a collection of software products designed specifically to assist software testers and software testing managers with different aspects of a testing project. The current commercial tool market has over 300 products. Each of these tools offers to assist the tester with one or more of the tester's activities. So far, no one tool has been proven to offer assistance with *all* tester activities.

There are testing situations in which the use of automated testing tools is inappropriate, disadvantageous, and expensive. There are also testing situations in which the use of automated testing tools is appropriate, advantageous, and cost-effective. Automated test tools that execute the AUT are designed to be used in a unique way. This unique way is referred to as "record/playback."

There are only two touchpoint paradigms that underlie the large number of available test tool products. A test tool touchpoint is the location of a test tool probe, either hardware or software, of the computer under test in order to measure some specific operational aspect of this test computer.

The first touchpoint paradigm is used by functional testing tools. The goal of this paradigm is to directly operate a computer as if the end-user was performing the actions from his or her chair. The second touchpoint paradigm is used by performance testing tools. The goal of this paradigm is to capture the messages and message timing passed between client computers and server computers that are all contributors to the AUT. The really good news for testers is that the two touchpoint paradigms do not conflict. Both touchpoint paradigms can be invoked by using functional test tools and performance test tools at the same testing time in the same testing environment.

Based on the previous sections in this chapter, you may conclude incorrectly that it is a good idea for a tester to *always* use automated testing tools. This would cause the tester to worry first about *which* test tool to use. Quite the contrary, one of the early development lifecycle decisions a test team leader must make is *whether* to include automated testing tools in the test environment plans. Only after the appropriateness of test tool usage has been determined does the question of tool choice arise.

KEY TERMS AND CONCEPTS

Automated testing tool
Eclipse
Hyades
Record/playback
Script file
Test script command
    language
Data-driven test execution

Test tool touchpoints
Foreground testing
Background testing
Test tool server
Test script library
    management
Test execution harness
    management

Expected values versus
    actual values
Pass/fail
Hidden results
Screen object coordinates
    versus screen object
    properties

Chapter 12

Analyzing and Interpreting Test Results

LEARNING OBJECTIVES

- to describe what successful test results tell about testing effectiveness
- to demonstrate how to exploit defect discovery beyond correcting individual defects

12.1 INTRODUCTION

This chapter describes the kinds of test execution results you might want to collect, the ways you might want to consider analyzing these results, and the interpretations you may place on your analysis outcome.

You are almost finished with your testing tasks. You have completed your test planning as described in Chapters 4 and 5. You have set up a testing environment as described in Chapter 10. With or without automated testing tools described in Chapter 11, you have started executing your testing scenarios designed in Chapters 6–9. With or without test management tools described in Chapter 11, you have started collecting the results of your test executions.

12.2 TEST CASES ATTEMPTED VERSUS SUCCESSFUL

The first step in discussing test execution results is to expect that you have done a thorough job of test planning. If you have unintentionally omitted certain application functions or business activities or structural components or performance aspects of your application from your test planning, then your test coverage will be inadequate. No amount of test execution of your planned coverage will give you test results for the "un"-covered testing. The extent of "un"-covered testing usually becomes

Software Testing: Testing Across the Entire Software Development Life Cycle, by G. D. Everett and R. McLeod, Jr.
Copyright © 2007 John Wiley & Sons, Inc.

apparent when customers start calling your HelpDesk with defects that eluded your testing. Customer-discovered software defects will be included in our analysis later in this chapter.

One planning key to successful test results analysis is the clear definition of success for each test case. It is common for a test case to have a number of expected results. If the actual results obtained from a test execution *all* match the expected results, then the test case is normally considered "attempted and successful." If only some of the actual results obtained from a test execution match the expected results, then the test case is normally considered "attempted but unsuccessful." Test cases that have not been executed are initially marked "unattempted."

The "unattempted" versus "attempted ..." status of each test case is tracked by testing management because this is the most obvious testing progress indicator. Ninety percent "unattempted" test cases indicates that the testing effort has just begun. Ten percent "unattempted" test cases indicates that the testing effort may be close to finished. The number of attempted test cases over time gives the test manager an indication of how fast the testing is progressing relative to the size of the test team. If you log 15 test cases attempts by your test team in the first 2 weeks of testing, this indicates an initial attempt rate of 1.5 test case attempts/day. If the test plan calls for a total of 100 test cases to be attempted, then you can calculate an initial estimate of 14 weeks for your test team to "attempt" all 100 test cases in the plan. Here are the calculations.

15 test cases attempted / 10 test work days = 1.5 test case attempts/day
100 test cases to attempt / 1.5 test case attempts/day = 67 days (14 workweeks)

Calculation 12.1   Estimating test execution schedule—first Draft

Some of the "attempts" will result in defect discoveries requiring time for correction and retesting. So the 14-week schedule really represents the expected completion of just the first round of testing execution. Depending on the number of "unsuccessful" test cases encountered during the 14-week period, a second, third, and possibly fourth round of correction and retesting may be necessary to achieve mostly "successful" results.

A test case may be "attempted but unsuccessful" because the actual results do not match the expected results or because the software halted with an error message before the test case was completed. The challenge to the test manager is to prioritize the unsuccessful test case results for correction. If a test case encounters an error that stops the test case before it can be completed, this is usually considered a severe defect sufficient to warrant immediate corrective action by the developers. Once that corrective action has been taken and the test case rerun, the test case may go to completion without further showstoppers and become marked as "attempted and successful." On the contrary, the test case may execute a few more steps and be halted by another defect.

If the application under test allows the test case to go to completion but provides actual results different from the expected results, the test manager needs to prioritize these unsuccessful test case results based on business risk to not correct. For example, if a functional test case shows that a set of screen input values produces an incorrect screen output value critical to routine business, then the unsuccessful test case presents a high business risk to not correct. An example of this kind of "attempted but unsuccessful" results would be an incorrect loan payment amortization schedule based on a loan principal value and annual interest rate. Testing can continue, but the application cannot be shipped or deployed to a business until the actual results match the expected results.

A low business risk example would be a "submit" message that appears in green in the lower right-hand corner of the screen instead of appearing in red in the upper left-hand corner of the screen. The actual execution result is different from the expected result, but the application is usable in business with the different outcome. The test manager needs to discuss this test finding with the application development manager to determine the priority of correcting the code that produces the "submit" message.

Testers tend to prioritize unsuccessful testing outcomes using the range of numbers from 1 to 4. Priority 1 is used to indicate the highest business risk. Priority 4 is used to indicate the lowest business risk. Historically, testers use the term "severity" instead of "priority" to convey relative business risk of unsuccessful tests. Figure 12.1a demonstrates how a test case execution schedule might appear. Figure 12.1b shows the analysis of the Figure 12.1a first week's test execution results.

	Test case execution schedule				
Date	Test case ID	Date atttempted	Outcome	Severity	Date corrected
Week 1	FT-001	5 Jul	Successful		
	FT-002	6 Jul	Successful		
	FT-003	6 Jul	Successful		
	FT-004	6 Jul	Unsuccessful	1	
	FT-005	7 Jul	Successful		
	FT-006	7 Jul	Successful		
	FT-007	7 Jul	Unsuccessful	2	
	FT-008	7 Jul	Unsuccessful	1	
	FT-009	7 Jul	Unsuccessful	1	
	FT-010	8 Jul	Successful		
Week 2	FT-011				
	FT-012				
	FT-013				
	FT-014				
...	...				
Week 14	FT-095				
	FT-096				
	FT-097				
	FT-098				
	FT-099				
	FT-100				

Figure 12.1a   A test schedule with first-week outcomes

Test case execution progress—week 1			
100	Total test cases to attempt		
10	Test cases attempted to date		
10%	Percent attempted to date		
6	Test cases attempted—successful		
60%	Percent test cases successful		
4	Test case attempted—unsuccessful		
40%	Percent test case unsuccessful		
	Severity 1s	3	75%
	Severity 2s	1	25%
	Severity 3s	0	0%
	Severity 4s	0	0%

Figure 12.1b   Analysis of first-week test execution outcomes

12.3   DEFECT DISCOVERY FOCUSING ON INDIVIDUAL DEFECTS

As we saw in the previous section, there are several possible reasons why the execution of a test case can be considered unsuccessful. The remaining sections of this chapter use the term "defect" for a confirmed software error discovered by test execution and requiring correction.

At its most basic level, testing discovers defects one at a time. Once the defect has been corrected and retested, the particular area of software under test may operate defect free throughout the remaining test case execution. More frequently, the correction of one defect simply allows the test case to proceed to the next defect in the software, resulting in a number of discovery/correction cycles that are required before the test case can run to successful completion. It is also likely that multiple test cases with different testing objectives in the same area of the software will discover different sequences of defects. The implication is that a single successful test case does not guarantee defect-free code in the area of the software being tested.

The incremental discovery and correction retesting of software defects is the primary way that software testers help software developers implement the development requirements. The fewer the latent defects in the delivered software, the closer the software comes to fulfilling the requirements. The success of incremental defect discovery is directly related to the management process used to track defects from discovery to correction. If defects are discovered but not reported to developers, then testing provides no real value to the development effort. If the defects are discovered and reported to developers but the corrective action not verified, then testing still provides no real value to the development effort. The success of incremental defect discovery requires defect tracking from discovery through correction to retesting and verification that correction has been achieved.

Defect tracking can be accomplished with a variety of reporting tools ranging from a simple spreadsheet to an elaborate defect management tool. Either way, the organized entry and tracking of simple information pays great dividends toward the success of defect correction efforts. Figure 12.2 demonstrates how an unsuccessful test case attempt causes one or more defect log entries that can be tracked to correction with simple metrics.

		Test case execution schedule						
Date	Test case ID	Date attempted	Outcome	Severity	Date corrected			
Week 1	FT 001	5 Jul	Successful					
	FT 002	6 Jul	Successful					
	FT 003	6 Jul	Successful					
	FT 004	6 Jul	Unsuccessful	1				
	FT 005	7 Jul	Successful					
	FT 006	7 Jul	Successful					
	FT 007	7 Jul	Unsuccessful	2				
	FT 008	7 Jul	Unsuccessful	1				
	FT 009	7 Jul	Unsuccessful	1				
	FT 010	8 Jul	Successful					
Week 2	FT 011							
	FT 012		**Defect tracking log**					
			Defect ID	Date discovered	Test case ID	Severity	Date assigned for correction	Date corrected
			SD-0001	6 Jul	FT-004	1		
			SD-0002	7 Jul	FT-007	2		
			SD-0003	7 Jul	FT-007	2		
			SD-0004	7 Jul	FT-007	3		
			SD-0005	7 Jul	FT-007	2		
			SD-0006	7 Jul	FT-008	1		
			SD-0007	7 Jul	FT-009	1		

Figure 12.2   Example defect tracking log from unsuccessful test case attempts

Because the severity code is meant to be an aid in determining which defects in the tracking log to correct next, at least three different kinds of severity codes can be found in use either singly or in combination. The first kind of severity code indicates severity relative to testing, that is, "Is this a testing showstopper?" The second kind of severity code indicates severity relative to development, that is, "Is this a development showstopper?" The third kind of severity code indicates severity relative to completing development, that is, "Is this a shipping/deployment showstopper?" The trend is toward capturing all three severity codes for each defect and use the one that makes the most sense depending on how close the development project is to completion. The closer the project comes to completion, the more important the shipping showstopper severity code becomes.

12.4   DEFECT DISCOVERY FOCUSING ON THE DEFECT BACKLOG

The first testing metric that we talked about at the beginning of this chapter was the number and ratio of planned test cases versus attempted test cases to give us a sense of how far we have progressed with our planned testing activities. The second testing metric that we talked about is the number and ratio of attempted test cases versus unsuccessful test cases to give us a sense of how defect free the testers are finding the software at that point in the testing schedule.

Successful incremental defect tracking can provide a third testing metric normally called the defect backlog. If your testing has discovered 300 software defects and development has successfully corrected 100 of these defects, then a backlog of 200 defects still needs to be corrected. The challenge for the development team is to determine if there is enough time and programming and testing resources available to reduce the defect backlog to zero before the development due date. Most times the answer is "no." The challenge then becomes one of the developers and testers reviewing the defect backlog to identify more severe defects for correction first. The hope is that when development time runs out, the remaining defects in the defect backlog are minor and will not adversely impact the software user's business. The residual uncorrected defect backlog typically becomes part of an interim fix pack or unfinished work for the next release.

In simple terms, the defect backlog is the list of all defects on the defect tracking log that have not been corrected by the reporting date, usually weekly. If the defect tracking log in Figure 12.2 is updated with a week's worth of developer correction effort, the uncorrected defects become the defect backlog shown in Figure 12.3.

Defect tracking log

Defect ID	Date Discovered	Test case ID	Severity	Date assigned for correction	Date corrected
SD-0001	6 Jul	FT-004	1	11 Jul	13 Jul
SD-0002	7 Jul	FT-007	2	11 Jul	14 Jul
SD-0003	7 Jul	FT-007	2	12 Jul	15 Jul
SD-0004	7 Jul	FT-007	3	12 Jul	15 Jul
SD-0005	7 Jul	FT-007	2		
SD-0006	7 Jul	FT-008	1	13 Jul	
SD-0007	7 Jul	FT-009	1		
	7 Jul				

Defect Backlog

Defect ID	Date discovered	Test case ID	Severity	Date assigned for correction	Date corrected
SD-0005	7 Jul	FT-007	2		
SD-0007	7 Jul	FT-009	1		

Figure 12.3   The defect backlog

The challenge for the backlog analysis team is that the backlog is a weekly moving target as defects are corrected and new defects are discovered. It is not uncommon for new defects discovered late in the development cycle to be immediately promoted to the top of the backlog as "must fix" backlog list.

At this juncture, fiery debates will arise over the quality of the software because "software quality" has no industry standard definition or measurements. For the purposes of this textbook, software quality goals and measurements for the software under test are included in the software requirements. The intended implication is that if the developer writes software that unequivocally meets all the development requirements and the tester successfully validates the software against all of the development requirements, then the software is considered to be of good quality. It is relatively easy to find publications that document how pervasive poor-quality software (using the above definition) is in the marketplace. [11] Those software products that do achieve this verified consistency with their development requirements are then challenged to define whether the requirements themselves are of good quality—a whole different quality issue beyond the scope of this textbook.

12.5   DEFECT DISCOVERY FOCUSING ON CLUSTERS OF DEFECTS

The metrics used to track the incremental discovery and correction of software defects can be leveraged for valuable test analysis beyond one-by-one defect review and backlog analysis. Consider the cost/benefit trade-off from adding one more column of information to the defect-tracking record: the identification of the code that contained the defect. We will call this the "code earmark."

The cost of adding this code earmark is not high, but it is usually not free either. First, the development team must agree on a standard way to identify the code in which defect corrections are applied. Programming specifications usually contain unique identifiers for the modules, subroutines, and classes that can also serve as code earmarks for defect tracking. Second, the development team must agree to take the extra time and effort to report back to the defect tracking log the code earmark

Defect tracking log						
Defect ID	Date discovered	Test case ID	Severity	Date assigned for correction	Date corrected	code earmark
SD-0001	6 Jul	FT-004	1	11 Jul	13 Jul	GL106
SD-0002	7 Jul	FT-007	2	11 Jul	14 Jul	AP234
SD-0003	7 Jul	FT-007	2	12 Jul	15 Jul	AP234
SD-0004	7 Jul	FT-007	3	12 Jul	15 Jul	AP236
SD-0005	7 Jul	FT-007	2			
SD-0006	7 Jul	FT-008	1	13 Jul		
SD-0007	7 Jul	FT-009	1			

Figure 12.4   Defect tracking log with code earmarks

for each defect that they correct. Up to this point, all of the defect tracking information has come from the tester who discovers and logs the defect. Now a reporting partnership is established where both test team and development team contribute data to the defect tracking log for defect analysis. Figure 12.4 shows how Figure 12.3 defect tracking log might appear with a code earmark column included.

This augmented defect tracking log can be used for root cause analysis. There are a number of good statistical textbooks available that provide the mathematical basis and practical application of root cause analysis to software defect logs. [48] The simplified explanation of root cause analysis for testing is the mathematical search for the "buggiest" code. This search can be accomplished by a simple frequency count of corrected defect code earmarks, ordered with the most frequently occurring code earmarks first. Clusters or groupings of defects will arise by code earmark. This kind of analysis is most helpful during the first third to first half of the software development cycle when the software is least stable and more susceptible to large numbers of corrections and updates.

Figure 12.5 shows the possible results of a ranked frequency count of 2,000 defects corrected by the end of the preliminary construction phase of a hypothetical software project.

Defect tracking log		
Root cause analysys of defects		
Corrected during preliminary construction		
May 1 thru Aug 15		
2000 total defects corrected during preliminary construction		
Code earmarks	Defects corrected per code earmark	Percent defects corrected per code earmark
AP234	450	22.5%
AP745	310	15.5%
GL106	150	7.5%
AR218	75	3.8%
PY512	10	0.5%
BK459	8	0.4%
DP113	8	0.4%
All others	989	less than 0.4%
Total	2000	

Figure 12.5   Using the defect tracking log for root cause analysis

The analysis shows that three or four code earmarks were the primary contributors to the defect log during the Preliminary construction phase of development. It would be very prudent for the testing team to urge a project team review of AP234, AP745, and GL106 before proceeding with the Final construction phase. A review of AR218 might pay dividends, but its defect contribution does not make as compelling a case for review as the other three code earmarks. This becomes a judgment call based on what else the testing team has learned about the AR module during testing. All earmarks below AR218 on the report were an order of magnitude less frequently occurring. Additional code review for the less frequently occurring code earmarks may not add much value.

There are three reasons for the recommendation to review the program code and design behind the top three code earmarks. The first and most obvious reason is the dominant discovery of defects in these code earmarks over all other code earmarks. The second, less obvious reason is that these three code earmarks account for 45.5% of all defects discovered during the Preliminary construction phase. The third and final reason is that two of the three top offenders come from the same major program module, the AP module. So a consolidated review of AP234 and AP745 could pay extra dividends.

These clusters occur due to a variety of development process influences such as incomplete or inaccurate design, inadequate code design, inadequate code writing, and inadequate debugging. More subtle influences are the coding standards that might actually encourage bad coding habits, or programmers with inadequate programming language skills for the complexity of the application.

Regardless of what might be causing the code earmark clustering in the defect log, the motivation for the reviews is to determine if there are, in fact, many more possible defects in the same earmark area that could be prevented or minimized by a design review, a specification review, or even a code walkthrough. Here is the payoff for the developer who takes the time to identify code earmarks for the defect log. The tester is able to say, "revisit this code one time thoroughly and you will probably reduce the number of times you must revisit the same code for additional corrections."

For the sake of demonstration, assume that the project team agrees with the testing team's root cause analysis. The team takes a couple of days to walk through the AP module and the GL module with AP234, AP745, and GL106 as their guide to potential trouble areas in the code. Sure enough, a major design flaw was discovered in the AP module. Additionally, subroutines in the GL module were found to violate programming standards regarding branching logic that left several dead end logic paths.

As a result of the review, the start of the Final construction phase was postponed 3 weeks to allow the developers to implement the review recommendations and the testers to rerun all their test cases for the AP and GL modules (regression testing). As with all coding revisions, the regression testing discovered 50 more defects that were added to the defect tracking log. Because none of the additional 50 defects were showstoppers, they were considered part of the defect backlog that could be corrected during the early part of the Final construction phase.

Halfway through the Final construction phase, the test team did another root cause analysis. This time the analysis focused on defects discovered and corrected thus far just in that phase. The test team was interested in seeing what effect the post-Preliminary construction code correction cycle had on the defects of the next phase. Recall that there is a human tendency to introduce new software defects during code correction. The team was also interested in seeing if other coding earmarks now arose as possible areas of review. Figure 12.6 shows the second root cause analysis report.

Defect tracking log			
Root cause analysys of defects			
Corrected during Final construction in progress			
Sept 15 – Nov 15			
1500 total defects corrected during Final construction in progress			
Code earmarks	**Defects corrected per code earmark**	**Percent defects corrected per code earmark**	
AR218	30	2.0%	
PY512	25	1.7%	
BK459	15	1.0%	
DP113	8	0.5%	
AP234	5	0.3%	
GL106	4	0.3%	
All others	1413	less than 0.3%	
Total	1500		

Figure 12.6   Second root cause analysis of defect logs

Several conclusions can be drawn from the second root cause analysis. The original top three code earmarks are no longer the major offenders. So the time and effort that went into the review, programming revisions, and retesting definitely reduced the number of hidden defects. The new top three code earmarks represent only 4.7% of the total defects corrected indicating a more even distribution of earmarks throughout the software observed as the software becomes stable. Therefore, there will not be much benefit expected from another 3-week effort to review, correct, and retest these new code earmarks in preference to other development activities. The fact that AP234 and GL106 are still on the list is neither alarming nor unexpected. Programming that starts out troublesome usually continues to be troublesome at some level for the duration of the development project.

Root cause analysis is normally less valuable during the middle-third of the development than it is during the first-third. There are two reasons for this reduced analytical value. First, by midproject most of the code has been tested several different times, which will tend to reinforce the earlier identification of particularly defective code with few new surprises. Second, by midproject the developers have little time or opportunity to fully review code design and structure that is well on its way to being finished code.

During the last third of the development, code earmarks tend to be used to prioritize the backlog of uncorrected defects rather than analyze the corrected defects. Recall that the code earmark is expected to come from the developer who corrects the code. By definition, the defect backlog has not been corrected; therefore, you do not expect to find code earmarks on the defect backlog entries. Consider doing a little guesswork on the most severe backlog defects. Have a brief meeting in which the developers are asked to guess which code earmark is most likely contributing each backlogged severe defect. Use this code earmark guess to see if there are clusters of high-priority backlogged defects based on code earmark. If clusters appear, then suggest that the developers concentrate on the first few in the cluster as their correction priority. Because the developers will be working on the most severe defects, no valuable (and scarce at this time in the development) correction time is squandered. After the first couple of most severe defects have been corrected, compare the actual code earmarks with the guesses. If the guesses are correct, continue to pursue the remaining code earmarks in that most severe defect cluster. If the guesses are incorrect, attack the first few defects in the next cluster. The risk is spending a little extra time up front with the developers when they are under the most pressure to complete the software. The benefit is giving them some analytical road signs that could make the remaining correction time and effort they have left most wisely spent from a quality perspective.

Figure 12.7 demonstrates what such a defect backlog root cause analysis might show for a backlog of 500 defects during Final construction.

Defect backlog		
Root cause analysys of defects		
Not corrected as of Dec 15		
1 Total defect—severity 1	Included in analysis	
24 Total defects—severity 2	Included in analysis	
475 Total defects—severity 3 and 4	Not included in analysis	
500 Total defects not corrected as of Dec 15		
Code earmark guesses	**Defects awaiting correction per code earmark**	**Percent defects awaiting correction per code earmark**
AR477 (includes severity 1)	13	52.0%
GL105	5	20.0%
PY632	3	12.0%
GL498	2	8.0%
GL551	1	4.0%
GL600	1	4.0%
Total	25	

Figure 12.7 Defect backlog root cause analysis

In this example, the development team is already concentrating on correction code around earmark AR477 because it has exhibited a Severity 1 defect. The development team might be surprised that so many of the Severity 2 defects are possibly colocated with the Severity 1 defect around earmark AR477 that they are already attempting to correct. Another possible conclusion of this analysis is for the test team to lend support to the development team that has been arguing with project management about the correction difficulties in this area of code due to vague or conflicting design specifications. One more possible conclusion of this analysis is what our Canadian friends would call "the dead moose on the table": The development team has been in denial that the AR477 earmark code area has major problems that present a real risk to the customer.

12.6 PRIOR DEFECT DISCOVERY PATTERN USEFULNESS

There is no current way to precisely predict beforehand how many or what kinds of defects your test team will discover in new software. The quest for such a prediction is often called looking for the "silver bullet." The software engineering researcher who finds the silver bullet will indeed strike gold!

Depending on the circumstances and maturity of the software development organization, predevelopment defect predictions can range from an educated guess to reasonably accurate predictions. Project managers are understandably hesitant to take any proactive steps based on educated guesses. Some historically based defect prediction techniques can yield answers $+/-10\%$ of the actual defect totals at the end of the project. Managers are more likely to take proactive steps based on historical defect prediction techniques that have proven to be credible over a series of projects.

The educated guess is used when the next software project is nothing like prior projects for the development and testing teams. There is no project history basis for gleaning predictions about the next project. The educated guess comes from the experts on the software development project that have "done something similar." If this explanation does not give you a warm, fuzzy feeling about the value of an educated guess, then you understand the implications correctly. The most generous statement one can make is that an educated guess in the absence of historical defect data is a better starting point than nothing … but not by much.

12.6.1 Prior Project Defect History as a Starting Point

If there is project history either from similar software applications or from previous releases of the same software application, then that project history can be leveraged for next project defect predictions. The value of the project history for defect prediction is directly proportional to the level of defect tracking detail that was captured in the project history. As we have seen in the previous sections of this chapter, the prior project can pick and choose what to include in the defect tracking log. As you would intuitively expect, the more the details in the prior project defect tracking log, the more useful that defect tracking log history becomes as a predictor for the next project. We will examine the usefulness of minimal historical detail in this section and conclude with a reference to a commercially available method that uses considerably more historical detail for defect discovery prediction.

The minimum useful historical defect information is a prior project's defect log that uniquely identifies each defect discovered and its date of discovery. An informative curve can be drawn on a two-dimensional graph showing numbers of defects discovered by week versus project week. Assume for the purposes of demonstration that the prior project was completed in 24 months and produced a software application containing 200,000 lines of code commonly referred to as 200KLOC. The defect log discovery curve by week might look something like Figure 12.8.

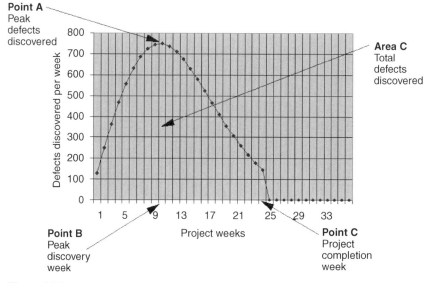

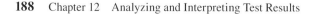

Figure 12.8   Prior development project defect tracking log

This curve demonstrates characteristics of most testing project results. There is an initial burst of defect discovery that peaks sometime in the first third of the project. Then the defect discovery rate trails back down as the software becomes more stable and exhibits fewer and fewer defects.

Point A is the peak (maximum) number of defects discovered during any week of the project. Figure 12.8 shows us that the discovery peak for this project was 749 defects. Point B is the week during the project in which the peak number of defects was discovered. Figure 12.8 shows us that the discovery peak for this project occurred during week 10. Point C is the week when the project was completed; in this example it is week 24. Finally, Area C under the curve from the project start date to the project completion date is the total number of defects discovered during the project. Figure 12.8 shows us that testing during this project discovered a total of 11,497 defects.

There is a body of research that suggests that the higher the defect discovery peak (Point A) and the earlier in the testing the discovery peak occurs (Point B), the fewer defects will be found by customers after project completion. [49] The implication is that if you compare defect curves from project to project and you see the defect discovery peak getting higher and occurring sooner in the project, then you are letting fewer and fewer defects get past the project completion to the customer. Recall from Chapter 1 that the most expensive defects to fix are customer-discovered defects. Any trend you see in testing results from project to project that suggests there will be fewer customer-detected defects also suggests that significant software support savings are being realized by your organization.

The same research suggests that if you extend the defect discovery curve beyond project software completion Point C to Point D on the x-axis, then Area D under the curve between Point C and Point D will approximate the number of defects found by customers. Figure 12.9 shows how the defect curve in Figure 12.8 might be extended to estimate Area D.

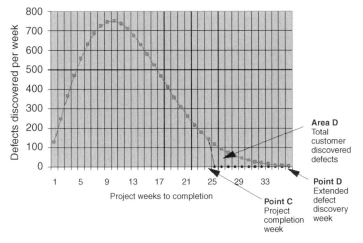

Figure 12.9   Prior development project defect tracking log extended beyond project completion

In this example, we have extended the prior defect history curve past the project completion week to the *x*-axis. Project week 36 becomes our Point D. Area D under the curve from Point C to Point D is 487 defects that customers might discover. Before acting on the 487 customer defects as a prediction, we need to consider additional information.

One additional graph from the prior development project defect tracking log can shed additional light. Consider stratifying the defect log data in Figure 12.8 by development showstopper severity codes. A graph something like Figure 12.10 might appear.

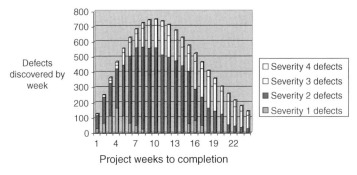

Figure 12.10   Prior project defect tracking log by development defect severity

The graph shows what you might already know. The more severe defects tend to be encountered early in the development cycle when the code is quite unstable. The severity of the defects declines as the code becomes stable. Generally speaking, the discovery of very severe defects at the end of the development project is truly bad news for any immediate plans to complete the software.

12.6.2   Leveraging Prior Project Defect History *Before* the Next Project Starts

This brings us to a second useful piece of defect prediction information that becomes available between the time the prior development project was completed and the time the next development project starts. This second piece of information is a HelpDesk log of customer-discovered defects. The number of customer-discovered defects will correlate somehow with the Area D prediction. This correlation may be 1 to 1 or 100 to 1 or some other number in between. For the purposes of demonstration, say there were 70 customer-discovered defects found in the Figure 12.9 release and reported to the HelpDesk. The customer defect discovery correlation is calculated by

$$\frac{\text{No. predicted}}{\text{No. actual}} = \text{No. predicted per actual}$$

For example:

$$\frac{487 \text{ Predicted from curve}}{70 \text{ Actual from the defect log}} = 6.9 \text{ predicted defects per actual defect}$$

The goal of the exercise is to be able to predict fairly accurately the number of customer-discovered defects that can be expected from the next development project as it concludes. The value of this prediction is the proactive economic implications for other parts of the organization like the HelpDesk and the software support groups. If HelpDesk and Support know to prepare for an estimated 70 customer defects in the next 6 months instead of 7,000 customer defects, then the HelpDesk and Support can be smarter about near-term staffing and hours of operation. Remember that this correlation of project defect discovery to customer defects is just an observation that can be useful.

Another interesting implication is the cost of correction represented by the customer-discovered defects. Chapter 1 places the average cost of correcting a customer-discovered defect at $14,000 per defect. If our customers found 70 defects in the last release of our software, the cost of correction to our software organization is

70 customer defects $\times$ $14,000 per correction = $980,000 in correction costs

When the customer defect logging system is established, consider requesting the inclusion of some elements from the development defect log such as a severity code when the call is received and a code earmark when the correction has been made by Support. This additional information will allow you to analyze the customer defects in the same way that we suggested analyzing the defect tracking log early in this chapter.

Figure 12.11 represents the HelpDesk log that corresponds to the customer defect discovery predictions in Figure 12.9.

HelpDesk tracking log		
Root cause analysys of defects		
Corrected after prior project completed		
before next project started		
2 Total defect—severity 1	Included in analysis	
13 Total defect—severity 2	Included in analysis	
55 Total defect—severity 3 & 4	Not included in analysis	
-----		
70 Total defects discovered by customers		
Code earmarks	**Defects corrected per code earmark**	**Percent defects corrected per code earmark**
AR477 (includes 2 Severity 1s)	7	46.7%
GL431	3	20.0%
DP268	2	13.3%
AP365	1	6.7%
BK663	1	6.7%
PY315	1	6.7%
Total	15	

Figure 12.11   Root cause analysis of customer-identified defects

From this analysis we see three code earmarks contributing the majority of the customer-discovered defects. If we return to the defect backlog analysis in Figure 12.7 and compare results with the customer-discovered defects, we learn two valuable facts.

First, the backlog analysis correctly identified concern with one particular code earmark as a dominant source of development defects, namely AR477. The fact that the same code earmark also appears as a dominant source of customer defects confirms the validity of the backlog analysis conclusions and, unfortunately, the fact that development did not take sufficient remedial action in AR477 before development was completed.

Second, the customer defect analysis identified code earmark GL431 that was not observed in the backlog analysis. It would be instructive for the next development project to determine the source of this surprise. The answer could be as simple as incorrect code earmark guesses prior to the backlog analysis. The answer could be as complex as incomplete test coverage whereby some aspect of the AR477 software under development escaped rigorous testing. Both answers may indicate process improvements that can be made during the next development project.

12.6.3 Leveraging Prior Project Defect History *As* the Next Project Starts

You have collected and graphed the prior project defect history and are ready to start your next project. You have learned three things from your last project that can be used as predictors for your next project effort: total defects, the defect discovery curve, and contour of defect severity.

First, you know the total defects discovered from the prior project testing results. If the next development project is of comparable size and complexity, then the total defects discovered last time is a reasonable initial predictor of the total defects you will discover next time. The size of the total defects will give you a viable basis for a first estimate of your test effort and resources if you have already derived rules of thumb for average numbers of defects discovered per test script, average numbers of test scripts per test case, and average time it takes to write and validate each test scenario. A word of warning at this point. The development manager, not understanding the sources of your prediction, may take the initial predictors as absolute and literally require your test team to find the same number of defects again. At most, this attitude will become a self-fulfilling prophesy, and the testers will find creative but not necessarily useful ways to discover that many defects. At least, this attitude will inhibit you from making adjustments to your predictors as the development project proceeds and you gain more information. Techniques for making these adjustments midway through the project will be discussed shortly.

Second, you know the curve of the defect discovery from the prior project testing results. As the test team begins executing testing scenarios and discovering defects, you should start plotting the next project defect discoveries on the same graph as the prior project curve as shown in Figure 12.12.

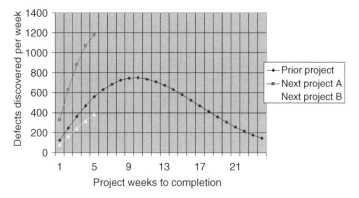

Figure 12.12   Defect tracking log comparison

Because no two projects are identical, the plot of the current project defect discovery will fall to either side of the prior project curve. Project A is an example of the curve for your next project if you started finding more defects faster than you did at the same time in your prior project. Recall that such a situation is a desirable trend, implying that your testing approach this time may find more defects over the life of the development.

The real value of predictors is to cause you to ask the right questions, not have the right answers. In this case, an early indication of more effective testing should cause you to ask why. What was consciously done differently in either the planning or test execution startup this time that is giving your testing effort this boost ? One possible answer is an investment in automated testing tools that is paying off with a faster, more complete defect discovery than your prior manual testing approach. If you cannot find evidence for this unexpected testing boost, then consider the curve difference nonpredictive at best and a warning that you may be getting a false indicator of success from your defect log reports.

Project B in Figure 12.12 is an example of the curve for your next project if you have started finding fewer defects later in the development cycle than you did in your prior project. Recall that situation is an undesirable trend, implying that your testing approach this time may be less effective in finding defects over the life of the development. In this case, an early indication of less effective testing should cause you to ask why. What was included in the prior project testing that may have been omitted or missed in either the planning or test execution startup this time ? After you have done this project-to-project comparison for several projects, a new exciting explanation could arise for Plot B. If the whole development team has actually taken the time and effort to find ways to improve the software development steps, then it is possible that Plot B is a clear, measurable indication that the development improvement effort is paying off with fewer defects to be discovered by testing. If you cannot find evidence for either a testing lag or a testing boost, then consider the curve difference nonpredictive, but consider the trend worth further scrutiny.

12.6.4   Leveraging Prior Project Defect History as the Next Project *Continues*

Continue to monitor and plot the defect discovery curve as the development project reaches each subsequent milestone. Sometime during the development project, usually about one-third of the way into the project, the defect discovery rate (number of defects discovered per week) will peak out and begin to decline. This point of inflection in the discovery curve tends to be a prediction anchor point for most defect analyses. Figure 12.13 includes the project curves from Figure 12.12 plotted to their defect discovery peaks that have been observed during all three development projects.

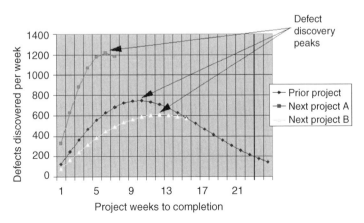

Figure 12.13   Defect tracking log comparison

Carrying the Project A analysis forward from the start of the project, we are expecting the Project A trend to continue to reinforce our interpretation that testing is doing a better job of finding defects during this project. Both coordinates of the Project A peak tend to reinforce our positive interpretation: The Project A peak occurs at a larger number of defects discovered—1213 defects for Project A compared with 749 defects for the prior project. The Project A peak also occurs sooner in the current than it did in the prior project: defect discoveries peaked at the 6-week mark for Project A compared with the 9-week mark for the prior project.

Carrying the Project B analysis forward from the start of the project, we are expecting the Project B trend to continue to reinforce our interpretation that testing is not necessarily doing a better job of finding defects during this project. Both coordinates of the Project B peak tend to reinforce our suspicions and begin to persuade us that the news is worse than originally expected: Testing is not as effective as last project at discovering defects. The Project B peak occurs at a smaller number of defects discovered: 607 defects for Project B compared with 749 defects for the prior project. The Project B peak also occurs later in the next project than it did in the prior project: Defect discoveries peaked at the 12-week mark for Project B compared with the 9-week mark for the prior project.

The critical success factor for the development team is to decide to minimize these undiscovered defects in a proactive, cost-conscious way. A starting point for minimizing undiscovered defects before development completion is to find ways to predict the approximate number of expected undiscovered defects. Recall from Figure 1.2 that these undiscovered defects cost $14,000 on average to correct after the customer finds them. The financial argument for redoubling the testing and correction effort before project completion would be different for a predicted 10–20 undiscovered defects (maximum estimated correction cost around $280K) than it would be for a predicted 300–500 undiscovered defects (maximum estimated correction cost around $7million).

One way to predict the approximate number of expected undiscovered defects is to extend the defect discovery curve in Figure 12.13 on out beyond the project completion date as we did with Figure 12.9. Determine the approximate area under the extended curve. The area under the extended curve represents a workable approximation. Figure 12.14 shows what the prior project, Project A, and Project B curves might reveal about predicted customer-discovered defects.

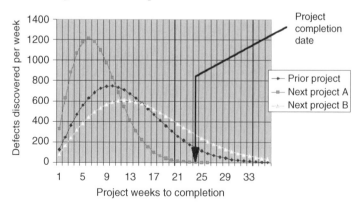

Figure 12.14   Defect tracking log comparison

Project A drops below the prior project curve after the peak because the better testing activity has left fewer defects to discover after the peak. The Project B curve stays above the prior project curve after the peak for just the opposite reason that the Project A curve dropped below. Project B testing is not finding as many defects as quickly as the prior project. Therefore, Project B will continue to find a large number of defects long after the prior project defect discoveries peaked and began to decline.

Recall that the prior project curve in Figure 12.9 extended beyond project completion to "zero defects" on the x-axis predicted 487 customer-discovered defects. The HelpDesk reported 70 customer-discovered defects, and for this reason, a prediction ratio of 7 to 1 will be our first guess for the next project.

Extending the Project A curve through the project completion date to "zero defects," we find the area under the extended curve to predict two customer-discovered defects. Applying the prior project prediction ratio of 7 to 1, we predict only one or two customer-discovered defects to be reported to the HelpDesk after Project A is completed. Applying our cost factors to get a grasp of the positive economic implications of this prediction, Project A testing results implies a $952,000 cost savings to the company as a result of investing in better testing for the next project. The negative economic implication is that even with improved testing, the development organization can still expect to spend $28,000 on customer-discovered defects from Project A. Here are the calculations behind these statements:

Prior project:
  70 customer defects predicted * $14,000 = $980,000 in correction costs
Project A:
   2 customer defects predicted * $14,000 = $ 28,000 in correction costs
   Possible Project A savings to company = $952,000 in correction costs

Extending the Project B curve through the project completion date to "zero defects," we find the area under the extended curve to predict 1377 customer-discovered defects. Applying the prior project prediction ratio of 7 to 1, we predict 196 customer-discovered defects to be reported to the HelpDesk after Project B is completed. Applying our cost factors to get a grasp of the positive economic implications of this prediction, Project B testing results implies a $1,764,000 additional cost to the company over the cost of the prior project customer corrections. This is due to the lack of emphasis on improving development and testing for the next project. The total cost of correcting customer-discovered defects rises to $2,744,000. There is no positive economic implication from Project B. Here are the calculations behind these statements:

Project B
  196 customer defects predicted * $14,000 = $2,744,000 in correction costs
Prior project:
  70 customer defects predicted * $14,000 = $980,000 in correction costs
   Possible Project B overrun to company = $1,764,000 in additional correction
                                                                        costs

Another interesting conclusion can be drawn from the project defect curve comparisons. Sometimes it is instructive to ask the question, "What is the risk/reward of shortening completion of the next project by 25%?" For projects like our examples that are 24 weeks long, a 25% schedule reduction would set the completion date back to week 16. The development team will raise a hewn cry that the project due dates are too short now for them to do their best job. The project defect curve comparison can inject some objectivity into the discussion.

Starting with the prior project, there were 70 customer-discovered defects. For the sake of discussion, consider that the economics and resources necessary to correct 70 customer-discovered defects are an unwelcome cost but not a financial showstopper.

If your next defect tracking log looks like Project A, then you can draw a vertical line at week 16 on the x-axis and predict how many more customer defects will occur because testing will be stopped short of the usual 24-week schedule. You can report back that by completing Project A on week 16 will result in about 70 more customer-discovered defects than the two defects originally predicted. The bottom line is the fact that your improved testing enables your company to consider completing development projects faster with no substantial increase in risk from the prior project testing perspective.

If your next defect tracking log looks like Project B, then you can draw a vertical line at week 16 on the x-axis and predict how many more customer defects will occur because testing will be stopped short of the usual 24-week schedule. You can report back that completing Project B on week 16 will result in about 650 customer-discovered defects, up from the 196 predicted for the 24-week completion date. Both numbers are substantially higher than the 70 from the prior project. The bottom-line is the fact that your less effective testing prohibits your company from considering completing development projects faster.

12.7   THE RAYLEIGH CURVE—GUNSIGHTS FOR DEFECT DISCOVERY PATTERNS

The first analytical hurdle for a software development project team is to capture, analyze, and compare enough defect discovery history that the in-progress project comparisons become credible. The second analytical hurdle is to find independent measures that indicate how close the project team is getting to industry-wide defect discovery rates. There is a dearth of published defect discovery rates because companies are reluctant to publicly admit any defect numbers because of its potentially damaging effect on the corporate image.

The only helpful source of industry-wide defect rates over the last 10 years has been a mathematical formula called the Rayleigh curve. If you are immediately skeptical that a mathematical formula could predict your company's defect patterns taking into account all the nuances of how you develop and test software, your skepticism is well founded and should not be suspended during this section. The reason we examine the Rayleigh curve for defect analysis is because worthwhile results are produced with intelligent use. "Intelligent use" is the key to success because anybody can crank out a Rayleigh curve for a project using zero or less intelligence and produce a meaningless curve.

The Rayleigh curve is a well-documented mathematical formula in a series of engineering formulas called the Weibul distribution. Although purely abstract in nature, the Weibul distribution seems to predict surprisingly well the behavior of a number of physical phenomena ranging from the flow of rivers to the bounce of ball bearings to the discovery rate of software defects. In the early 1990s, engineering researchers applied the Rayleigh curve to software development project defect discovery rates and found to their delight that the Rayleigh curve was more predictive than any other method attempted to date. [48] Prediction accuracies within +/− 10% were seen in several large research projects over a 3–5-year defect discovery comparison. Because the Rayleigh curve is pure mathematics and the actual defect discovery curve is purely behavioral (developer processes and skills, tester processes and skills, development and testing environments, tools, and so forth), then the key to successfully using the Rayleigh curve on your project is to also apply a healthy dose of judgment, experience, and intelligence.

Here is one approach found effective in applying the Rayleigh curve to your testing results by comparing it to the defect discovery curve plotted during your most recent project. For the purposes of demonstration, consider Figure 12.15 to be your prior project.

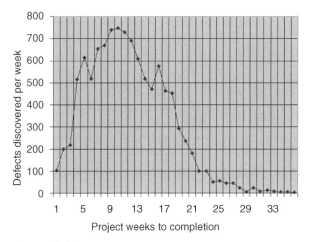

Figure 12.15   Prior development project defect tracking log

The prior project curve has a familiar contour although it is not as smooth as the idealized curves in previous examples. The main peak of 749 defect discoveries occurs during week 10 of the project. There are a couple of secondary peaks that appear at week 6 and week 15. These peaks are expected because the testing team doubles their effort twice: at the end of the Preliminary construction phase and again when all of the software components are integrated for the first time during the Final construction phase. Because these peaks are so pronounced and because they appear very regularly across several prior projects, the testing team is convinced that their testing has maximum effectiveness.

To compare the prior project defect discovery curve with the Rayleigh curve, first place an imaginary gunsight on the prior project defect discovery curve at the discovery peak as in Figure 12.16.

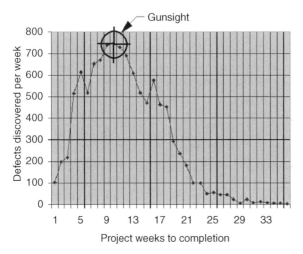

Figure 12.16   Prior development project defect tracking log

Write down the gunsight x-coordinate as the number of weeks in the project, in this case week 10. Write down the gunsight y-coordinate as the peak discovery rate, in this case approximately 750 defects. The Rayleigh curve formula requires any *two* of the following three inputs:

1. peak defect discovery rate
2. project week that the peak defect discovery occurred
3. total number of defects discovered

Notice that you have inputs 1 and 2 from the prior project curve gunsight; furthermore, you would like the Rayleigh curve to tell *you* input 3. Figure 12.17 shows you the results of your inputs to the Rayleigh curve formula plotted on the same axis as your prior project defect curve.

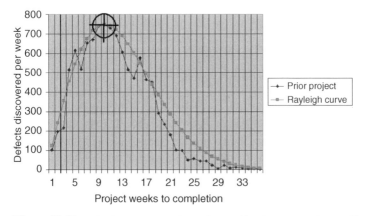

Figure 12.17   Prior development project defect tracking log compared to a calibrated Rayleigh curve

Visually, the Rayleigh curve shows you that when the testing team doubles its effort, they do indeed "push the envelope" or find more defects in the software than normally expected at that time in the project based on the Rayleigh formula. The fact that the prior project curve then falls below the Rayleigh curve shows you that the follow-up testing effort may have been less effective than expected at finding the defects also based on the Rayleigh formula.

Now that you have a sense of what the curve comparison tells you, look at the total defects discovered by each curve. The prior project discovered a total of 10,682 defects. The Rayleigh curve formula predicts 12,328 defects, 15% more defects than the prior project found. The next question you ask is, "How can we find 15% more defects with our testing ?" You may find one area of the software that test planning consistently misses across the projects like security or backup/recovery that could account for the majority of the 15% missed defects. You may find several areas of the software that test planning consistently misses across the projects that collectively begin to approach the missing 15% of defect discoveries. You may find that your test planning is very comprehensive, but the way you execute some of your tests may allow some defects to go undiscovered. Finally, you may find that your testing is planned well and executed well, leading you to conclude that the Rayleigh curve is simply not predictive for your projects. The purpose of the Rayleigh curve comparison is to prompt you to ask probing questions about your testing effectiveness, then act on any findings to improve your testing.

Finally, we need to show you one example of a kind of prior project defect curve that defies Rayleigh curve comparison from the outset. Instead of looking like Figure 12.15, assume that your prior project defect curve looks like Figure 12.18.

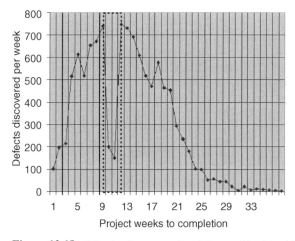

Figure 12.18   Prior development project defect tracking log with a gap in defect discovery

The challenge in comparing the Rayeigh curve to these results is the accurate placement of the gunsight. Instead of a clearly defined peak, defect discovery dropped off dramatically between weeks 9 and 13. The proper location of the gunsight becomes problematic in the area of the dotted box.

12.8 MORE DEFECT TRACKING METRICS

It is worthwhile to take inventory of the metrics that we have found to be helpful in analyzing defect discovery trends and prioritizing defect backlogs.

Development metrics discussed and demonstrated

1. unique development defect identifier

2. development defect discovery date

3. development defect severity

4. development defect correction date

5. development defect correction code earmark

HelpDesk metrics discussed and demonstrated

1. unique customer defect identifier

2. customer defect discovery date

3. customer defect severity

4. support defect correction date

5. support defect correction code earmark

These metrics come from four sources: the test team, the development team, the HelpDesk team, and the software support team. As simple as this list of metrics appears, the effort to establish uniform collection and reporting of this list is intensive and nontrivial. Many software organizations think that the value of the results do not justify the effort. Consider a small pilot project to establish the value of these metrics to your organization. Then make an informed decision about continuing the metrics collection and analysis on a progressively larger scale.

Some software organizations have proven to themselves that the value of the results do justify extending the list of metrics further, thereby adding effort but also providing additional analysis opportunities. One of the more successful techniques for adding to the above list of metrics is IBM's Orthogonal Defect Classification which is called "ODC." [50] ODC is the result of IBM software defect research started around 1994 and has become a mature technique. ODC suggests adding two more metrics to the defect log that the testing team provides at defect discovery time and four more at defect correction time. IBM has developed a complementary analysis and reporting tool called JMYSTIQ (*Java—managing your software to improve quality*) to help the ODC user analyze this formidable list of metrics over thousands of defects. Expect further development of tools and techniques in software defect analysis, a rich area of practical research that just might produce our silver bullet.

12.9   PUTTING TEST RESULTS IN PERSPECTIVE

The analysis of testing results can benefit a development project in two different ways. The first and most obvious way is to track individual defects to correction. This tracking provides the development manager with the number of defects discovered, the number of defects corrected, and the number of defects awaiting correction. From these tracking reports, the development manager can make informed decisions about the effort and advisability of correcting all known defects before the development is declared completed.

The second and less obvious way that test results analysis benefits a development project is by noting trends and trend comparisons that can indicate possible issues with successful testing completion. These possible issues can take the form of unusually buggy software components, testing effort that may not keep pace with the development effort, and anticipation of numbers of defects that may escape the development project and be discovered by end users. These analytical results represent additional management decision inputs available while the software is being developed.

12.10   SUMMARY

This chapter describes the kinds of test execution results you might want to collect, the ways you might want to consider analyzing these results, and the interpretations you may place on your analysis outcome.

The first step in discussing test execution results is to assume that you have done a thorough job of test planning. If you have unintentionally omitted certain application functions or business activities or structural components or performance aspects of your application from your test planning, then your test coverage will be inadequate.

One planning key to successful test results analysis is the clear definition of success for each test case. It is common for a test case to have a number of expected results. If the actual results obtained from a test execution *all* match the expected results, then the test case is normally considered "attempted and successful." If only some of the actual results obtained from a test execution match the expected results, then the test case is normally considered "attempted but unsuccessful." A test case may be "attempted but unsuccessful" because the actual results do not match the expected results or because the software halted with an error message before the test case was completed. Test cases that have not been executed are initially marked "unattempted."

The incremental discovery and correction retesting of software defects is the primary way that software testers help software developers implement the development requirements. The fewer the latent defects in the delivered software, the closer the software comes to fulfilling the requirements. The success of incremental defect discovery is directly related to the management process used to track defects from discovery to correction.

Successful incremental defect tracking can provide a third testing metric normally called the defect backlog. If your testing has discovered 300 software defects and development has successfully corrected 100 of these defects, then a backlog of 200 defects still need to be corrected. The challenge for the development team is to determine if there is enough time and programming and testing resources available to reduce the defect backlog to zero before the development due date.

The metrics used to track the incremental discovery and correction of software defects can be leveraged for valuable test analysis beyond one-by-one defect review and backlog analysis. Consider the cost/benefit tradeoff from adding one more column of information to the defect tracking record: the identification of the code that contained the defect.

This augmented defect tracking log can be used for root cause analysis. There are a number of good statistical textbooks available that provide the mathematical basis and practical application of root cause analysis to software defect logs. The simplified explanation of root cause analysis for testing is the mathematical search for the "buggiest" code. This search can be accomplished by a simple frequency count of corrected defect code earmarks, ordered with the most frequently occurring code earmarks first.

There is no current way to precisely predict beforehand how many or what kinds of defects your test team will discover in a new software. Depending on the circumstances and maturity of the software development organization, predevelopment defect predictions can range from an educated guess to reasonably accurate predictions. If there is project history either from similar software applications or from previous releases of the same software application, then that project history can be leveraged for next project defect predictions.

KEY CONCEPTS

Attempted versus
   unattempted test cases
Business risk to not
   correct
Code earmarks

Customer defect
   discovery correlation
Defect backlog
Defect log discovery
   curve

Successful versus
   unsuccessful test cases
Rayleigh curve
Root cause analysis
Severity codes

Chapter 13

A Full Software Development Lifecycle Testing Project

LEARNING OBJECTIVE

- to demonstrate the testing concepts, strategies, and techniques described in previous chapters using a real software development project from beginning to end

13.1 INTRODUCTION

We have presented fundamental software testing concepts, strategies, and techniques in the first 12 chapters. The final ingredient for successful software testing is your knowing when and how to correctly apply these strategies and techniques.

The examples we have given you so far have been intentionally simple to clarify the specific concepts, strategies, and techniques in a very limited context. Simply lifting these examples out of context and applying them ad hoc to a software testing situation will give you disappointing results. As with all technical professions, it requires intelligence to determine which strategies and techniques can be successful for the situation at hand. Stated another way, no two testing projects are identical; therefore, no "cookbook approach" to testing can succeed for very long.

The challenge for this chapter is to walk you through a case study that will demonstrate ways to make intelligent choices of strategies and techniques that are successful time after time when there is no single formula for success. We will answer that challenge by repeatedly applying the SPRAE method to a series of situations that arise during a software development case study. As you read each subsequent SPRAE discussion, you may find yourself coming to a different conclusion. You are encouraged to think through the outcome you might expect if you were to act on your conclusion instead of ours. Because there is no single "right answer," you may determine that your conclusion is just as viable as ours. This is a good indication that you have begun to internalize the topics in the earlier chapters.

Software Testing: Testing Across the Entire Software Development Life Cycle, by G. D. Everett and R. McLeod, Jr.
Copyright © 2007 John Wiley & Sons, Inc.

The case study chosen for this chapter contains some intentional simplicity. One reason for this simplicity is ease of demonstration and discussion. Another reason for this simplicity is to set the stage for Chapter 14 that will show how more complex testing situations can be attacked successfully by decomposing the complex situation into the simpler, more familiar situations from this chapter. The case study development activities follow the phased development methodology. Testing at each stage is conducted using the SPRAE methodology. You will find all of the case study artifacts discussed in this chapter stored on the textbook publisher's Web site as Case Study B: The DriveSafeAmerica (DSA) System.

13.1.1 Case Study Background

The software development project chosen for Case Study B is a real software development project in which one of the authors was a primary participant. The company name, staff, and location have been changed to honor the company's confidentiality.

Introductions are the first order of business. DSA is a U.S. company in Denver authorized by the State of Colorado to provide automobile driver training. The scope of the driver training includes unlicensed driving students and licensed drivers who are taking refresher training in lieu of paying traffic ticket fines for moving violations. DSA sells classroom driver training that provides the successful student with a completion certificate that satisfies the State of Colorado requirement for classroom instructions prior to behind-the-wheel testing. The same completion certificate also satisfies the Colorado traffic court obligation for refresher training in lieu of paying certain traffic ticket fines.

DSA is experiencing healthy business growth. From a modest start of 2,000 certificates issued the first year of business to last year's 32,144 certificates, DSA has written over 62,000 certificates. The DSA business is doubling each year. If this trend continues, DSA can expect to write over 64,000 certificates next year.

13.2 PRELIMINARY INVESTIGATION STAGE

Tom Thompson, the DSA President, is worried. His company is preparing and tracking all DSA completion certificates manually. The completion certificates are filled in from class rosters using a typewriter. A carbon copy of the completion certificates are filed away in cabinet drawers in the DSA home office. When the company started, one clerk could easily manage the 2,000 certificate production and archiving. As the annual workload grew, Tom added more clerks, more typewriters, and more file cabinets. He sees this year as a break point for the manual process. Not only does the forecast workload increase call for a substantial increase in certificate preparation staff but also for a substantial increase in certificate archive staff. The certificate preparation staff increase can be offset by the expected proportional increased revenue from the certificates. The certificate archive staff increase represents pure overhead because by law there is no charge for searching the archives or mailing out duplicate certificates to replace lost originals.

Tom meets with Frank Fouchet, the company Financial Manager, and Lisa Lemoine, the company Operations Manager. They determine that it is time to automate the certificate production and archiving process. The numbers tell them that a computer-assisted certificate system might allow them to defer a preparation staff increase for several years and possibly allow them to reduce the current archive staff while sustaining revenue growth and increasing profit. As with all automation projects, there is no "free lunch." It will take money to save money. DSA must invest some of its profits now in a computer system in order to realize both the revenue growth and increased profit later. Lisa also observes that there will be costs and effort beyond the computer system implementation per se to convert the current manual archives to computer-searchable archives. There may need to be a transition period in which some certificates will be computer searchable and printable while other certificates will remain searchable and printable only by hand.

DSA contacts Computing Perspectives, Inc. (CPI), a local computer consulting company, and requests a bid from CPI for a turn-key computer-assisted certificate production system that will completely replace the DSA manual certificate system. The CPI consultant team visits the DSA offices and interviews Tom, Frank, and Lisa to understand the scope and requirements of the new system. Then, the CPI team asks to see the written office procedures and watch the certificate staff manually produce completion certificates using these procedures. Afterwards, CPI replies with a turn-key bid that includes

- computer hardware
- computer software
- written guides for users and administrators
- training for the administrators

The CPI team highlights the following specific risks that the automated certificate system implementation will present to DSA business. Most of these risks have been mitigated so far by the manual certificate system in place.

- ability to produce State approved original certificates that conform to State of Colorado legislation
- ability to archive all DSA original certificates produced and mailed for the legislated 3-year duration
- ability to search the DSA certificate archive and either confirm certificate originals or print approved certificate duplicates

The CPI team also points out DSA risk due to the nature of the required manual-to-automated system skills transition because the current certificate production staff is not accustomed to doing more than word processing and spreadsheets on computers.

DSA accepts the CPI bid and sets the date to begin the formal development process for the new automated DSA Certificate Processing System (DCPS).

13.3   ANALYSIS STAGE

13.3.1   Initial Meetings and Conclusions

CPI holds several Analysis stage meetings with the DSA management to formulate an appropriate high-level technical approach for the DCPS. The following initial analysis conclusions are reached:

1. The new certificate software will be implemented using an off-the-shelf database management system that provides simple navigation menus, screen management, structured data storage and retrieval, and formatted printing of records.

2. No prior technical experience will be required to operate the new certificate software.

3. Although there can be flexibility in the screen designs and database structure, the print format must align exactly with the Colorado State approved continuous-form blank certificates already stockpiled in quantity by DSA.

4. In addition to the normal monitor, keyboard, mouse, and multifont printer, the workstations will need largest available capacity hard disks for certificate archives and high-volume tape drives for regular archive backups and searches.

5. Because all the workstations will be located in a lockable DSA office and none of the workstations will be connected to computers outside of the DSA office, chassis lock and key is a sufficient security measure to keep the DAS certificate data safe from intrusion and theft.

6. The workstations will be connected peer-to-peer for the simplest file-sharing operations possible with the least amount of computer equipment possible (no network servers) and no required technical staff (network administrators).

7. The only new computer hardware needed will be desktop PC workstations that replace the current typewriter stations one for one.

This is the first computer application for DSA beyond simple clerical activities, so everything about the system will be new to DSA management and staff. They will not have any experience with prior computer systems that can be leveraged when designing or learning the DCPS. The only computer experience on the project will come from CPI and the previous business systems that CPI teams have implemented.

You are the test team manager for CPI. You have been included in all the Analysis stage meetings to date as an observer. This meeting participation allows you to gain an initial understanding of the issues and decisions around the DCPS. During the Analysis meetings, you reach for a blank testing strategy chessboard and start making notes. As the first round of Analysis stage meetings with DSA concludes, your testing strategy chessboard looks like Figure 13.1.

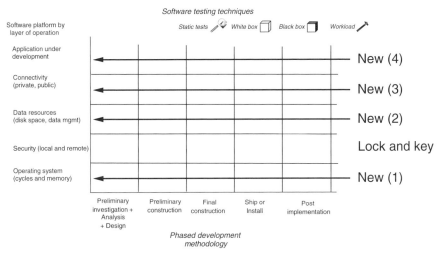

Figure 13.1   First cut testing strategy chessboard for the DSA certificate processing system

Your testing strategy chessboard indicates a high number of new support systems required for the DCPS, which, in turn, represents a substantial implementation risk to the development team. Of all the possible support systems, only Security is a trusted technology because it is a physical lock and key used frequently in everyday life. If any one of the other support systems cannot deliver the specified kind of functionality at its level, then the DCPS will fail to deliver its overall business functionality.

Your testing strategy chessboard also indicates that there is a critical sequence of early testing activities prerequisite to a successful Design stage. The chessboard is intentionally laid out to dramatize the priority of testing from bottom to top when any of the support systems below the application under test are not trusted.

Following this priority, the operating system with its central processing unit speed and memory capacity must be the first support system to identify and evaluate (validate by testing) against the DCPS requirements. The next support system to identify and evaluate will be data resources, which for this project means the hard disk capacity for the certificate archives, the archive backup capability, and the database that will support all master file activities. The last support system to identify and evaluate will be connectivity necessary for the certificate workstations to swap/share/aggregate weekly data files of printed certificates. Notice that significant failure of any of these support systems to pass the required evaluation tests could cause major redesign of the application before the first line of application code is written. With all the support systems passing their evaluation tests, the development team is in position to start the application level Design stage activities.

You alert the development project manager that from a successful testing perspective you will need the Analysis stage to produce detailed requirements for the new support systems as well as the application itself; furthermore, you will need to test these new support systems requirements very early in the Design stage. Your request will be a little surprising to the development manager because the manager is so intensely focused on the functional requirements and probably has not realized the full impact of improperly chosen support system components on successful functionality.

There is one troublesome issue for the test team that arises from the initial analysis conclusions. Conclusion #3 contains a hard and fast application print format requirement. Absolutely everything else about the DCPS and its support systems may function perfectly; however, if the system cannot correctly print the results on approved completion certificate forms, then DSA is in violation of the law.

The normal approach for developing new application reports is for the development team to design the reports in the Design stage and write the report programs in the Preliminary construction stage. The timing of report development and testing is usually much closer to the end of the Preliminary construction stage than the beginning because report development tries to leverage the application program structure and data file structures after they are written and stable, as well as have valid data loaded for report testing. Then, the testers execute the report programs during the later part of the Preliminary construction stage and compare actual report results against expected results.

Initial analysis Conclusion #3 mandates a test strategy that validates the technical reporting capability of the database management system during the Design stage, well before the Preliminary construction stage is begun. If the reporting capability of the database management system chosen for the DCPS is found to be inadequate during the Design stage, the dollar and time impact of changing technical approaches during the Design stage is substantially lower than making the same discovery at the end of the Preliminary construction stage. You alert the development project manager that database management report testing will need to be advanced in the schedule to the *beginning* of the Design stage along with the new support systems.

This is about as far as you can go with your test planning until the development team documents the requirements. Once the requirements are written, your test team can static test the requirements for completeness and correctness. Then, your test team can begin to apply the SPRAE method to each requirement (*Specification*) to complete your testing strategy and draft your test plans (*Premeditation*).

13.3.2 Requirements Writing and Review—Use Cases

CPI begins the requirements research and documentation in earnest. The primary sources of requirement information are the DSA manual procedures, the continuous-form completion certificates, and the DSA class rosters showing who completed the classes. Refer to Case Study B Document Repository on the publisher's Web site to see a blank completion certificate and a blank DSA class roster.

From this information and further discussions with Lisa and her certificate support staff, CPI develops the following DCPS use cases.

Sky-level use cases—DSA procedures to remain manual

> Use case-01: DSA Roster Sign-In
> Use case-02: DSA Roster Completion

Sea-level use cases—DSA procedures to be automated

> Use case-03: DSA Roster Input
> Use case-04: DSA Certificate Printing
> Use case-05: DSA Certificate Record Searching
> Use case-06: DSA Certificate Printing—requests for Duplicates
> Use case-07: DSA Certificate Records—weekly Management
> Use case-08: DSA Certificate Records—yearly Management

When the development team publishes the use cases, you compare the requirements to your testing strategy chessboard and detect that none of the new support system risks or requirements have been formally documented. You urgently request the development team to draft an architecture design that captures the known support system requirements. They comply with your request by drafting an architecture design for the support system components.

13.3.3   Requirements Static Testing

You and your test team closely review each use case and the architecture design, comparing them with the DSA manual procedures, DSA blank completion certificate, the DSA class roster, and the Preliminary investigation stage meeting results. Your testing goal is to confirm the completeness and correctness of each use case individually, all use cases collectively, and the architecture design for subsequent Design stage use. Once you complete the requirement static testing, you have correctly established the "S" (Specification) in the SPRAE testing method as the basis for all subsequent testing activities in this development project.

13.3.4   Using Static Testing Results to Correct or Improve the Requirements

You and your test team carefully read and review all of the requirements documents in static testing walkthrough meetings. During each meeting, you log which areas of the requirements cause questions to arise among the test team. The questions may be answered by clarification from DSA management or the CPI development team and no further action need be taken. The questions may be answered by the identification of needed requirement revisions. The questions may be answered by the identification of needed new requirements. At the end of each meeting, you and your team specifically think about and log anything you suspect is missing or incorrect.

The goal of the review meetings is to determine what, if any, changes are needed before the requirements are considered valid for Design stage activity. You invite the DSA management team, the CPI development team, and your test team to a series of review meetings to discuss the test team's static testing review results for the requirements. Depending on which area of the system is reviewed first, second, and so forth, you may need to extend an invitation to specialists in the topic covered by the requirements. For example, when data entry is the review meeting topic, it would be very helpful to have one of the more experienced DSA data entry operators/certificate writers included in the meeting discussion. Similarly, when database searching is the review meeting topic, it would be very helpful to have one of the more experienced CPI database designers included in the meeting discussion.

Here is an example of what might happen during one of the static test review meetings. On the surface, it looks like the instructor certification code listed on the class rosters is incidental to entering and printing each student's completion certificate. When the situation is discussed with Lisa Lemoine, the DSA Operations Manager, she indicates that DSA has several legal obligations to the State regarding DSA instructors.

First, each DSA course instructor must be certified by the State of Colorado before the instructor can deliver driver training and vouch for successful student completion. The State of Colorado assigns each instructor a unique code after the instructor passes the State examination. DSA must track the certification code for each instructor and ensure that the instructor successfully completes initial certification and recertification every 2 years. The penalty for out-of-certification instructors vouching for successful student completion is a fine of $25,000 for each instance. So far, DSA has not been fined for out-of-certification instructors. A penalty that DSA has incurred is a fine of $1,000 for each instructor name on a completion certificate that does not match exactly the instructor name on the State instructor certification document. DSA has paid an average of $5,000 per year in non-matching instructor names on completion certificates for a total of $10,000 in fines. This problem will most likely reoccur as long as DSA workstation employees must retype the full instructor name onto each completion certificate.

CPI suggests a modest extension to the current system design to provide an instructor code lookup feature. Once the absolutely correct instructor names and codes have been entered into a system file, the workstation operator need only enter a valid instructor code and a guaranteed correct instructor name can be provided to the input process via automated lookup. Furthermore, if the instructor code is stored on the student completion master record in lieu of the instructor name, there is a possible disk storage savings because the instructor code is much shorter than any instructor name. Although the lookup action will require a small amount of additional processing per student completion master record, the value of the increased accuracy of instructor name spelling is expected to more than offset the additional processing cost. As a result of this static test discussion, the following additional use cases are documented:

Use case-09: DSA Instructor Certification Input

Use case-10: DSA Instructor Certification Update

You know when to stop your requirements review meetings by the completion of your static test review item list. When all review items have review resolutions, you are finished with the review meetings. There can be at least three different kinds of review resolutions:

1. The requirement is correct as stated; no further action is needed.

2. The requirement is correct but needs additional written clarification.

3. The requirement needs content update or new documentation that may impact other requirements.

Before reading further in this chapter body, please review the Analysis stage documents provided in Case Study B. Case Study B contains four sets of documents, one set for each development stage. All of the primary documents in each set are suffixed by the development stage number and name as

Development stage	Primary document filename suffix
Preliminary investigation	(none in this case study)
Analysis	-2analysis
Design	-3design
Preliminary construction	-4precnst
Final construction	-5fincnst
Installation	(none in this case study)

You will find six primary documents in each stage except Analysis (no user interface documentation). These six primary documents are

Use case suite (high-level description with lists of use cases)

Use cases (each use case documented in detail)

Design architecture (support systems and data flow)

Test plan (high-level description with lists of test cases)

Test cases (test case skeletons—see Case Study A for details)

User interface (menus and screens)

Most of the high-level primary documents have links to related detailed documents. Here is a roadmap of that primary document linkage:

Use case suite links to use cases

Design architecture does not link to other primary documents.

Design user interface does not link to other primary documents.

Test plan links to test cases.

Each test case links to its related use case(s), its design architecture, or its user interface.

All of the primary documents for the developers except use cases have been omitted from the testing case study. Please refer to any reputable textbook on software development for examples of the omitted documents.

Revisiting the impact of UC-09 on the data volumetrics in the Analysis architecture design, we see that storing the instructor certification code in lieu of the instructor name reduces the original estimate of the 3-year completion certificate master file by about 57 Mbytes in hard disk storage. The offsetting increase in hard disk storage due to the new certified instructor master file is only 140 Kbytes. The real downside is expected to be the additional processing time necessary to validate instructor certification codes on each student completion input and convert instructor certification codes to instructor names for all certificate printing.

13.3.5 Completion of the Test Strategy

Your last testing step in the Analysis stage is to begin the "P" (Premeditation) in the SPRAE testing method by completing your test strategy. Based on the bathtub model of test planning, you know that your test plans will start with details from the development team's Design stage. Figure 13.2 shows a likely test strategy based on the ten use cases and draft architecture design.

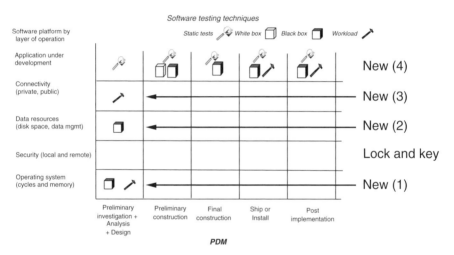

Figure 13.2 Testing strategy chessboard for the DSA certificate processing system

This strategy shows that the first concern will be the speed and capacity of the workstation hardware as described in the draft architecture design.

The second concern will be the functionality of the database management system as described in the draft architecture design. Of particular concern is the architecture support of use case-04 for printing student completion records on the approved completion certificate form. These concerns will drive the choice of the database management system before any detailed design work can be started by the development team. All other use cases have quite a bit of latitude in their actual implementation.

The third concern is the speed of architecture connectivity that will adequately support use cases -07 and -08.

The fourth and final concern is the set of use cases -03 to -06 that define the software application primary functionality to be developed. This row of the test strategy will follow familiar testing patterns for new applications under test.

Successful static testing of all requirements represents a key step in completing the Analysis stage before the Design stage is started. Part way through the requirements static testing, the development team can get the irresistible urge to start the Design stage with the tested but uncorrected requirements. Knowing that 85% of software development defects come from bad requirements, the CPI project executive defers all Design stage development activities until the requirements static testing is completed. The static testing emergence of new use cases -09 and -10 along with their positive impact of reducing the major file size requirements reaffirms the value of thorough static testing before design work is begun.

13.4 DESIGN STAGE

With the Analysis stage completed, the Design stage is begun. CPI initiates several concurrent activities that must dovetail before the design is completed. Here are the activities initiated by CPI in priority order:

(a) a search for database management software that provides

1. printing the completion certificate forms specified in the the draft architecture design to support use cases -04 and -06,
2. master file and index file size support specified in the draft architecture design, and
3. general user navigation capabilities in the draft architecture design.

(b) a search for workstation hardware that has the file storage capability, backup capacity, and connectivity specified in the draft architecture design and runs the chosen database management system.

(c) technology independent logical design of the DCPS functionality (normally the only priority of the Design stage).

13.4.1 Support Systems Design

The search for database management software is undertaken by a joint team of senior members from the development team and the test team. With a list of most promising database management software packages, the team takes the following repeated evaluation approach until a package is found that meets all of the support requirements. First, the developers hand build a small file of real DSA certificates using the database package. Then, the developers use the database package to write a certificate report program. The developers and testers together use the report program to align and print the hand-built data onto the blank DSA completion forms. If the forms cannot be printed correctly, then the database management package is rejected before the other capabilities are attempted. If the forms can be printed correctly, then the developers and testers move on to write and test representative menus, data entry screens, and control screens.

If all of these application capabilities pass the tests, then the final evaluation focuses on the maximum file size the database management package will build and maintain. The database package vendor may claim maximum file size support beyond the application requirements. It is prudent business to actually test the database package against the application requirements if the evaluator (CPI in this case) has not seen that the database package supports files that are large elsewhere.

The maximum file size testing process is straightforward and will run many hours. The tactic is to write a simple program that adds dummy records to a database file through the database management package's ADD function. The dummy records have a unique record ID started at 1 and incremented by 1 until the desired number of records have been stored based on the estimated maximum number of records required for the new application. The dummy records can all be blank but should approximate the expected record size for the new application. Anticipate file test problems if your maximum number of records or maximum file size parameters are within 10% of the database vendor's published maximums. Commercial software does not have a sterling track record when marketing claims meet technology boundaries.

The database management software preferred by CPI is evaluated first and soon rejected because the wysiwyg (pronounced "wizzy wig," standing for "what you see is what you get") report design tool of that software package cannot keep the print registered on the blank DSA certification form as the printing proceeded down the form. The second choice database management system has less sophisticated development tools (no on-screen report designers or screen designers), but it keeps the printing registered within the entire length of the blank certification form. The second choice database management package candidate also provides all the remaining required capabilities as verified through developer and tester execution.

The search for appropriate workstation hardware is easier than the database management software search because the workstation capabilities are commonly available off-the-shelf. Pricing rather than capability of comparable workstations becomes the workstation hardware selection yardstick.

13.4.2   Application Logical Design

While the database management software and workstation hardware are being evaluated, CPI also starts the logical design of the application. This is possible because the logical design is dependent neither on the choice of database management software nor the workstation hardware. The first draft of the logical design is reflected in the Case Study B Design stage primary document about the user interface. As each logical design component is completed, the CPI development team walks (static testing) the CPI testing team through the design component to verify that it fulfills the associated requirements.

Only some of the components in the new system are included in the user interface design. The CPI developers choose representative components to design first. After the developers get confirmation from DSA and the testing team that the logical design of the representative components is on track, the developers design the remaining components.

13.4.3 Logical Design Static Testing

How do you go about static testing the application logical design? Because we now have a basis for logical design, namely the requirements, the static testing approach is cross-validation.

First, we validate the logical design against the requirements by asking the following kinds of questions.

- Does every component of the logical design correctly represent its referenced requirement in the use cases?

- Are there logical design components that do not reference requirements? If so, why have these components been included in the logical design or, conversely, did we miss some requirements?

- Does the logical design make sense in the context of the overall scope and purpose of the application?

An example of the first bullet can be demonstrated by comparing the simple menu structure requirement in the use case suite supplemental requirements with the user interface design menu/screen hierarchy. The simple menu requirement implies that the completion certificate action screens should be found immediately behind the main menu. The proposed menu/screen hierarchy locates the completion certificate action screens behind a secondary menu behind the main menu. When asked to reconcile the two approaches, the development leader replies that the new secondary menu structure for completion certificate action provides economies of main menu screen real estate without any expected decrease in ease of use.

If this design change caused the completion certificate clerk to revisit unnecessary menus many times during the workday, then the longer screen navigation path would not offset the main menu real estate considerations. The developers expect the completion certificate clerk to navigate the menus once at the beginning of the workday and stay in the completion certificate data entry screen most of the day. Therefore, this interface design change does not really conflict with the overall architecture goal of a simple menu structure.

Second, we validate the requirements against the logical design by asking the following question.

- Have all requirements been represented by at least one logical design component?

As with requirements static testing, we will expect a few user interface design static testing defects to be discovered. These defects must be corrected in the documentation and retested before the Design stage can be considered completed. The completed, verified logic design is the next documentation step that represents the "S" in *SP*RAE.

13.4.4 Design Test Planning

When the logic design is drafted, the testing team starts writing the test plan, the next step after the testing strategy in the "P" of S*PRAE*. As the logical design is refined, the test plan is refined and the test cases are written. The Case Study B Design stage section shows you what the test plan might look like by the time the logic design is completed.

At the beginning of the logical design phase, the design details are sketchy at best. Rather than trying to guess the design details and start writing test cases, consider blocking out groups of test cases that you will most likely need to write as the details become available. The authors have found two patterns of test case groups to be useful as starting points.

The first pattern of test cases is for the use cases. Regardless of the actors involved, you can anticipate some kind of user process to be executed with some kind of results captured in some kind of data file. Many times, the speed with which the software allows you to complete the process is also of interest. Therefore, our first draft list of test cases for use cases is a group of four test cases per use case: FTPOS-*nn.m*, FTNEG-*nn.m*, ST-*nn.m*, and PT-*nn.m*. The *nn.m* notation indicates use case UC-nn process path m where m=0 is the main path or "happy path" and *m*=1 is the first alternate path, *m* = 2 is the second alternate path, and so forth.

The FTPOS-*nn.m* test case will use positive functional testing techniques described in Chapter 7 to validate the operation of the input data fields and actions on each screen. The FTNEG-*nn.m* test case will use negative functional testing techniques described in Chapter 7 to try to "break" the operation of the input data fields and actions on each screen. The FTDAT-*nn.m* test cases will use database testing techniques described in Chapter 7 to validate the associated use case ADD, CHANGE, DELETE, and SEARCH data file activity hidden from the user's view. The PT-*nn.m* test cases will use performance testing techniques described in Chapter 9 to verify that the search times are not linear with respect to the increasing size of the master files; the backups can be accomplished within the available business day window; and the record archiving can be accomplished within the available business day window.

The second pattern of test cases is for the user interfaces and architecture design, which may not be associated directly with any use cases. As we have seen from the testing strategy, the test planning activity must pay attention to the support levels of hardware and software in addition to the application software being developed.

Our draft list of test cases for the user interfaces is a group of test cases prefixed by UI for "user interface." The draft list will contain test cases designated IUFTPOS-*nn* for positive menu tests, IUFTNEG for negative menu tests, and UIERMSG-*nn* for menu error message tests. The *nn* is an arbitrary sequential number usually beyond the range of the use case numbering. For Case Study B, we started numbering the user interface test cases at 20.

Our draft list of test cases for the architecture design is a group of test cases prefixed by ST for "structural test." The draft list will contain test cases designated STHWR-*nn* for hardware test cases and STSWR-*nn* for software test cases. The *nn* is an arbitrary sequential number usually beyond the range of the use case numbering. For Case Study B, we started numbering the structural test cases at 30.

The Case Study B Design stage test plan contains a draft schedule for writing test cases to be executed in the Preliminary construction stage as the code becomes available. To a great extent, the testing schedule is always dependent on the development schedule because you cannot test what has not been written.

Where does the development schedule come from? Normally, the development plan includes the order in which the new application components will be constructed plus a construction effort estimate. Having developed a number of software applications, the CPI development team knows ways of prioritizing component development that leverages each prior component completed to expedite the development of the next component. Specifically, the CPI developers recommend the following priority of component development for DCPS.

1. data entry screens
2. search screens
3. print screens
4. backup and archiving
5. menus

This priority allows the developers to achieve a certain amount of programming momentum. Once the data entry screens are finished, they can be used to enter enough correct data to expedite the search screen coding and debugging. Once the search screens are finished, there is sufficient data reported to expedite the print screen coding and debugging. The print screen output availability expedites the coding and debugging of the backup, record transfer, and archiving features. Menus are last to be constructed because they are needed only at the end of the development effort to "package" all the action screens into a free-standing application that nonprogrammers can operate.

The priority list above does not track with the Case Study B Design stage test plan schedule. What happened to the CPI developers' priority recommendation ? In this case, DSA intervenes with its business risk concerns. Because completion certificate printing is *the* reason for the software development project, DSA presses the CPI team to show early achievement of this printing capability in the software. Instead of seeing proof of the software's print capability later in the developer schedule, DSA wants to see this proof very early in the developer schedule, perhaps as early as week 2 or 3. Furthermore, the DSA management wants to operate the certificate print screens themselves as a final verification of the print capability. Here are the development priorities finally negotiated between DSA and CPI to address the certificate printing business risk.

1. print screens
2. data entry screens
3. search screens

4. backup and archiving

5. menus

This priority list and attendant developer effort estimates drive the testing schedule you see in the test plan.

The testing schedule is represented by a development task followed by a series of testing tasks. Almost all of the testing tasks extend beyond the development task timelines because the testers cannot make a final evaluation of this particular component until after the developer is finished. At a more summary level, this project is expected to take 10 calendar weeks of development effort, but the combined Preliminary construction test plan and Final construction test plan show a 12 calendar week effort.

The other aspect of the test plan worth mentioning is the test case list for each development stage. This section of the test plan responds to the testing accountability, the "A" in SPRAE, by delineating in advance what will be tested and in which order. This minimizes the wasteful tendency to test "until you get tired of testing."

As we document the list of performance test cases, some of the performance test limits are immediately apparent from the use cases. For instance, the weekly backup process must complete within a 4 hour window on Friday afternoons. Other performance test limits are not mentioned in the use cases but have obvious implications for the DSA business. Test case PT-03.0 is troublesome at this juncture. PT-03.0 is supposed to measure how quickly a data entry screen can be completed.

The business question for the testers is "How quickly *must* the data entry screen be completed?" This question is directly related to the manual processing bottleneck that prompted DSA to consider a computer system in the first place. DSA recognizes that all of the data entry staff are currently working at maximum capacity and any increase in completed certificate production will require additional data entry staff to handle the increased load. The point is that DSA does not need to do a time–motion study to see that its data entry staff is maxed out. The flip side of this point is that the test team needs to know the current manual process time–motion numbers in order for performance testing to target computer response times fast enough to level the staffing load for several years.

CPI meets with DSA to request a time–motion study of the manual system before it is replaced by the new computer system and before the new computer system is completed. Here are the metrics that CPI requested from DSA.

- Take several timing samples of the completion certificate typing process over the next 3 weeks (before the data screen programs are due to be finished).
- Consider sampling work levels of a few of the most proficient data entry staff, usually longest employed. Use these numbers as the upper range of certificate production.
- Consider sampling work levels of a few of the lesser proficient data entry staff, usually newer employees. Use these numbers as the lower range of certificate production.

- Consider performing the sampling on Tuesdays, Wednesdays, and Thursdays. Mondays represent a work week startup challenge from the weekend and might not portray the sustained work levels accurately. Fridays represent a workweek closedown for the weekend and might introduce inaccuracies similar to Mondays.

- Consider sampling a couple of times midmorning and midafternoon to get a good representative day-long work level.

- Consider timing the actual start/finish of four or five completion certificates in a row once the measurement has started. The average time for completing certificates will be the number that the new computer system data entry screen must beat.

CPI also alerts DSA to reenforce the data clerks' understanding that the time–motion study is to gain measurements for "tuning" the new computer system, not for evaluating their current job performance. Lacking that reenforcement, the data entry clerks might view the study as "testing" them to see how much work they can do, which will completely skew the results.

When DSA does the time–motion study, they find out that the manual completion certificate typing takes from 10 min per certificate for experienced data entry staff to 15 min per certificate for inexperienced data entry staff. The testing team suggested that a fourfold decrease in time per certificate is a minimum goal to keep the data entry staff size flat for at least the next 2 years because the workload seems to be doubling each year. Using the DSA time–motion study numbers, the PT-03.0 slowest data entry screen response time for an experienced data entry clerk is 2.5 min per certificate. An inexperienced data entry clerk needs to be able to complete certificate entry using the same screen in no more than 3.75 min per certificate. Because all DSA data entry clerks will be "inexperienced" on the new system, the 3.75 min per certificate goal is expected first. If the data entry screen is designed for ease of use, then the more experienced data entry clerk should be able to demonstrate increased speeds approaching the 2.5 min per certificate in less than 2 weeks of practice. All of these measurements and assumptions need to be documented in PT-03.0 for execution measurement in the Preliminary construction stage.

13.5 PRELIMINARY CONSTRUCTION STAGE

13.5.1 Static Testing

With the Design stage completed, the Preliminary construction stage is begun. The development team writes detailed specifications and starts coding the application in the database management screen and process languages. Your testing involvement in these activities is fairly indirect. You convince the development manager of the value of static testing both the specifications and the code. Of the two, static testing the code via walkthroughs is the most familiar kind of static testing to the developers. The requirement continues to be the authority document for this testing. Someone must validate the software specifications against the requirements they are supposed to fulfill. Then someone must validate the software code against the software specifications and, by implication, validate the code against requirements. With encouragement and support from the test team, the development team performs these static tests. The more the testers are invited to participate in the developer testing, the more the testers can learn about the system to be tested. This increased tester knowledge tends to shorten the test case detail writing effort.

13.5.2   Test Environment Setup and Test Data Preparation

While the developers are writing the program specifications, some of the testers are writing test cases and other testers are setting up the testing environment and collecting test data. See the Case Study B Preliminary construction stage architecture design for the DCPS production environment and the test plan test environment. It is decided to set up two of the new DSA workstations for the test environment: one for clerk user testing and one for administrator user testing. This decision gives the test team an exact copy of the intended production environment in which to test. If automated test tools are to be used, now is the time to acquire the tools and install them in the test environment. This approach provides the controllability and repeatability of all DCPS testing in conformance with the "R" in SP*R*AE.

When the developers start writing code, the testers will start collecting and creating test data. Because there is no DSA computer data to collect from prior certificate printing, the testers will need to create all the computer readable test data from scratch. The Case Study B Preliminary construction test plan calls for test data to be created from the following DSA data sources:

1. current list of all certified instructors who work for DSA
2. current list of all DSA class teach locations
3. copy of all DSA class rosters used last month to manually prepare completion certificates.
4. copy of last year's search log from municipal court and student requests that resulted in requests for duplicate certificates

The first application module to be tested is the print screen (DSA1.02S). So the testers responsible for test data preparation create data files of certified instructors (data source 1), DSA class teach locations (data source 2), and DSA completion certificates (data source 3) during Weeks 1 and 2. The search log (data source 4) will not be needed for testing until Week 4 when the search screen (DSA1.03S) is written. These test data files must be hand-built and visually verified from printouts because none of the new system input or reporting functions will be available until later in this development stage.

Usually the tester has a choice of test data building approaches: brute force or equivalence classes. An example of brute force test data building for this application would be to create a certified instructor file of all 200 DSA instructors, a class location file of all 75 locations, and a completed certificate file of all 1,267 certificates issued last month. A total of 1,542 test data records would be manually built using the brute force approach. An example of the equivalence class approach would be to start by creating 20 certificates records representative of different ages, different sexes, different instructors, and different classroom locations. Then create only the 10 or so instructor records needed to print the 20 certificate records. Then create only the 5 classroom location records needed to print the 20 certificate records. A total of 35 test data records would be manually built for first testing using the equivalence class approach. Once testing is begun, the number of certificate records can be increased, the number of associated instructor records can be increased, and the number of associated classroom location records can be increased to meet the specific volume and variety testing needs. Lower volume, wider variety of records are needed first for functional testing. Higher volume, fairly similar records are needed second for performance testing.

13.5.3 Functional Testing

Chapter 7 identifies six functional testing techniques classified as white box testing, that is, testing with the source code available. These techniques are

1. Statement coverage technique
2. Branch (Single condition) coverage technique
3. Compound condition coverage technique
4. Path coverage technique
5. Loop coverage technique
6. Intuition and experience

As the developers write and debug the DCPS screen programs, the test team encourages the developers to strive for 100% coverage of their code using each of the first five techniques. The more coverage the developers achieve, the fewer defects are expected to be discovered later by the testers. The intuition and experience techniques include

1. dates
2. zero length anything
3. buffer overflow

and any aspects of the chosen database management system known to be troublesome. Dates will play a major role in the DCPS from a data entry standpoint (student birthdate, date class completed) and from a record management standpoint (completion records entered today, certificate records printed this week, instructors with certifications about to expire, and so forth). Because most data entry fields are required, the "zero length anything activity" will apply more to data records and data files than to data fields. Buffer overflow may not be a significant area of risk for the DCPS because the overwhelming majority of process activity is single thread, that is, one user performing one task at a time on one workstation.

Chapter 7 identifies four functional testing techniques classified as black box testing, testing with the source code *not* available. These techniques are

1. Equivalence classes technique
2. Boundary value analysis technique
3. Expected results coverage technique
4. Intuition and experience

There will be ample opportunities to apply equivalence class techniques to the testing of data entry screens (FTPOS-03.0, FTNEG-03.0, FTDAT-03.0, FTPOS-09.0, FTNEG-09.0, and FTDAT-09.0). Student names and instructor names provide a rich opportunity for testing allowable alpha and special character string classes as a more cost-effective alternative than entering all the names in a phone book. Mailing address zip codes represent another interesting test class of values. The tester could attempt all 100,000 values in the range 00000–99999 or the tester could start with 150 zip codes: three valid zip codes for each state (lowest, middle, and highest value).

The DCPS will not be very rich in boundary value testing because it is neither a true inventory control application that would have many opportunities to count and calculate things nor a true financial application with many opportunities to track money. The two boundary value testing opportunities in the DCPS arise from the completion student's birth date. The birth date itself offers some interesting boundary value testing around days in a month, months in a year, and days in February for leap years and leap centuries. If the developer has not already included this kind of date component check, it is appropriate for the tester to suggest a reasonableness check on the student birth date.

Because there is no independent way of checking the validity of the birth date beyond confirming that it is a legitimate calendar date, you can use an age calculation that traps at least century entry errors. For example, if the State of Colorado does not issue driver licenses before the student age of 14, then use the input birth date and today's system date to calculate the student's age. If the student is 13 years old or younger, display a warning message suspecting a lower boundary birth year error. If the State of Colorado has a cap on the age of drivers, say 80 years old, or the State can tell you the oldest living driver, then use that age as a birth year upper boundary warning.

One testing area of the DCPS that could benefit from expected results test thinking is search screen execution (FTPOS-05.0, FTNEG-05.0, and FTDAT-05.0). A larger class of names will be allowed for searching than for data entry, especially if wildcard characters are permitted. For example, if you are searching for a last name that could be spelled Smith or Smyth or Smithe, a wild card search on "Sm?h?" should find all three spellings, so should "Sm*," but the second search criterion would return a much longer list: every name that starts with "Sm" regardless of the remaining letters. Related expected results issues arise between data entry and searching of last names when the question is asked, "How are trailing blanks treated in the stored record name field versus how are trailing blanks treated in a search criterion?"

13.5.4 Structural Testing

The majority of the DCPS structural testing is focused on creating, printing, backing up, and aggregating files of certificate records. Chapter 8 identified six structural testing techniques:

1. Interface testing
2. Security testing
3. Installation testing
4. Smoke test
5. Administration testing
6. Backup and recovery testing

Of the six techniques, security testing, installation testing, and smoke test do not apply to the DCPS as it is currently designed. Security testing will arise if DSA finds it needs more than physical lock-and-key security on the workstation chassis. Installation testing and smoke test will probably never arise because the DCPS will be installed by the CPI system developers and only on DSA workstations.

Taking the testing techniques in the order that they are expected to be used, administration testing will be first by virtue of use cases -07 and -08 whose actor is administrator. The high-level goal of administration testing here will be to ask the question, "Does the Admin Menu contain all the activities necessary to support the DCPS on a daily, weekly, monthly, and yearly basis?" The low-level goal of administrative testing will be to validate the functionality of the administrative processes provided.

Next, interface testing will occur as an extension of use cases -07 and -08 as files of student completion records are selected and moved from local database files to transfer files that can be sent from one workstation to another. These test cases are represented by the FTXXX-08.0 series. If transfer files of student completion records cannot be properly built, then there is no value in testing backups, transfers, or archiving of bad transfer records.

Finally, backup and recovery testing will occur after the transfer file validation is completed. These tests are represented by the FTXXX-07.0 series. They validate the destination file updates caused by moving the transfer files via the administrative screens. Notice that these tests involve two or more workstations (see the preliminary construction architecture design). The multiple workstation test requirement introduces the additional test environment dimension of peer-to-peer connectivity. The primary developer challenge is to make these backup and archive processes rerunable if the process fails. For example, if the peer-to-peer transfer process fails while testing FTPOS-08.0, the software must provide a retry capability without duplicating records on either the transfer file or the destination file.

13.5.5 Performance Testing

Although there are several data entry screens in the new application, the data entry screens for use case-03 class roster input have the most critical performance role with respect to previously identified high business risk. This performance measurement must validate that the new screens do enable the DSA data entry personnel to complete each certificate entry faster than before with the manual system. The target screen completion speed from our time–motion study at the end of the Analysis stage is 2.5 min, a fourfold faster completion than the manual system. The first set of test case PT-03.0 execution results show a certificate screen completion time of 4.6 min, a little over twice as fast as the manual system but not fast enough. The screen developer and performance tester walk through the data entry screen design and find no obvious ways to speed up the code. The screen code is really straightforward.

At the tester's suggestion and with DSA's permission, the developer and tester sit down side-by-side with one of the senior DSA entry staff members and more closely observe the typing of a dozen or more completion certificates. The tester notices that the DSA employee makes extensive use of the typewriter's Tab key to move the typewriter to the next field on the certificates. Reflecting on the current operation of the data entry screen, the developer realizes that the user is forced to move his or her hands from the keyboard to the mouse in order to position the screen cursor on the next data entry field. After further discussion, the developer decides to add code to the data entry screen that provides directed tabbing through the screen in class roster data field sequence.

When the new tabbing code is added, the test team first performs a regression test on the data entry screen using test cases FTPOS-03.0 and FTDAT-03.0 to ensure that the added code does not disturb any of the validated functionality. The test team then reruns the data entry performance test case PT-03.0 and finds that the new, tab-enable screen can be completed in 3.5 min. This is faster than before but still shy of the needed fourfold speed increase. The developer and tester returned to the DSA manual data entry employee and observed some more certificate typing.

The tester observes that numeric fields on the typewriter do not require the Shift key, whereas the data entry screen does. Furthermore, there are several screen fields that accepted only digits (class date, instructor code, address zip, and social security number). The developer agrees to add code to the data entry screen that placed an automatic NumLock on those number-only screen fields to eliminate the user's need to manually press the NumLock key for those fields. Again, the test team regresses the functional tests and reruns the performance tests. This time the new, tab-enabled, auto-NumLocked screen is completed in 2.0 min, a fivefold speed increase!

13.5.6 Defect Tracking and Analysis

As coding is completed and test execution is begun, software defects are discovered and tracked to correction. The relatively small size of the DCPS allows the developers to correct defects usually within 36 hours of detection and logging. With larger software projects completed over several months, it would not be surprising to experience a 5–10 day correction cycle. The intent should be to have all of the severe defects corrected and most of the important defects corrected by the Preliminary construction stage completion date.

CPI previously developed several software applications that are about the same size and complexity as the DCPS using about the same size project team. As a result, CPI has defect history that can be used as an expected pattern for the DCPS defect discoveries. As we saw in Chapter 12, if the DCPS defect log tends to follow the CPI project defect histories, then we gain a certain level of comfort that the testing is proceeding well. If, on the contrary, the DCPS defect log diverges from the CPI project defect histories, then we begin to ask "why?" Figure 13.3 shows the CPI defect histories and the DCPS defect log progress as of Week 5, a little more than half way through Preliminary construction.

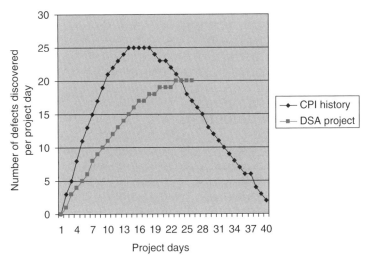

Figure 13.3   Comparison of CPI defect history with DSA project defect log

Before raising any issues from the comparison, you first need to recognize that both plots represent small numbers of defects discovered on any given day. This recognition should temper the issues and conclusions that you derive from the comparison.

The most obvious conclusion you can draw from the defect discovery comparison is that DSA testing is finding fewer defects and finding them later, normally not a desirable situation. After conducting discussions with the developers, you surmise that the later defect peak might be attributable to the fact that the print screen was developed and tested before the data entry screen in the DSA project. It is reasonable to expect that most defects will be found in the screens with the largest number of input or output data fields; therefore, the delayed defect discovery peak might be attributable to the delayed testing of the data entry screen relative to other CPI project screen development sequences. Recall that DSA did request a change in the intended sequence of software development.

Regardless of the sequence of screen development and testing, you would expect to see the same or very similar defect detection peak in both plots. The comparison is trending toward the DSA having a lower defect discovery peak (20) than the other CPI projects (25). Although the relative difference is 20%, the actual difference is only five defects, which may be too small a difference to prompt further investigation.

At day 26 the plots intersect. Based on the lag in the peak of DSA discoveries, it is reasonable to expect the DSA plot to remain higher (larger number of defects discovered per day) than the CPI projects for the remaining DSA project days. Although this trend strongly implies missed defects by DSA project end, it does not indicate what kinds of missed defects there might be. A root cause analysis of the 334 defects discovered so far might shed some light on the expected nature of the missed defects. Figure 13.4 shows a rough analysis of the code earmarks for these 334 defects on the DSA defect log.

Root cause analysy of defects

334 total defects corrected to date

Code earmarks	Defects corrected per code earmark	Percent defects corrected per code earmark
DSA1.01S	122	37%
DSA1.02S	70	21%
DSA3.01S	61	18%
DSA3.02S	56	17%
All others	25	7%
Total	334	

Figure 13.4   DSA Project showing defect tracking log corrected as of a day 28

As stated before, the screens with the largest number of input or output fields such as the certificates data entry screen (DSA1.01S) are expected to contribute the largest number of defects. Having said that, the screen with the second largest number of defects is expected to be the certificate search screen (DSA1.03S) or instructor data entry screen (DSA2.01S), but neither code earmark appears at the top of the list. Instead, the screen with the second highest number of defects is the certificate print screen (DSA1.02S). The picture becomes even more puzzling with the weekly certificates backup (DSA3.01S) and weekly certificates transfer (DSA3.02 S) screens having the third and fourth highest defect counts. When you discuss your analysis results with the development team, you discover that they have become worried about the basic certificate record processing flow design. The design is complex and not stabilizing quickly. If this design is faulty, it could contribute to the defect counts for all the top scoring screens.

On a hunch, you check with the testers assigned to test case PT-04.0 and -07.0, which measure the response times of certificate record counting, printing, and backing up. The performance tester alerts you that when small numbers of certificate records are tested (less than 10), the process completes within the specified maximum response time. However, when a larger number of certificate records are tested, the response time for each process becomes unacceptably slow as the number of records increases. The specified maximum response time is exceeded when the certificate master file grows to 230 records, well before the 311 records per week expected during next year.

The puzzle pieces begin to fall into place. The basic certificate record processing flow design presents two significant risks to CPI if only piecemeal action is taken against the defects found so far. The first risk is that the design code will not stabilize regardless of the amount of effort the developers invest in trying to make it work. The second risk is that when the design code stabilizes, it will always fail the performance requirements. Based on these two risks, you recommend that a new basic certificate record processing flow design be implemented in the Final construction stage and that a moratorium be imposed on any further testing and correction of the current design in the Preliminary construction stage.

This process of analyzing test results and inferring the usefulness (economy) of further testing responds to the "E" in SPRA*E*. The test team begins to see patterns of test execution results that imply continued program code instability. As a result, the testers recommend stopping testing the unstable code in lieu of redesign or reprogramming. This tester recommendation provides economy of project resources by minimizing any further time spent on code that may never stabilize sufficiently to be used in production.

13.5.7 Exiting the Preliminary Construction Stage

Several events occur during the Preliminary construction stage that will shape the plans for the Final construction stage. The first event is the root cause analysis of the majority of the Preliminary construction defects. Based on the root cause analysis conclusions, the development manager decides to have the basic certificate record processing flow redesigned in an attempt to stabilize the code. Because the use cases state *what* needs to be finished and not *how*, the redesign does not cause a requirement modification, only a specifications modification at the next level of development detail. The authors recommend that a defect log entry be made against the certificate record processing flow specification in order to fully document and track the redesign effort and outcome.

The next completion shaping event is CPI asking DSA for suggested approaches to cut over to the new automated system from the manual system. The CPI project team asked the DSA representatives about possible cutover plans during the Design stage, but DSA deferred cutover discussions until DSA management could see the new system in action. One of the customer relationship benefits of including DSA in the data entry screen tests is to gain credibility that the new system could replace the old system. With the DSA management fully "on board," a meeting is held around week 6 to define the cutover plans.

During the static testing of use case-05: DSA certificate record searching, one of the testers asks the question, "When and how should we transfer the current file cabinets of completion certificates to the new computer system for historical searching?" This question leads to a lively discussion. As long as there are manual records to search, DSA incurs the overhead of staff to search them and 5 years worth of file cabinet space to store them. With the new data entry process five times faster than the old typing process, the current data entry staff should be able to finish the weekly class roster workload and have some time to spare initially for historical data entry.

The first suggested approach is for DSA data entry personnel to start with the day one DSA completion certificate and enter all of them in ascending numerical order as time permits until all of the precutover certificates have been entered into the new computer system. One of the CPI testers put on her "boundary analysis hat" and observed that the oldest DSA certificates (first 2 year's worth) fall outside the 3-year retention rule for searching and entering these certificates would be a waste of time and effort.

The suggested approach is amended to start with the first certificates that are less than 3 years old from the cutover date and proceed forward in time toward the cutover date. Then the tester observed that some of the data entry effort under the amended approach would still be wasted because the first certificates that are less than 3 years old from the cutover date fall outside the 3-year retention rule the month or so after they are entered.

Finally, the CPI tester suggests that the historical data entry start from the last completion certificates typed before the cutover and proceed back through the certificates in descending order. Using this approach, the certificates with the longest retention time hence the most valuable to DSA are entered first.

The third event occurred because of legislative changes in other states during the development startup. The States of California, Arkansas, and New York notified DSA that their new laws required DSA to report all students who take DSA classes and reside in one of these three states. With CPI's help DSA contacts the data processing department of each state and negotiates an electronic file format for sending this report to each state. Each state wants a different format (naturally). Because California is usually the trendsetter in new kinds of state legislation, DSA suspected that over time most of the other 48 states will impose similar reporting demands on driver training companies nationwide. Whatever solution CPI proposes must allow for later expansion of the capability to encompass additional state reports with minimal effort.

The developers and testers meet to discuss the best overall approach to complete the remaining work in the shortest schedule. The agreed approach will start with the development and testing of the historical data entry screen. As the historical data entry screen task is launched, a second task to address the redesign and redevelopment of the basic certificate record processing flow design will be started. This second task is expected to take the lion's share of the CPI development and testing resources. The third task to develop and test the new out-of-state reporting capability will be started after the historical data entry screens are finished. When all three Final construction tasks have been completed, an additional week of regression testing will be scheduled to ensure that the three newly completed tasks have not adversely affected any of the previously tested code.

Here is a recap of the additional use cases that impact the Final construction use case suite, the test plan, and the test cases.

Use case-11: DSA Certificate Records—out-of-state Reporting

Use case-12: DSA Completion Records—historical Completions

Use case-13: DSA Completion Records—production Cutover

One final suggestion is made by the testing team. Because the development and testing of the current certificate record processing flow will be curtailed in preparation for the redesign, the Final construction stage can begin a week early, the last planned week of the Preliminary construction stage. The revised development and testing schedule are reflected in the Final construction test plan.

13.6 FINAL CONSTRUCTION STAGE

13.6.1 Static Testing

The static testing of Final construction documentation follows the same pattern we saw in Design and Preliminary construction. The first documents tested will be the new use cases and process flow in the architecture design. Then the programming specifications derived from the requirements are static tested. Then the programming code written from the specifications are static tested. The new static testing for this stage will be the DSA end user documentation: User Guide and Administrator Guide. Because CPI will install the new system, there will be no formal Installation Guide for DSA.

The pivotal document for this stage will be the architecture design, which contains the redesign of the basic certificate record processing flow. The tester's job is focused on asking hard questions like, "How do you know that this new design will be more stable and works better than the original design?" If the developer does his homework, he can give the tester very concrete reasons why the new design is better. If the developer has not done his homework, then he will most likely become defensive with answers like, "because I'm the design expert." Specific deficiencies are discovered in the old design and, as a tester, you know it will take specific deliberate action to correct these deficiencies.

13.6.2 Functional Testing

As soon as the new and revised documentation is declared correct by static testing, the Final construction stage programming, code debugging, and code testing begin. The first code to be functionally tested in this stage is the historical data entry screen. Many parts of the completion data entry screen test script should be reusable here. Most of the data entry fields are the same. Hence, the same testing details will apply. The two main differences will be the certificate number and instructor name field. In the completion data entry screen, the certificate number does not appear because the print program assigns the certificate number at print time based on the continuous forms being used. Additionally, the certificate number input value test must be numeric only and fall within a specific value range (greater than 0 and less than 10,000,000,000). The instructor information is entered on the completion data entry screen as an instructor code that is used to look up the instructor name from a table of certified instructors. The instructor information is entered on the historical data entry screen as the instructor name that needs to be validated against the instructor list instead of the instructor code. Finally, the historical data entry screen changes the student name validation criteria somewhat because the name components are entered in a different order than the completion data entry screen.

13.6.3 Structural Testing

The structural testing finished in the Final construction stage will be as complex as it is critical. The Preliminary construction stage was halted a week earlier than planned because the originally designed structural components that support the basic certificate record processing flow would not fully stabilize, and the parts that did stabilize exhibited poor performance. The testing challenge is to adapt the test cases to the redesign. The fact that the original design could not withstand the structural testing before "going live" is a very desirable testing outcome. We have all experienced software systems that seem to need many patches (not enhancements) over the lifetime of the software. It is likely that the original testing of this software was not sufficiently rigorous to force the kind of redesign decision during development that has occurred on the DSA project.

There is one more structural consideration worth highlighting at this point in the project. We have a new requirement for student reports to out-of-state agencies. This requirement could have been addressed by new structural components (file extracts, file backups, and file transmissions) independent of the basic certificate record processing flow redesign. In this case, there is a benefit to delaying the development and testing of the out-of-state reporting until after the process flow redesign is finished. The out-of-state reporting designers might be able to convince the process flow redesigners to adopt design strategies that make some aspects of the out-of-state reporting easier to implement or faster to execute without sacrificing process flow effectiveness.

13.6.4 Performance Testing

The performance testing activities during the Final construction stage will focus on two main objectives. The first objective is to ensure by performance regression testing that none of the new or redesigned code adversely affects the response times of the screens that achieved their performance goals in the Preliminary construction stage. The Preliminary construction screens are not scheduled for many changes beyond menu additions. Therefore, the basic screen operation should perform the same at the end of Final construction. Because the process flow redesign will probably influence the way data files are built and updated, the original screen operation may experience new file processing overhead. This new file processing overhead could unexpectedly cause the screens to run too slow. If the screens are not regressed for their performance objectives after the process flow redesign has been implemented, unacceptable performance might be discovered after implementation by DSA.

The second objective is to collect first time performance statistics on the redesigned process flow when it becomes stable. As with all performance testing, you should expect the first results to miss the mark. Be prepared from a testing perspective to characterize as much of the performance problem as many ways as possible so that the developers can more quickly determine if the performance problem lies with the redesign code or the redesign itself.

Unlike structural testing in this stage, the Preliminary construction performance testing scripts should require very few changes because the overall response time objectives and strategies for achieving them remain the same in the Final construction stage.

13.6.5 Defect Tracking and Analysis

We continue to plot the defect discoveries for the overall project on the same axis that we used during Preliminary construction. We are still looking for that peak around 25 defects per day that we were not able to achieve because, we think, the basic process flow instability interfered. Figure 13.5 shows the results of our defect tracking as we approach the end of the Final construction stage.

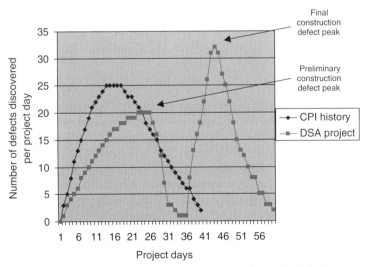

Figure 13.5 Comparison of CPI defect history with DSA project defect log

The first peak of defect detection was already seen during Preliminary construction. The peak quickly falls off as Preliminary construction activity is curtailed early to prepare for the Final construction development. A small period around Day 32–Day 36 shows minimal defect detection as the CPI development team goes back into "design mode" for the new requirements and process flow redesign. Most of the defects found during this period are static defects in the new documentation.

The defect detection rate increases dramatically starting with Day 38 as testing begins on the new historical data entry screen and the redesigned process flow. The higher peak of 32 defects during Final construction is more in keeping with previous CPI experience and higher than the 20 defect peak discovered during Preliminary construction. After the Final construction peak at Day 44, the rate of defect discovery drops as expected.

In summary, the Final construction defect pattern looks much more like prior CPI projects. Unless the regression testing during the last week of Final construction uncovers drastic problems, Final construction will be completed successfully around Day 60 as planned. When the CPI development team meets with DSA management after Day 60 and presents the development and testing results, DSA accepts the system and schedules the "go live" date the first week of the next calendar month in accordance with use case 11: DSA completion records—production cutover.

13.7   IMPLEMENTATION STAGE

During the first week of the next calendar month after Final construction, CPI installs the new software system on all of the DSA workstations purchased and configured during the Preliminary construction stage. The two workstations used as test environments are included in the production software installation but are held back from production by DSA at CPI's request. The intent is to use these two test workstations, now with the full production loads, as a quick way to diagnose any problems arising in the critical first couple of weeks of production. Everybody crosses their fingers and DSA "goes live." Two weeks later, DSA and CPI declare the system fully in production based on use case 11 production results and DSA management's own assessment. CPI testers release the two test workstations to DSA for full production use. CPI developers are scheduled to be "on call" until DSA has successfully completed a full month's worth of data entry, certificate printing, backups, and master file updating. CPI testers are scheduled to return in 3 months to do a postimplementation performance checkup to confirm that the performance objectives are still being met.

13.8   POSTIMPLEMENTATION STAGE

One month after DSA "goes live," the CPI project team meets at the CPI offices and conducts a "postmortem" or "lessons learned" discussion of the DSA software development. The primary focus for the developers is the contributing factors to the original process workflow design failure and how these factors might be avoided the next time.

The primary focus of the testers is the difficulty they encountered as they adapted some of the Preliminary construction test cases to the new but similar screens added in Final construction. Testers also recalled that they had difficulty with the regression testing because of rerun challenges with the test cases.

When the time comes for the testers to return to DSA for Postimplementation testing, the testers request the use of one workstation, the time of one of the more experienced DSA certificate preparation staff, and the time of the DSA Operations Manager, Lisa Lemoine. Testers repeat their Final construction performance testing with the DSA staff operating the workstations and software. In accordance with the postimplementation test plan, the testers start by measuring the data entry screen response times. Then the testers move on to measure the printing response times. Finally, the testers measure the weekly certificate file transfers to the master file. Each round of tests takes most of a workday. At the end of each day's tests, the testers show DSA the measurements collected over the day and how these measurements compare with the Final construction testing measurements. At the end of the week, the CPI testers and DSA staff agreed that the DCPS continues to operate as well as it did the first days after "going live."

13.9 CASE STUDY CLOSURE

The software system that is the basis for this chapter's case study was implemented in 1988 and was still in production in 2000 as originally implemented without any major fixes. The customer felt that the software achieved all of the original design objectives with nominal disruption to business and continued to meet its business requirements three times longer than the originally hoped 4-year return on investment period.

13.9.1 Summary

The challenge for this chapter is to walk you through a case study that will demonstrate ways to make intelligent choices of strategies and techniques that are successful time after time when there is no single formula for success. We will answer this challenge by repeatedly applying the SPRAE method to a series of situations that arise during a software development case study.

The case study chosen for this chapter contains some intentional simplicity. One reason for this simplicity is ease of demonstration and discussion. Another reason for this simplicity is to set the stage for Chapter 14 that will show how more complex testing situations can be attacked successfully by decomposing the complex situation into the simpler, more familiar situations from this chapter. The case study development activities follow the phased development methodology. Testing at each stage is conducted using the SPRAE methodology.

The software development project chosen for Case Study B is a real software development project in which one of the authors was a primary participant. The company name, staff, and location have been changed to honor the company's confidentiality.

The resulting software system the basis for this chapter's case study was implemented in 1988 and was still in production in 2000 as originally implemented without any major fixes. The customer felt that the software achieved all of the original design objectives with nominal disruption to business and continued to meet its business requirements three times longer than the originally hoped 4-year ROI period.

13.9.2 Case Study—Disclaimer

We suspect that as you read the unfolding story of the case study, you attempted to guess which computer equipment and software were involved in the certificate processing system development project. We intentionally omitted sufficient details to confirm your guesses. There are two reasons for these omissions. The first reason is that the best choice of hardware and software for the certificate processing system may be the worst choice for your next project. The second reason is that the worst choice hardware and software for the certificate processing system may be the best choice for your next project. By not revealing either the details or the brand names involved, we force you to consider the testing strategies and approaches that would reveal the best choices instead of allowing you to jump to conclusions based on your own experience. We would be glad to tantalize you with more case study details over a couple of beers or a glass of good chardonnay.

Chapter 14

Testing Complex Applications

LEARNING OBJECTIVE

- to demonstrate a repeatable approach to simplifying the test planning of complex applications

14.1   INTRODUCTION

This chapter describes an approach to testing complex applications that builds on the strategies, tactics, and techniques that you used in Chapter 13 for simple application testing. This approach is basically "divide and conquer." *Divide* the complex application into manageable application components that can be *conquered* by familiar testing techniques.

As with most technical approaches, you run the risk of extremes when you do the dividing. Divided application components can still be too large for manageable test planning and execution. Divided application components can become too small for effective test planning and execution. Finding the right division of application components is definitely a skill sharpened by experience rather than by any rote procedure.

If you have been attracted to reading this chapter, then you probably have been asked at one time or another to test an application with an architecture that looks something like Figure 14.1.

The testing task looks daunting because there appear to be so many moving parts. We will discuss some underlying similarities among the application components that you can leverage to reduce the testing task from daunting to challenging.

14.2   1-TIER APPLICATIONS

Where do you start your test planning for a complex application ? Start at a familiar starting point: the testing strategy chessboard. The testing strategy chessboard served us well with

Software Testing: Testing Across the Entire Software Development Life Cycle,   by G. D. Everett and R. McLeod, Jr.
Copyright © 2007 John Wiley & Sons, Inc.

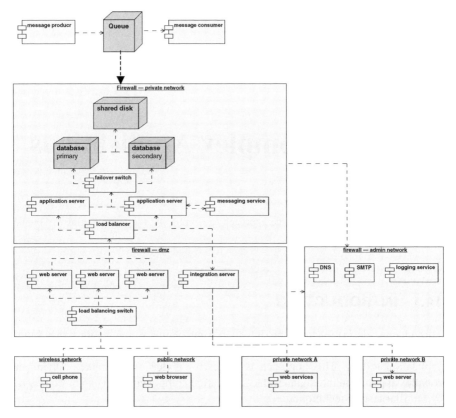

Figure 14.1 Architecture for a complex application

our test planning and execution of Case Study B because the application is what we call a "1-tier" application. This term means that although multiple workstations are involved, each workstation is the same hardware platform running the same version of the application software. Figure 14.2 shows the architecture of the Case Study B 1-tier application.

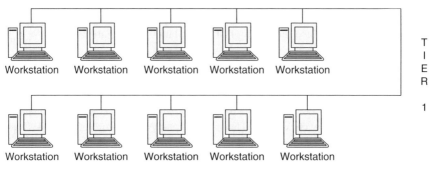

Figure 14.2 Architecture of a simple 1-tier application

The network connectivity is simple peer-to-peer, another way of saying that each workstation does the same business tasks even though certain designated workstations house the master file of all completion certificates. The interworkstation communication is strictly to aggregate new certificate records weekly and store them in one place for later searching and archiving. As a point of review, Figure 14.3 shows the testing strategy chessboard that we used for our Case Study B 1-tier test planning and execution.

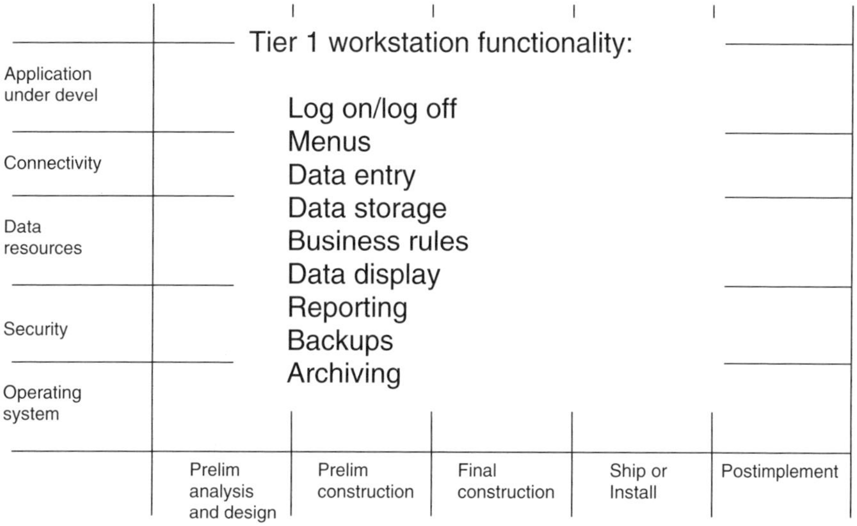

	Tier 1 workstation functionality:			
Application under devel	Log on/log off			
Connectivity	Menus Data entry			
Data resources	Data storage Business rules			
Security	Data display Reporting Backups			
Operating system	Archiving			
	Prelim analysis and design	Prelim construction	Final construction	Ship or Install	Postimplement

Figure 14.3 Test strategy example for a simple 1-tier application

Recall that the test planning started at the top layer in the tier and went down as needed into the support layers. Then the test execution started at the bottom layer in the tier and went up to confirm that each successive layer could deliver the required cumulative support functionality.

The bottom-line is that you have seen how to plan and test 1-tier applications. We now add a tier to the application complexity and the test planning.

14.3 2-TIER APPLICATIONS

The classic example of a 2-tier application is any client/server application. Figure 14.4 shows a typical client/server architecture.

The main difference between Figure 14.2 and Figure 14.4 is that there are two distinctly different groups of computers with distinctly different tasks. A useful approach is to first consider developing a separate testing strategy chessboard for

Local area network (LAN)/wide area network (WAN)

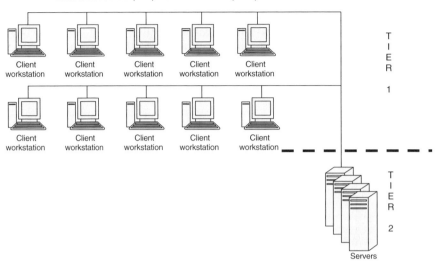

Figure 14.4   Architecture for a fairly simple 2-tier application

each tier. The client tier testing strategy chessboard will reflect the client computer support structures and the client application that normally provides the user interface functionality, that is, logon screens, data entry screens, data search screens, and data report screens. The server tier testing strategy chessboard will reflect the server computer support structures and the server application that normally provides the business rules and data management, that is, customer files with customer discounts and payment terms, inventory files with pricing and quantities on hand, purchase orders, and payment records.

The actual way the client/server application will distribute functional and nonfunctional responsibilities between the two tiers will differ from application to application. It will be the development team's responsibility to determine the distribution of responsibilities during the Preliminary design stage. This distribution must then be reflected in the specific kinds of tier testing planning done by the test team. Another way to state the situation is to say that client test strategies from prior application development are not guaranteed to be completely appropriate for the new client design. The statement is also true for the server test strategies.

The benefit of splitting the testing strategy into two separate chessboards is to provide more efficient test planning and execution focus. For example, this approach narrows the client tier test team to focus on data presentation functionality to the exclusion of data management. Similarly, this approach narrows the server test team focus on data management and business rules to the exclusion of data presentation functionality. Both test teams can readily identify the parts of the system they can ignore from a testing perspective early in the planning process. This simplifies and reduces the total effort each test team must invest to be successful by minimizing testing effort overlap. Figure 14.5 shows how these two chessboards might look.

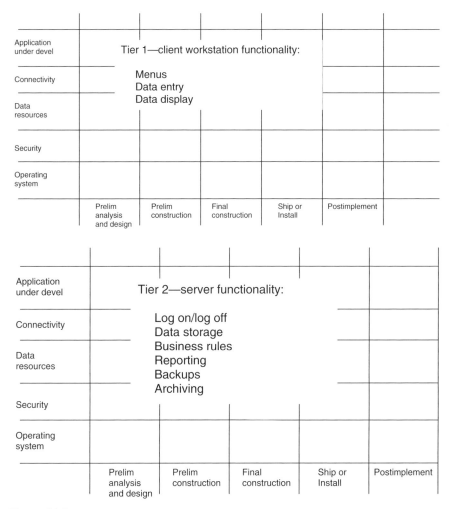

Figure 14.5   First step in 2-tier test planning

Somehow, we must account for the connectivity between the client tier and the server tier. The planning discussion has initially ignored this linkage in order to start the planning activities as simple as possible. Turning to the linkage testing issue, consider stacking the tier 1 client testing strategy on top of the tier 2 server testing strategy with an additional connectivity layer of testing between the two tiers as shown in Figure 14.6.

The order of stacking these strategies deliberately suggests that the server test execution should be started before the client execution if we are to follow the bottom-up execution strategy of 1-tier applications. At first blush, this would appear to be the more challenging execution order for the test team. Using data management as an example, it seems like it would be significantly easier for the test team to test purchase orders on the tier 2 server database structures if the purchase order screen is already

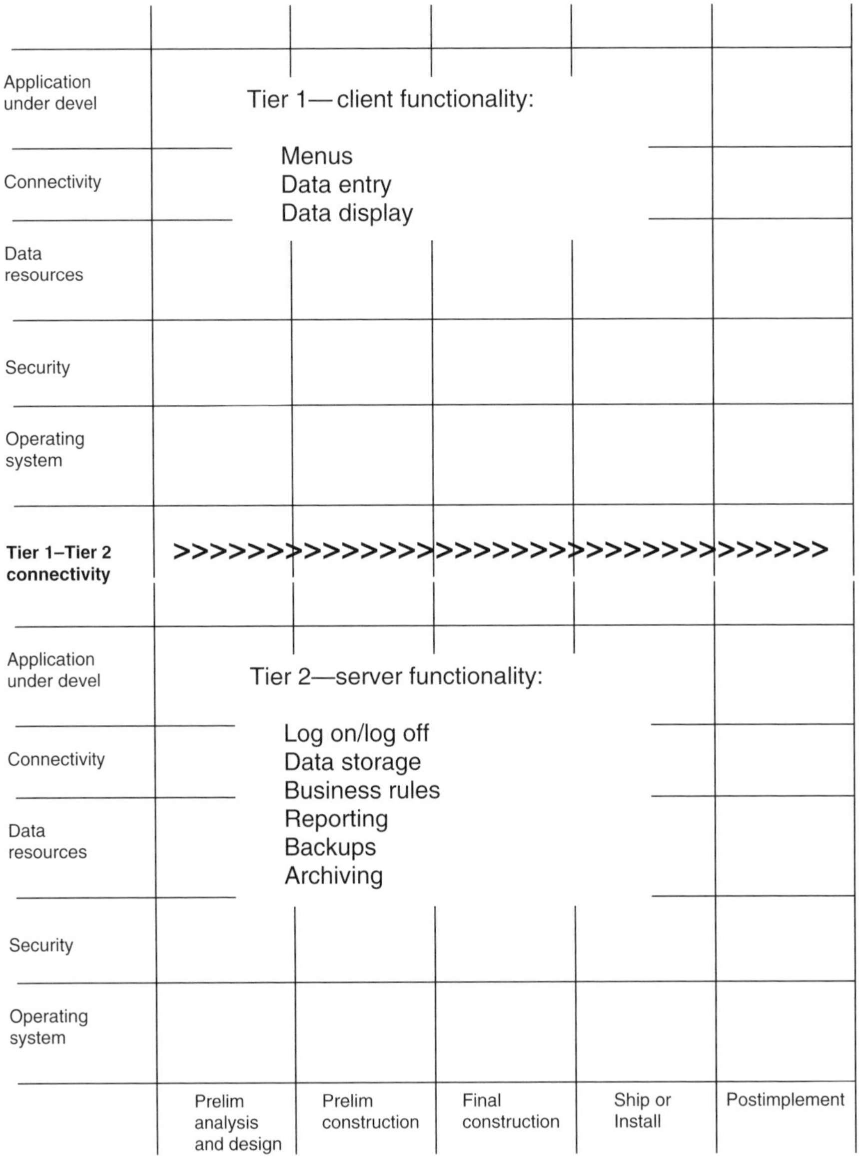

	Prelim analysis and design	Prelim construction	Final construction	Ship or Install	Postimplement
Application under devel		Tier 1—client functionality:			
Connectivity		Menus Data entry Data display			
Data resources					
Security					
Operating system					
Tier 1–Tier 2 connectivity	>>				
Application under devel		Tier 2—server functionality:			
Connectivity		Log on/log off Data storage Business rules Reporting Backups Archiving			
Data resources					
Security					
Operating system					

Figure 14.6   Second step in 2-tier test planning

available on the tier 1 client. The problem with testing the client first and the server second arises as soon as the first defect is discovered. The diagnostic challenge is to determine which tier (if not both tiers or both tiers and the connectivity) is the source of the defect. Extraordinary resources from both the test team and the development team can be consumed diagnosing defects under these circumstances.

Alternatively, consider the situation when the tier 2 server is tested first. The server data management functionality can be tested directly. This usually involves building simple test harnesses that support business function activity via native Data Manipulation Language (DML) calls. The most common form of DML for accessing and manipulating databases is the ANSI Standard Query Language (SLQ), which is supported by all major database management systems such as Oracle, DB2, Sybase, Informix, Microsoft SQL Server, Microsoft Access, and others. The extra effort needed to build and run the test harness is more than offset by identifying application database design defects long before the client software attempts to use the databases.

Once the application database design has been validated on the server, the test team then moves the test harness from the server to a client. This positions the test team to validate the tier-to-tier connectivity next. The SQL commands that worked correctly on the server *should* now produce the same results on a client *if* the tier-to-tier connectivity layer is working correctly. If defects arise during the tier-to-tier connectivity testing, the diagnosis effort can focus just on the connectivity components because the server side has been validated and is known to work correctly.

Once the server side and tier-to-tier connectivity have been validated, then the test team is ready to test the client side user screens and functions. If defects arise now, the diagnosis effort can focus just on the client side application software because both the server side and tier-to-tier connectivity have been validated and known to work correctly. This represents a relatively advantageous situation of introducing only one new variable at a time compared to the relatively disadvantageous situation where the testing is started on the client side; a defect is discovered, and none of the tiers can be excluded from the diagnosis.

The development team receives an additional benefit of this tier 2-to-tier 1 server-to-client testing strategy. Recall that the test team uses a testing harness and SQL to test the server side. When the development team writes the client side application code, they will eventually need to use some derivative of the test SQL. Whether the chosen development language supports SQL calls directly or SQL calls by means of Application Program Interfaces (APIs), the same business task must be accomplished from the user screen that was accomplished by the test harness. So the development team is given a substantial programming starting point with the tested and verified harness SQL.

14.4   3-TIER APPLICATIONS

The classic example of a 3-tier application is any Internet business application. Figure 14.7 shows a reasonably mature Internet business application example.

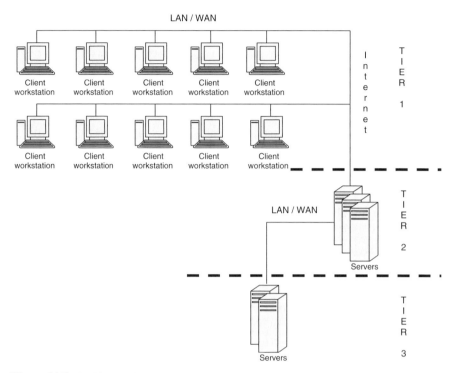

Figure 14.7   Architecture for a complex 3-tier application

The main difference between Figure 14.4 and Figure 14.7 is that there are more distinctly different groups of computers with distinctly different tasks. The identification of the different groups becomes more difficult as the number of different tasks multiplies and, in some cases, overlap. We suggest an approach to identifying these groups that works well but is not the only successful way. As long as the rationale behind your approach is technically consistent and reasonably unambiguous, your test planning can succeed.

We suggest grouping the Figure 14.7 components into three tiers: browser tier, security tier, and application tier. Figure 14.8 shows the grouping of components into these three tiers.

The browser tier in the 3-tier example is analogous to the client tier in the 2-tier example. It provides the end-user screen interface for running the application. The security tier in the 3-tier example is analogous to expanded tier-to-tier connectivity functionality in the 2-tier example. The application tier in the 3-tier example is analogous to the server tier in the 2-tier example.

As we saw with the 2-tier example, the secret of test planning success is the test team's involvement in and understanding of the development team's functional design of each tier. For example, some development teams might design the web home page server as mainly a security function like logging onto the web application, basically

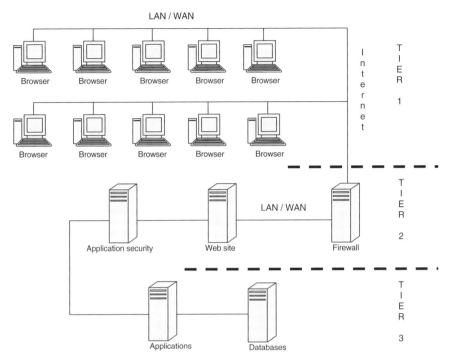

Figure 14.8   Tier identification for a complex 3-tier application

a tier 2 activity. Other development teams might design the web home page server as a logon function and some of the search/view application functions, basically a tier 3 activity. One design is not inherently better than the other. Each design requires commensurate test planning.

We take the first test planning step for 3-tier applications similar to our first step with 2-tier applications: Develop a separate strategy for each tier. Figure 14.9 shows how these separate tier strategies might look.

The second test planning step for 3-tier applications also follows the second planning step with 2-tier applications: Stack the tiers with a sandwiched tier-to-tier connectivity layer. Also, following the 2-tier planning model, we will place the application (third tier) on the bottom of the strategy followed by the security (second tier) next followed by the end user (first tier) on top. Figure 14.10 shows the completed second step in our 3-tier test planning.

The 3-tier test execution approach will be to complete the third tier testing first, the second tier testing second, and the first tier testing last. As with the 2-tier testing, test harnesses will probably be needed for the lower layer tiers to simulate/emulate the tiers above for testing purposes. Any useful information that the developers can glean from the testing harnesses about the design and coding of higher layers is an added testing contribution to the project.

Application under devel	Tier 1—browser functionality:			
Connectivity	Menus			
Data resources	Data entry Data display			
Security				
Operating system				
	Prelim analysis and design	Prelim construction	Final construction	Ship or Install	Postimplement

Application under devel	Tier 2—web access functionality:			
Connectivity	Firewall			
Data resources	Web site Application log on/log off			
Security				
Operating system				
	Prelim analysis and design	Prelim construction	Final construction	Ship or Install	Postimplement

Application under devel	Tier 3—application functionality:			
Connectivity	Data storage			
Data resources	Business rules Reporting Backups			
Security	Archiving			
Operating system				
	Prelim analysis and design	Prelim construction	Final construction	Ship or Install	Postimplement

Figure 14.9   First step in 3-tier test planning

	Prelim analysis and design	Prelim construction	Final construction	Ship or Install	Postimplement
Application under devel		Tier 1—browser functionality:			
Connectivity		Menus			
Data resources		Data entry Data display			
Security					
Operating system					
Tier 1–Tier 2 Connectivity		>>>			
Application under devel		Tier 2—web access functionality:			
Connectivity		Firewall Web site			
Data resources		Application log on/log off			
Security					
Operating system					
Tier 2–Tier 3 connectivity		>>>			
Application under devel		Tier 3—application functionality:			
Connectivity		Data storage Business rules			
Data resources		Reporting Backups			
Security		Archiving			
Operating system					

Figure 14.10   Second step in 3-tier test planning

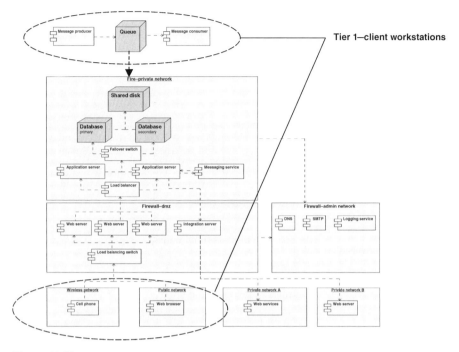

Figure 14.11   Tier 1 identification for a complex n-tier application

14.5 n-TIER APPLICATIONS

We return to the starting point of our discussion, the complex application in Figure 14.1. We approach the test planning for this application by applying what we have learned from the previous, increasingly complex applications. We start by identifying the different testing tiers in the application with the development team's assistance. Figures 14.11–14.14 show one such possible planning approach.

Application components that seem to provide the input/output functionality of the application to the external world are "lassoed" first as seen in Figure 14.11. These components and their activities will be included in the tier 1 test strategy chessboard.

Application components that seem to provide the security layers between the external world and the web services are "lassoed" next as seen in Figure 14.12. These components and their activities will be included in the tier 2 test strategy chessboard.

Application components that seem to provide the basic web service layers between the security layer and the application are "lassoed" next as seen in Figure 14.13. These components and their activities will be included in the tier 3 test strategy chessboard.

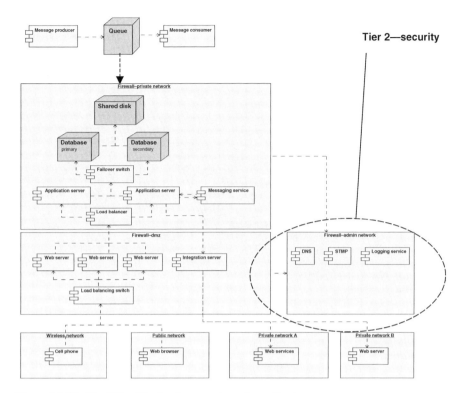

Figure 14.12   Tier 2 identification for a complex n-tier application

Application components that seem to provide the business functionality layers on the other side of the web services are "lassoed" last as seen in Figure 14.14. These components and their activities will be included in the tier 4 test strategy chessboard.

From this tier identification, we develop the individual tier testing strategy chessboards. Then we stack the chessboards starting with tier 4, then tier 3, then tier 2, then tier 1 with tier-to-tier connectivity layers in between each pair of tiers.

Finally, we review the overall testing strategy with the development team to confirm that the strategy represents the most logical testing progression of the tiers and their components. It is possible that this review may reveal some alternate approaches to the overall development that can take advantage of the test results as they are completed. It is equally possible that one or more of the tier components were not correctly described to the testers or some component activities have been redefined. The design changes probably imply test planning changes. The good news is that you have been able to address these development changes very early in your test planning, minimizing disruption and rewriting of test cases later in the "throes of battle."

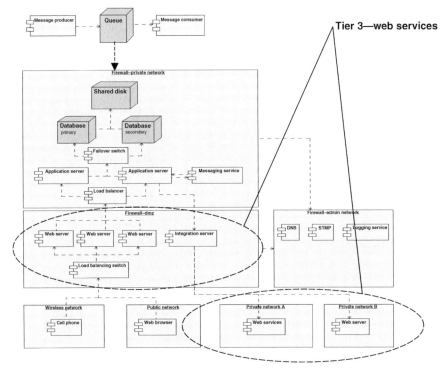

Figure 14.13 Tier 3 identification for a complex n-tier application

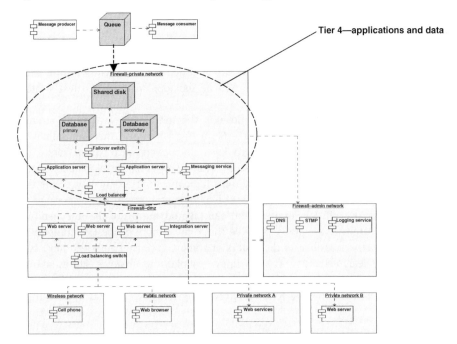

Figure 14.14 Tier 4 identification for a complex n-tier application

14.6   PUTTING TESTING COMPLEX APPLICATIONS IN PERSPECTIVE

The advent of major commerce on the Internet has brought with it very complex, business critical software applications. These applications challenge the software tester to identify as many traditional testing approaches as possible that are still appropriate and effective for e-commerce testing. Where traditional testing approaches fail, the software tester is challenged to find a minimum number of new, reusable testing approaches that fill the traditional testing approach gap.

Because e-commerce is surely not the last frontier of software development, the way we extend our traditional testing approaches to e-commerce applications may give us a clue about the way we can approach the next software development frontiers and resist the temptation to discard all of our traditional testing approaches and experience.

14.7   SUMMARY

This approach is basically "divide and conquer." *Divide* the complex application into manageable application components that can be *conquered* by familiar testing techniques.

Where do you start your test planning for a complex application? Start at a familiar starting point: the testing strategy chessboard. Split the testing strategy into multiple separate chessboards corresponding to major application components for more efficient test planning and execution focus. Finally, account for the connectivity among the separate chessboards by planning appropriate linkage testing.

KEY TERMS

1-Tier application	Tier 3	Tier-to-tier connectivitty
2-Tier application	Tier 4	
3-Tier application	Client tier	Test harness
n-Tier application	Server tier	DML
Tier 1	Security tier	SQL
Tier 2	Web services tier	API

Chapter 15

Future Directions in Testing

LEARNING OBJECTIVES

- to predict the kinds of opportunities that might arise for experienced software testing professionals in the future

15.1 INTRODUCTION

It is time to gaze into our testing crystal ball and divine some of the new opportunities and directions that software testing will take in the next 10 years. First, we will look at trends in software development to augur the implications for the software testing profession. Then, we will look at trends in applications to prognosticate the implications for software testing research.

15.2 FUTURE DIRECTIONS IN SOFTWARE DEVELOPMENT THAT COULD INCREASE THE NEED FOR TESTING PROFESSIONALS

There are two trends in software development that are of interest to software testing professionals. The first trend is "get the code out quickly, we can fix it later." This trend seemed to start in the 1990s and was pushed to the extreme by the dot-com boom. Recall how unstable the first versions of this quick-release software were. However, because the concept and marketing were so exciting and innovative, companies purchased the poor-quality software by the hundreds of licenses anyway.

Fast-forward 15 years. The patches and fixpacks that used to be provided reluctantly by these software vendors over a period of months are now boldly announced by icons daily on my desktop computer. Some of the patches fix problems so severe that my current employer *requires* me to apply these patches *immediately*! We can

---

Software Testing: Testing Across the Entire Software Development Life Cycle, by G. D. Everett and R. McLeod, Jr.
Copyright © 2007 John Wiley & Sons, Inc.

only conclude that this quick-release software development model is a long-term technology failure.

Further devaluation of the quick-release software development model comes from a simple observation. With the number of patches and fixpacks increasing almost exponentially (from once a month to three times a day!), the authors find the software vendors' response to this avalanche of software defects to be most interesting and most telling about their technology priorities. Instead of a reemphasis on quality (fewer bugs = fewer fixes and fixpacks = better quality software), they have chosen to invest development dollars into software that alerts the software customer quicker that a fix needs to be applied and, if the customer chooses, the new software will install the software fixes either in the background or as the computer is shut down so as to minimize interference with productive activities. These software vendors have made a conscious decision to invest in more sophisticated fix alert actions as a priority over investing in development or testing models that produce software with the need for fewer fixes in the first place.

Even with the public evidence of the quick-release software development technology model failure, the phenomenal success of the associated business model is like the Siren Song to other software development companies and software development organizations within large corporations. One of the resonant lessons learned is that more and better testing tends to mitigate the quick-release software development model failure. Throughout the IT industry, we predict an increasing demand for experienced professional software testers to mitigate this "Quick-Release Syndrome" in the software market. This demand for experienced testers will easily exceed the availability of experienced testers if colleges and universities do not start offering software testing curricula.

At some time in the future, the major software vendors who have enjoyed business success with quick-release software products will implode. This situation is somehow reminiscent of the children's story that ends with an observant child remarking, "the king has no clothes!" Entrepreneurs who fully understand and embrace the lessons learned from the quick-release development technology model will have a real chance to offer cost-effective software with significantly better quality (fewer patches and fixpacks) to a market hungry for good-quality software. If they succeed, then the software testing profession will really take wings. Quality software requires more testing than just the "stop the bleeding" approach these quick-release proponents seem to take. Testing will become an integral part of the entire software development and deployment model from day one. We expect that the demand for experienced software testing professionals under these circumstances will double or triple worldwide.

15.3 SOFTWARE TESTING CHALLENGES ALREADY UPON US

Over the last 5 years, wireless communication devices have entered the mainstream of computing environments. Only within the last couple of years has this industry begun to standardize the messaging that can contain text, voice, music, and images.

252 Chapter 15 Future Directions in Testing

The standardization challenges have been exacerbated by the diversity of computing devices that support wireless communication.

The software development challenges to extend the current applications into the wireless environment have been enormous. The plethora of viable devices running a wide range of successful applications attests to the software development profession's creativeness and persistence. The approach to software test planning and execution described in this textbook is appropriate for the wireless environment but with some warnings. At the moment, testing wireless applications is very work intensive for two reasons. The first reason is the complexity of the test environment and test data needed. The second reason is the absence of tools in the market for automatically managing and executing wireless test scripts.

Although the needs for wireless software testing are not academically rigorous enough to be termed "testing research," there is a clear need for pioneers to extend current approaches and find new approaches that assist the testing profession to keep up with the wireless development technologies.

15.4   SOFTWARE TESTING NEAR FUTURE CHALLENGES

The next quantum leap in software development after wireless applications is autonomic computing. The term, as it is currently used in the industry, means a computing system that can "heal itself." The concept is gaining in importance because of the complexity of very large-scale computing platforms being designed for the scientific arena. The challenges in writing operating systems for such "self-healing" systems are significant. These significant challenges increase as "self-healing" applications are designed to run on the "self-healing" operating systems.

Testing autonomic systems would be sufficiently challenging if all we had to achieve was validation that the "healing" process was correct, that is, the expected "healing" matches the actual "healing." Basic testing approaches will need to be carefully extended to address the "healing" paradigm in a manner similar to the wireless application testing extensions.

We believe that successfully testing autonomic systems will require a testing paradigm shift to validate the feature of autonomic systems not present in other software, namely the ability to "self-diagnose." In order for the software to start a "healing" process, the software must somehow detect that it is "injured." It is this detection process that will need either new testing approaches or a new testing paradigm ... or both. We suggest that this is a fertile area for both practitioner and academic software testing research.

15.5   SOFTWARE TESTING CHALLENGES TO COME

Stand back from the immediate and near-term software development challenges for a minute and consider where the challenge combinations might take you. One possible combination would be the remote testing of autonomic systems that are physically inaccessible. Physical inaccessibility is used here to mean the system is operating in an environment hostile to human beings. Two examples quickly come to mind.

The first example is outer space such as earth orbiting satellites. Self-healing communication of navigation or scientific satellites seem very desirable when considering the alternative cost of sending humans into orbit to repair a satellite. Some of the software testing challenges would be sufficiently valid testing before satellite launch and a sufficiently robust test monitoring after satellite launch.

The second example is inner space such as ocean going submersibles. Self-healing exploration systems seem very desirable when considering the cost and time required to bring a submersible vessel to the ocean surface from a depth of several miles. Two of the software testing challenges would be sufficiently valid testing before submersion and sufficiently robust test monitoring during a dive.

One final prediction arises out of a movie the late 1960s of "2001–A Space Odyssey." [53] One particularly interesting sequence shows the hero Dave deactivating a series of memory cells in a runaway computer system named HAL that control's Dave's spacecraft. As each successive memory module is deactivated, HAL degenerates from a sophisticated, voice-activated, chess-playing, 3-D object recognizing, and lip-reading mega computer to a nursery rhyme singing desktop computer.

What challenges the imagination is the implication that HAL "learned" all his supercomputer abilities starting from the simple ability to sing the tune "Daisy, Daisy." There are a number of articles in the Artificial Intelligence research arena that propose how such "learning" might occur. No overtly successful efforts have been reported to date. Showing a bit of optimism in the hardware and software developers' genius, we expect that "learning" computers will come into existence. At this time, we can only wonder at the testing challenges posed by software that "learns."

15.6 PUTTING FUTURE TESTING DIRECTIONS IN PERSPECTIVE

Technology professionals always have a nagging question in the back of their mind, "What is the useful lifetime of my current technical expertise?" Some technologies tend to grow and mature over time, offering the experienced professional a long, prosperous career with appropriate continuing education. Other technologies become a dead end because something leapfrogs them and becomes dominant in the industry.

Software testing clearly falls in the former category of growth and maturity. We see vast opportunity for basic software testing skills because the current and foreseeable software development methods remain highly reliant on correct human behavior. When (hopefully not if) software development methods truly mature, then software testing professionals will have vast opportunity for developing more advanced software testing skills to match the challenge of new technology arenas.

Clearly, the software testing profession has a very promising future.

15.7 SUMMARY

First, we will look at trends in software development to augur the implications for the software testing profession. Then, we will look at trends in applications to prognosticate the implications for software testing research.

There are two trends in software development that are of interest to software testing professionals. The first trend is "get the code out quickly, we can fix it later." With the number of patches and fixpacks increasing almost exponentially (from once a month to three times a day!), the authors find the software vendors' response to this avalanche of software defects to be most interesting and most telling about their technology priorities. Instead of a reemphasis on quality (fewer bugs = fewer fixes and fixpacks = better quality software), they have chosen to invest development dollars into faster alerts that a fix needs to be applied. Entrepreneurs who fully understand and embrace the lessons learned from the quick-release development technology model will have a real chance to offer cost-effective software with significantly better quality (fewer patches and fixpacks) to a market hungry for good-quality software. If they succeed, then the software testing profession will really take wings.

The software development challenges to extend the current applications into the wireless environment have been enormous. The plethora of viable devices running a wide range of successful applications attests to the software development profession's creativeness and persistence.

The next quantum leap in software development after wireless applications is autonomic computing. We believe that successfully testing autonomic systems will require a testing paradigm shift to validate the feature of autonomic systems not present in other software, namely the ability to "self-diagnose."

There are a number of articles in the Artificial Intelligence research arena that propose how software "learning" might occur. No overtly successful efforts have been reported to date. Showing a bit of optimism in the hardware and software developers' genius, we expect that "learning" computers will come into existence. At this time, we can only wonder at the testing challenges posed by software that "learns."

KEY CONCEPTS

"Get the code out quickly, we can fix it later"

Software development technology model

Software development business model

Testing for and in hostile environments

Software that is "self-healing"

Software that "learns"

Wireless environment

References

[1] Gregory Tassey, *The Economic Impacts of Inadequate Infrastructure for Software Testing*. National Institutes of Standards and Technology, May 2002.

[2] ibid.

[3] G. J. Meyers, *The Art of Software Testing*, John Wiley & Sons, 1976.

[4] B. Beizer, *Software Testing Techniques*. Van Nostrand Reinhold, 1990.

[5] Cem Kaner, Jack Falk, Hung Quoc Nguyen, *Testing Computer Software,* 2nd edition. International Thompson Computer Press, 1993 (ISBN 1-85032-847-1).

[6] James A. Whittaker, *How to Break Software: A Practical Guide for Testing*. Addison-Wesley, 2003 (ISBN 0-201-79619-8).

[7] Cem Kaner, James Bach, Bret Pettichord, *Lessons Learned in Software Testing*. Wiley Computer Publishing, 2002, 286 pp. (ISBN 0-471-08112-4).

[8] James Schafter, *All Corvettes Are Red*. Simon & Schuster, 1996, 384 pp. (ISBN 0-684-80854-4. Academic permission granted to copy excerpts from the following pages for class: pages 243, 246, 254, 287, 295–296, 297).

[9] Elsa Walsh, Court secrecy masks safety issue. *The Washington Post*, 1988, A1.

[10A] Basili and Boehm, Software Defect Reduction Top 10 List, IEEE Computer Society, vol. 34, (No. 1), January 2001, pp. 135–137.

[10B] Capers Jones, *Applied Software Management: Assuring Productivity and Quality,* 2nd Edition, McGrah-Hill, 1996 (ISBN 13 978-0070328266.

[11] Mark Minasi, *The Software Conspiracy*. McGraw-Hill, 2000, 271 pp. (ISBN 0-07-134806-9).

[12] James Martin, *Rapid Application Development*. Prentice Hall, New York, 1991.

[13] Raymond McLeod, Jr. Eleanor Jordan, *Business Systems Development: A Project Management Approach*. John Wiley & Sons, 2002, pp. 328–338.

[14] O. Flaatten, Donald J. McCubbrey, P. Declan O'Riordan, Keith Burgess, Per *Foundations of Business Analysis*. Dryden Press, Fort Worth, TX, 1991, pp. 210–218.

[15] McLeod and Jordan, ibid.

[16] Michael O'Leary, *B-17 Flying Fortress, Production Line to Front Line, vol. 2* (Chapter 1). Osprey Aviation, 1998 (ISBN 1-85532-814-3).

[17] Edward L. Jones, SPRAE: A Framework for Teaching Software Testing in Undergraduate Curriculum, NSF Grant EIA-9906590, 2001.

[18] James A. Whittaker, What is software testing? And why is it so hard? *IEEE Software* (No. 1), 2000, 70–79.

[19] Website that contains the Software Engineering Institute description of their Capability Maturity Model Integration (CMMi): www.sei.cmu.edu/pub/documents/02.reports/pdf/02tr011.pdf.

[20] James Bach, *Rapid Software Testing*, Satisfice Inc., www.satisfice.com.

[21] The IEEE Computer Society web site www.ieee.org.

[22] The Tigris Open Source Software Community project ReadySET web site http://readyset.tigris.org/.

[23] M. Ramachandran. Requirements-Driven Software Test: A Process Oriented Approach, *Software Engineering Notes* 21(4), 1996, 66–70.

[24] Alistair Cockburn, *Writing Effective Use Cases*. Addison-Wesley, 2001 (ISBN 0-201-702258).

[25] James A. Whittaker, *How To Break Software: A Practical Guide To Testing*. Addison-Wesley, 2003 (ISBN 0-201-79619-8).

[26] H.K. Leung, L.A. White, A Study of Regression Testing. *Proceedings of the 6th International Conference on Testing Computer Software*. USPDI, Washington, D.C., May 1989.

[27] G. Rothermel, M.J. Harrold, Analyzing Regression Test Selection Techniques, *IEEE Transactions on Software Engineering*, 22(8), 1996, 529–551.

[28] John Watkins, *Testing IT: An Off-the-Shelf Software Testing Process*. Cambridge University Press, 2001 (Chapter 11, *Regression Testing*, ISBN 0-521-79546-X).

[29] A. Bertolino, M. Marre, Automatic generation of path covers based on the control flow analysis of computer programs, *IEEE Transactions on Software Engineering*, 21(12), 1994, pp. 885–899.

[30] C.S. Chou, M.W. Du, Improved Domain Strategies for Detecting Path Selection Errors. In: *Proceedings of the Conference on Software Maintenance*, IEEE Computer Society, Los Angeles, 1987, pp. 165–173.

[31] P.G. Frankl, E.J. Weyuker, Provable improvements on branch testing. *IEEE Transactions on Software Engineering* 19(10), 1993.

[32] R.D. Craig, S.P. Jaskiel, *Systematic Software Testing*. SQE Publishing, 2002 (Chapter 5 section "White Box Science", ISBN 1-58053-508-9).

[33] B. Beizer, *Software Testing Techniques,* 2nd Edition. International Thomson Press, 1990 (Chapter 3 "Flowgraphs and Path Testing", ISBN 1-85032-880-3).

[34] B. Biezerk, *Black Box Testing*. John Wiley & Sons, 1995.

[35] R.D. Craig, S.P. Jaskiel, *Systematic Software Testing*. SQE Publishing, 2002 (Chapter 5 section "Black Box Art", ISBN 1-58053-508-9).

[36] B. Beizer, *Software Testing Techniques,* 2nd Edition. International Thomson Press, 1990 (Chapter 4, Transaction-Flow Testing, ISBN 1-85032-880-3).

[37] Ronald L. Rivest, *Testing Implementations of DES*. MIT Laboratory for Computer Science, Cambridge, Mass., February 1985.

[38] Lawrence E. Bassham III, *The Advanced Encryption Standard Algorithm Validation Suite (AESAVS)*. National Institutes of Standards and Technology, November 2002.

[39] Steven Splaine, *Testing Web Security*. Wiley Publishing, Inc., 2002 (ISBN 0-471-23281-5).

[40] *Ixia Introduces Gigabit Line Rate Encryption Test Solution, Enterprise*

Networks & Servers. PCI Publisher (August 2004 Issue).

[41] Troell, Burns, Chapman, Goddard, Soderlund, Ward, *Data Encryption Performance: Layer 2 vs. Layer 3 Encryption in High Speed Point-to-Point Networks*. The Rochester Institute of Technology, October 2005.

[42] Tim Richardson, Cowboy computer glitch blamed for construction slump. *The Register* 2004.

[43] Eclipse organization homepage www.eclipse.org.

[44] Hyades project homepage www.eclipse.org/hyades.

[45] Mercury Interactive Software testing tools and training homepage www.merc-int.com.

[46] Rational Software testing tools, testing processes, and training homepage www.rational.com.

[47] Segue Software testing tools and training homepage www.segue.com.

[48] Stephen H. Kan, *Metrics and Models in Software Quality Engineering*, 2nd Edition, Addison-Wesley, 2002, ISBN 0-201-72915-6.

[49] ibid, Chapter 7.

[50] *IBM Center for Software Engineering*, T.J. Watson Research Laboratory, http://www.watson.ibm.com/

[51] Please refer to Case Study B in website http://www.wiley.com/WileyCDA/Section/id-2925.html

[52] Computing Perspectives, Inc. is a Texas corporation (#1054978-0) chartered to provide computer consulting services. The DriveSaveAmerica case study is a customer project completed by CPI and is used in this textbook with the permission of Gerald D. Everett, President of Computing Perspectives, Inc.

[53] "2001 — A Space Odyssey", a motion picture by Stanley Kubrick, MGM, 1968.

Index